DEBUNKERY

FISHER INVESTMENTS PRESS

Fisher Investments Press brings the research, analysis, and market intelligence of Fisher Investments' research team, headed by CEO and *New York Times* best-selling author Ken Fisher, to all investors. The Press covers a range of investing and market-related topics for a wide audience—from novices to enthusiasts to professionals.

Books by Ken Fisher
Debunkery
How to Smell a Rat
The Ten Roads to Riches
The Only Three Questions That Count
100 Minds That Made the Market
The Wall Street Waltz
Super Stocks

Fisher Investments Series
Own the World by Aaron Anderson
20/20 Money by Michael Hanson

Fisher Investments On Series
Fisher Investments on Energy
Fisher Investments on Materials
Fisher Investments on Consumer Staples
Fisher Investments on Industrials
Fisher Investments on Emerging Markets
Fisher Investments on Technology
Fisher Investments on Consumer Discretionary

FISHER
INVESTMENTS
PRESS

DEBUNKERY

Learn It, Do It, and Profit From It—
Seeing Through Wall Street's
Money-Killing Myths

KEN FISHER
with Lara Hoffmans

WILEY

John Wiley & Sons, Inc.

Published by John Wiley & Sons, Inc., Hoboken, New Jersey.
Published simultaneously in Canada.

Important Disclaimers: This book reflects personal opinions, viewpoints, and analyses of the authors and should not be regarded as a description of advisory services provided by Fisher Investments of performance returns of any Fisher Investments client. Fisher Investments manages its clients' accounts using a variety of investment techniques and strategies not necessarily discussed in this book. Nothing in this book constitutes investment advice or any recommendation with respect to a particular country, sector, industry, security, or portfolio of securities. All information is impersonal and not tailored to the circumstances or investment needs of any specific person.

Limit of Liability/Disclaimer of Warranty: While the publisher and author have used their best efforts in preparing this book, they make no representations or warranties with respect to the accuracy or completeness of the contents of this book and specifically disclaim any implied warranties of merchantability or fitness for a particular purpose. No warranty may be created or extended by sales representatives or written sales materials. The advice and strategies contained herein may not be suitable for your situation. You should consult with a professional where appropriate. Neither the publisher nor author shall be liable for any loss of profit or any other commercial damages, including but not limited to special, incidental, consequential, or other damages.

For general information on our other products and services or for technical support, please contact our Customer Care Department within the United States at (800) 762-2974, outside the United States at (317) 572-3993 or fax (317) 572-4002.

Wiley also publishes its books in a variety of electronic formats. Some content that appears in print may not be available in electronic formats. For more information about Wiley products, visit our Web site at www.wiley.com.

Library of Congress Cataloging-in-Publication Data:
Fisher, Kenneth L.
  Debunkery : learn it, do it, and profit from it—seeing through Wall Street's money-killing myths / Ken Fisher with Lara W. Hoffmans.
    p.   cm.
  "Fisher Investments Press."
    Includes index.
  ISBN 978-0-470-28535-0 (cloth); 978-0-470-94417-2 (ebk); 978-0-470-94418-9 (ebk)
  1. Investments. 2. Investments—Decision making. 3. Portfolio management.
I. Hoffmans, Lara. II. Title.
  HG4521.F5847 2010
  332.6—dc22   2010032752

Printed in the United States of America
SKY10036069_091622

CONTENTS

ACKNOWLEDGMENTS

I've always been fortunate to do something I love professionally—grapple with capital markets—and also engage seriously in my two favorite hobbies: writing and redwoods. And when the professional day is over or on the weekends, when it's too dark to tramp around the woods, I enjoy turning to my typewriter. (Which has been, for a very long time now, the computer.)

This is my seventh book—and a fun one to write. Easy, too! My editor won't like me saying this—thinking "easy" means maybe I didn't put in much effort, so you won't get much benefit. Not true! Hopefully you will get huge benefit. What I mean by "easy" is these are all short lessons that are near and dear to my heart. Many are ones I've even written on before—in different ways and formats and venues—some of which have been previously published and many of which haven't. A lot are ones I've written about before in short pieces for use by my firm. Some I haven't written on but are things I've said repeatedly to clients, in client seminars, in media interviews, etc. Others are newer but still vital core lessons I think about or apply near constantly—or advise others to think about and apply.

There were many topics I considered, but 2010 seemed a particularly good time to attack common investing myths and misperceptions—and how to debunk them. The bad 2008 bear market is still fresh for most investors. And bear markets make people's brains go haywire like nothing but an extreme bull market. Bear markets are emotionally trying and can make folks seek to reduce the near-term pain. That can mean making a radical change to investing strategy; one that may feel better now, but may not be appropriate long term. Ironcially, it can end up hurting folks far worse than the pain they feel now—but far down the road when it's too late (or almost too late) to do anything about it. Or, folks seek the safety and comfort of crowds—following "rules of thumb" or those things that "everyone knows"—and that's when you can get into real, lasting trouble (as you'll see in the book). So I decided a book that directly counters common, widely held myths and misperceptions that rob folks of better long-term results was especially relevant now.

And though writing this book was "easy"—it's never really easy. Which is why I'm fortunate to be graced with a huge supporting cast. Not many authors have vast amounts of smart, talented people chasing down data, confirming facts, and otherwise making sure what I say is what I mean—making my job easier still. (There's that word again.) Lara Hoffmans was again pulled from her normal duties writing for my firm's website MarketMinder and overseeing my firm's imprint with John Wiley & Sons, Fisher Investments Press, to assist me in drafting chapters, checking my edits, and running interference with the research folks to make sure all our statements were supported and factually accurate. So all I had to do was the fun part, writing.

And, as will become quickly apparent, this book is littered with data and analysis. For that, I must thank my firm's tireless research team, headed by Andrew Teufel—one of the brightest people you can ever meet—and his fearless admirals, Bill Glaser and Mike Hanson. Contributing analysis to the book were Austin Fraser, Akash Patel, Charles Thies, and Jarred Kriz.

And then there are all those graphs—nearly every chapter has one if not more. All that data had to be pulled and checked, then the chart created and formatted. Then checked and re-checked and re-checked again and reformatted again. That takes attention to detail, time, and patience—vast amounts of patience. Leading the charge was the Team Leader of my firm's Research Analytics and Production team, Matt Schrader, along with analyst Jessica Wolfe. Jessica did the lion's share of the graph grunt work, has a great eye for detail, and had a terrific attitude throughout—for that I thank her heartily. Also contributing heavily were Brad Rotolo, Jason Belsky, Andrew Bates, Scott Botterman, Lindsey Skopal, Tom Holmes, and Karl Wonstolen.

Not all the graphs were data-driven—we had some hypothetical drawings done by our in-house graphic designer, Leila Amiri. Leila also designed the cover (which I think is pretty cool), and in general is great at putting a creative spin on abstract concepts. Also helping develop cover concepts (for this and my last few books, as well as the Fisher Investments Press books) was Molly Lienesch, who heads up Branding for my firm. She has a terrific eye for detail and understands the consumer experience better than anyone I know. Maybe she's tied with Marc Haberman, my firm's Chief Innovation Officer. I don't know of any other investment firm that has an Innovation department—at least not one as deep as ours, or as sure. Marc was instrumental in helping our folks kick around titles and book concepts. And as always, Fab Ornani, our Web guru, and Tommy Romero, our head of Marketing, help get the books noticed. If the book doesn't sell, you don't have a book.

Helping pick up the slack in writing client-facing content while Lara was otherwise occupied were Aaron Anderson, Elizabeth Anathan, Jason Dorrier, Carolyn Feng, and Todd Bliman. And backing up Lara in doing fact-checking, citations, and copyediting was Evelyn Chea—who always does a top-notch job catching our goofy typos. Giving the book the legal "look-over" (and providing me with some good editorial feedback as well) were Fred Harring, Nicole Gerrard, and Tom Fishel.

Thanks also, as always, to my agent Jeff Herman. And I must thank the crew at John Wiley & Sons—David Pugh, who shepherded me through my first three books with Wiley (my fourth, fifth, and sixth books)—*The Only Three Questions That Count* (2006), *The Ten Roads to Riches* (2008), and *How to Smell a Rat* (2009). These were all *New York Times* best sellers (as well as hitting other best seller lists—the *Wall Street Journal, BusinessWeek, USA Today,* and various smaller lists) thanks in no small part to David's fine work, and the fine work of the Wiley team. Laura Walsh has since replaced David, and working with her has been a pleasure. I must also thank Kelly O'Connor and Adriana Johnson, as well as Joan O'Neil, executive publisher at Wiley, who kindly lets me say whatever I want to say.

I must also thank my firm's senior managers—Andrew Teufel (again), Steve Triplett, and Damian Ornani—three of the brightest, most diligent young men (they are younger than me, and therefore will always be "young men") anyone could have the pleasure of working with. They didn't contribute directly to the book, because they were busy running the moment-to-moment management of my firm, but their contribution is vital to the firm's success—and without my firm's success, I doubt people would want to read what I have to say. Also, many thanks to Jeff Silk, Vice Chairman, whose introspection and insight make the firm—which is my core responsibility—what it is.

Finally, all my gratitude goes to my wife Sherrilyn. Time I spend writing is time spent away from her. The redwoods don't mind when I spend time away from them on weekends. Hopefully she does forever. This book was a blast to work on, and I hope you have a blast reading it.

Ken Fisher
Woodside, CA

INTRODUCTION
Debunkery Made Easy

What is "debunkery"? It's a *comberation*. Decades back my wife started calling all the semi-understandable words I made up "comberations"—an operation that is part combination, part abomination and yet you know largely what it means. With debunkery, I hope you intuitively get that it's myth debunking—with a twist.

The twist is that it's a game, of sorts. Don't take that to mean it's not serious. In this book, we're dealing with capital markets, investing, and money—serious topics. But games and play are part of how we learn. And debunkery—particularly in investing—is a game requiring dedication and practice. Why not have some fun on the way, if you can? So *debunkery* means unearthing truths or, at the very least, overturning common but widespread and frequently harmful market untruths, myths, and misperceptions most investors fall prey to.

But before going further, let me say that this book is not about some "how-to" system for beating the market. It doesn't have a market-beating formula or even specifically tell you *how* to invest. If you want a serious primer on overall investing strategy, I refer you to several of my other books. This one is about improving your odds and making fewer mistakes by deploying debunkery.

If you read my 2006 book, *The Only Three Questions That Count*, this can be a companion book—more examples of those three questions at work. Or it can be an introduction for how to (correctly) stand conventional wisdom on its head, where and when appropriate.

Reduce Your Error Rate . . . If You Can

A huge part of successful investing is just avoiding common errors most folks make repeatedly—that's the focus of this book. Most folks can't accept, in their bones, that investing isn't a certainties game. Can't be. Capital markets are far too complex. Instead, investing is a probabilities game—like medicine, engineering, and most sciences. We accept this about medicine—we know the risks of medications or procedures. There are no fail-safes, no guarantees. And yet, for some reason, investors demand absolutes from investing. This leads to serious errors.

All investors make mistakes. Even the very best—repeatedly. I make mistakes—lots of them. Some huge ones! I'll make more in the future—I promise. If you think you won't, you're wrong. If you think you haven't, you either haven't done much or you're delusional. My father was an admirer of Herbert H. Dow, the founder of Dow Chemical (America's largest chemical company) who famously said, "Never promote someone who hasn't made some serious mistakes because you would be promoting someone who hasn't done enough." That applies equally to investing. The very best—and those who have been the very best the longest—still have made lots and lots of mistakes. Pretty much no long-term investor has been right in their decisions more than about 70 percent of the time. If you get up close to those levels over the long term, you become a living legend. Plenty of folks think Warren Buffett is the all-time best investor—and I'm not being critical of him in any way, but even he's had some famous doozies. Everyone does. The goal isn't to be error-free; it's to be right more than wrong over time.

Overwhelmingly, most investors are wrong more than they're right. When you're wrong more than right, you lag the market. When you're right more than wrong, you can become one of the small percentage of investors, amateur or professional, who beat the market. So reducing your error rate is a worthy goal.

If you can accept that you're going to make mistakes—lots of them—you will be a better-adjusted investor (and your spouse will like you better, too). But if you can accept you will make mistakes, *and* aim to try to lower your error rate, you can be better adjusted, but also probably get better future results. Far better than most! That's what this book is about—showing you some common misperceptions—ones that can lead to serious errors. Knowing about them means you can learn to better avoid them. But more importantly, in the process, I hope you see it can be fun to figure out even more of these misperceptions for yourself, enabling you to do more debunkery on your own.

Getting It So Wrong

Many folks find it hard to believe that a huge swath of investors—professionals, pundits, academics, and even seasoned individual investors—frequently see the world completely wrong. And basically have done so and will do so forever—repeating the same silly mistakes over, and over, and over.

But you know it's true—why else do the bulk of professional investors fail to beat the market? It isn't because they have a low IQ. They don't. (Most are smarter than I am, to be sure, which isn't that hard to do). And why else do so many investors, among those who lag markets, do it so extremely? Why do folks pile heavily into so-called "hot" areas just in time for them to go cold and then do it again and again, repeating their error? And why do they sit idly by and miss the huge booms off bear markets bottoms while waiting for a "more clear" future that never comes?

Maybe you think you don't see the world wrong, and you do pretty well—that it's those other people who do badly. Great! (Though, keep in mind, overestimating one's investing skills is a common cognitive error.) But even if you're already a very good investor, you can still benefit from lowering your error rate. Everyone can. I'm 60 years old and I'm still working on it. Let me say that again. I've got a long-term history of being among the few to have beaten the market in the long term,[*] run a big firm managing over $32 billion,[1] have written the "Portfolio Strategy" column at *Forbes* for 26 years now, have written seven books (including this one), three of

---

[*]The Fisher Investments Private Client Group (FI PCG) Global Total Return (GTR) strategy was incepted on January 1, 1995 and is managed against the MSCI World Index. For the period from inception through December 31, 2009, performance returns (net of advisory fees, commissions and other expenses, and reflecting the reinvestment of dividends and other earnings) of the FI PCG GTR composite have exceeded the total returns of the MSCI World Index as well as the S&P 500 Index. Past performance is no guarantee of future returns. Investing in stock markets involves the risk of loss.

which were *New York Times* bestsellers—and I have a lot less of my career ahead of me than I have behind me. But still I'm trying to learn continuously how to lower my error rate because it is one of the only things you can do that really makes impact.

So why do people so commonly see the investing world so wrongly and become so error prone? A big part is our brains didn't evolve to deal with capital markets. Humans are intuitive creatures, but markets are inherently counterintuitive. "Common sense" thinking as well as gut instinct—fundamental in so many other parts of our lives and, in fact, often crucial—frequently hurts you big with investing. Folks are also blinded by biases, ideology, or any number of cognitive errors (which we will delve into). Behavioral finance, a now-maturing school of thought, looks at the many ways our ancestral brains trip us up in investing.

Another problem: Sometimes, things change. They used to work and stopped working. Or they work at some times, but not others. Why? The stock market is an efficient discounter of widely known information. But folks have a hard time shifting their views, particularly when for so long so many smart people believed something. And the longer something seems to be working, the less likely those who believe in it seem to be able to contemplate that it may stop working. Never take anything on faith.

For example, decades ago, access to information was hard to get and expensive to come by. If investors could get key information somehow—any which way—that often gave them real power. Now, anyone anywhere can get firm earnings, balance sheets, valuations, and more information than most people's brains can process—nearly instantly.

My first book, *Super Stocks,* was about using the price-to-sales ratio (PSR) to find super stock bargains. It was a concept unknown and hence not understood before then. And it worked! For a while. But over time, the PSR became popular and easy to find (back in the day, I had to pay to get the data, then basically derive the ratio myself). Today, you can get all the PSRs you want free on the Internet. So PSR, on its own, has lost much of the predictive power it once had. It can still help you at times, but you must know when those times are. (I discuss this more in *The Only Three Questions That Count.*) That's why you can't always rely on something that once worked to keep working like it did. What markets do and don't price into current stock prices evolves. Always.

Another reason investors get it wrong: The financial services industry sometimes teaches investors they need things they really don't. Why? Products with big paydays can be very bewitching to sell. Stop-losses (Bunk 12), covered calls (Bunk 13), dollar-cost averaging (Bunk 14), variable and equity-indexed annuities (Bunks 15 and 16) are all sold, usually, as ways to mitigate risk. But as applied, they're bunk, as you will see. And they can increase risk badly. But they certainly do increase commissions to the sales person. There is no doubt about that, and I'll show you that clearly.

Debunkery 101

There is an age-old saying Warren Buffett has re-popularized in recent decades: "You should be greedy when others are fearful and fearful when others are greedy." Good advice and particularly true at sentiment extremes. But in between those times, there's a vast muddiness of sentiment that often confuses. What if half the people are greedy and half fearful? Which half do you believe? Who? And why? Maybe you run with one pack or the other. But what are the odds you're right? And how might you measure that? That is just when you need the clarity that debunkery can provide.

Once you intuitively accept that 1) lots of commonly accepted investing wisdom isn't wise, and 2) you will still make mistakes anyway but can aim to lower your error rate and improve your results, actually doing debunkery can be easy. Simple really! To do debunkery, you can:

- **Scale.** Big numbers are always scary! That's the Stone Age part of our still-evolving brains. But if you consider big numbers in proper context, they may not only seem not-so-scary, but can become downright cuddly.
- **Be counterintuitive.** Ignore common sense as a guidepost and instead think counterintuitively.
- **Check history.** Endlessly, you hear in the media, "XYZ happened, and that's bad." Or, "ABC would be good!" But is there any evidence that XYZ historically led to bad or ABC to good? It's usually easy to check, yet few think to. If something hasn't reliably led to the expected outcome in the past, then folks need to explain why this time will be extraordinarily different. They usually can't.

- **Think globally.** It's amazing how distorted investors' world-views can be, simply because they don't think outside their home borders. If you think globally, a lot of misconceptions melt away. Substitute thinking "outside the box" with "outside your country."
- **Check data yourself.** This is like checking history. Now, ample free historic data exists so you can examine almost everything on your own.
- **Run some simple correlations.** Learn to use Excel. If you read that X leads to Y, check it yourself and see. Very frequently, when most people believe X leads to Y, it doesn't. Maybe it doesn't lead to anything at all, or it leads to something totally different—like Q!
- **If most people believe something is true—question it.** Flip common knowledge on its head. If everyone says something is bad, dare to ask, "What if it's good?" Then check historic data and run correlations to see. (And vice versa—see if something everyone thinks is good is really bad.)
- **Do a "four-box" to check outcomes.** I'll teach you how. Example: It's common to hear a down January foreshadows an overall down year. Check the four possible outcomes historically—down January and down year, down-up, up-up, up-down—to see if this myth holds water. (We do this in Bunk 24 and elsewhere.)

I'll show you how to do all these things (and more) in this book. Sometimes you can attack misperceptions with just one of these, sometimes a combination. But learn to do them all. Practice! Take what you learn here and apply it in different ways to different investing beliefs. Or start by disproving what I show in these pages. That would be great practice.

Standing Convention on Its Head

When I was young and first went to forestry school hoping to be a forester, we learned that my beloved redwoods needed summer fog baths to successfully reproduce via cone (which is true). The presumption was that more fog was better—a linear function. Partly this was from the common sense observation that the tallest and biggest redwoods were toward the north of the California coastal range, where the fog is heaviest. This became common wisdom. In the last few years, my young friend Steve Sillett (a professor at Humboldt State University—smack dab amidst the best redwood groves) proved that up to a point that's true.

But after that point, too much fog is counterproductive, and more sunlight becomes more important. That's just been shown in the last few years, standing 100 years of conventional wisdom on its head. That's what investing should be like, looking for things you can challenge—that stand conventional wisdom and common sense on their heads, whether that becomes uncomfortable for you (or fun).

A sidenote: You needn't believe everything or anything I say here. Not at all! After all, I've just told you to not take anything on faith. So you don't have to take what I say on faith either. But then, just because you don't accept what I say, don't simply respond, "That's silly! I don't believe it!" That's just using your intuition, gut instincts, and common sense, all the things the stock market—or rather, by its proper name, The Great Humiliator—wants to use against you (and which most investors do so terribly with). No— instead, take the time to prove you're right and I'm wrong, using the same basic statistical and analytic tools. It's a worthwhile exercise. Besides, I'm going to make lots of strong claims later on, so proving me wrong could be both rewarding and fun for you.

Also, remember, because capital markets are incredibly complex, things don't always work the way you think—even if you've successfully debunked a market myth. Again, investing is a probabilities game, not a certainties game. Not often, but sometimes, the low probability thing happens—you can get 100 heads in a row when flipping a coin. It happens. Doesn't mean you should bet on 100 heads in a row. Highly unlikely! But when the unlikely happens, you dust yourself off, learn what you can, and move on.

Misperceptions on Parade

Like two of my earlier books, *The Wall Street Waltz* (1987) and *100 Minds That Made the Market* (1993), this book is meant to be read in bite-size chunks—where you can read one chapter or many—and not necessarily in any particular order. Feel free to skip around! Dive in anywhere. Some chapters link to others and provide further background—and point to each other—but I'll tell you when that happens. Ultimately, this book is meant to deliver short lessons in just a few pages that are applicable right away. Or the book can be several hours of continuous reading. Your choice!

And as you read and start practicing, you'll find all the chapters fit pretty nicely into one of five categories:

1. **Basic Bunk to Make You Broke**: These are the biggest, most basic misperceptions about the very fundamentals of capital markets and Capitalism. Start here, and if you read nothing else, read this section.
2. **Wall Street Wisdom**: Sometimes the industry itself is set up in a way that helps you fail. Seeing through these myths helps you determine what's real, what's costly (though overall fairly harmless) tradition, and what's downright deadly.
3. **"Everyone Knows"**: Rules of thumb and other "common wisdoms" can feel comforting, but that doesn't mean they're right. These are all bits of bunk everyone knows but shouldn't.
4. **History Lessons**: A lot of harmful bunk persists because folks fail to check if what they believe is true with a simple scan of historic data.
5. **It's a Great Big World!** It's amazing how much bunk endures because people fail to think globally. Do so, and you won't fall for any of these.

In each section you'll use all the standard debunkery tactics—and more I'll introduce in the book. But this book is by no means exhaustive, nor is it intended to be. I could write 10 encyclopedias on market myth and misperceptions and barely scratch the surface. But no publisher wants to publish a 2,000-page book, and you can learn enough in these few pages to get the rest on your own, which is the most valuable thing I could possibly give you.

Included here are those misperceptions I've run into most in recent years—hearing them on TV, seeing them in headlines, hearing them from clients or my *Forbes* readers, in conversation with other professionals, etc.—and therefore the ones I think you'll run into most now and immediately ahead. Some are timeless, others are newer and more pertinent in 2010 (and beyond).

And some flip in and out of favor. You might go years without hearing folks gripe about our too-big trade deficit, then that fear comes roaring back (Bunk 48). And some fears flip-flop regularly—sometimes folks fear a too-weak dollar, then shift to fear a too-strong dollar, as if some perfect state of dollar balance exists. (It doesn't—or at least not that can be discerned circa 2010. See Bunk 27.) So this book serves as a handbook to potential error-inducing misperceptions, but also as a workbook to learn how to do debunkery on your own afterward and forever.

And whether you believe some, most, or none of these yourself, this book is still useful because these are mistruths that, overall, most investors believe—at least I think they are. There's real power in seeing the world more clearly than most.

With that, it's time for some debunkery. I hope you enjoy the book, and I hope you enjoy playing the very tough but rewarding game of investing. It can be even more rewarding if you see the world more clearly with debunkery.

PART ① BASIC BUNK TO MAKE YOU BROKE

T here are myriad reasons investors fail, long term, to get the returns they want. Folks have a romantic notion about "beating the market." A lofty goal—and possible, though difficult—but most investors not only fail to beat the market; they don't match the market or come anywhere close.

You'd think with all of today's technology and instant information, we'd have banked on all that past collective wisdom and do better at investing—overall and on average. Yet, overwhelmingly, investors don't.

There's no one reason, but a major reason—maybe the primary one—is our brains aren't set up to do this stuff right. (I'll talk about this more in future chapters.) Our brains evolved to keep us warm, dry, fed, and safe from charging beasts. That helps us in our quest to build taller, stronger, safer buildings and develop life-saving vaccines, but it does nothing in our quest to conquer capital markets. In fact, it can hurt us. Humans are intuitive creatures; markets are inherently counterintuitive.

Simply, the way our brains evolved can make us see the world completely wrong. We see heightened risk exactly when risk is actually least. (Bunks 7, 9.) We seek patterns where there are none (Bunk 10)—we want to see order in something that is inherently and beautifully chaotic. Then, despite our innate desire to assign meaning when there is none, we completely ignore obvious patterns—even mock them! (Bunks 1, 2.)

Part 1 deals with the most basic fundamental misunderstandings. These aren't mere theoretical disagreements—these are misperceptions that can cause investors to make lasting, costly errors. For example, despite decades—centuries even—of historic evidence, investors overwhelmingly cannot get, in their bones, that stocks rise more than fall. (Bunks 1, 2, 6, 8.)

Investors are also compelled to think too short term. Humans are obsessed with near-term survival—have to be! That helped us survive the colder months and stay fed, but it makes humans think about the investing future all wrong—to their detriment. (Bunks 3, 4, 8.) And though most investors (those with long-term growth goals, i.e., almost everyone reading this book) *know* they should think long term—and even say so in cooler moments—all that can go out the window once volatility kicks up. (Bunks 1, 6, 7, 8.) And once you make one or a few strategy shifts driven not by rational, cool-headed, long-term goals but by greed, fear, anxiety, indigestion, insomnia, what-have-you, you can seriously erode the chances you get anything near equities' long-term average growth. (Bunks 2, 5.)

And volatility! Drives folks crazy—because they can't train themselves to think long term. But volatility is normal. Even the most grizzled old investor can forget: In capital markets, averages are just that—averages. Reality can be wildly extreme—and that's normal. (Bunks 5, 7, 9.) Folks who fail to understand that may not only get unnerved and end up missing the likely superior long-term return of stocks—they can even get robbed blind! (Bunk 11.)

Ultimately, these are misperceptions that fade away if you can get, in your bones, the power of Capitalism—that human ingenuity is boundless, and that ingenuity eventually shows in future firm earnings, which goad stock prices higher over the long term. And that if you exchange the future uncertainty of likely higher returns from stocks for the nearer-term certainty of guaranteed returns—through a risk-free investment like a Treasury—finance theory and history both say you get a lower return. That's the risk/reward trade-off. (Bunks 1, 2, 3, 4, 5, 6, etc., etc., etc., etc.)

And if you don't believe in the power of Capitalism, that's fine—you don't have to—it believes in you. Still, if you think, as many perma-pessimists do, that Capitalism is broken, can't work anymore, or is somehow morally wrong, I'm sorry for you, but also you shouldn't be investing in stocks anyway and you probably wasted your money on this book. Many are prone to look at the current environment as I write in 2010 (or anytime, really) and fear Capitalism is unable to overcome the anti-capitalistic forces in our government and from other governments. But ultimately, Capitalism is a bigger force than any of those anti-forces. You may not believe that, but it's true.

Investing, inherently, requires faith that Capitalism isn't perfect in the near term but eventually gets darn close in the longer term—and is the best way (we currently know) to ensure capital flows to where it can be best used to create near-infinite future wealth. (Bunk 10.) Therefore, investing success requires grit, discipline, alligator skin, and the clearer vision you can get through debunkery. On with it!

BUNK ① BONDS ARE SAFER THAN STOCKS

Bonds just feel safe. The very name even implies safety—as in, "My word is my bond." Far too many investors with long-term growth goals load up on bonds, presuming they're safer than scary stocks. But are they? Depends largely on how you define "safe."

Does "safe" mean a high probability of lower long-term returns with less near-term volatility? Or is "safe" increasing the probability your portfolio grows enough to satisfy your long-term growth and/or cash flow needs? If you need a certain amount of growth to maintain your lifestyle in retirement, you might not feel so "safe" when you discover having too little volatility risk for too many years later means you must subsequently dial back your lifestyle. And you may not feel "safe" when you must explain that to your spouse—particularly if in that future there is any huge inflation spurt (always possible).

Bonds Can Be Negative, Too

Yes, stocks can be pretty darn volatile and scary—near term. But people forget: Bonds do sometimes lose value in the near term too. In 2009, bonds not only suffered relative to stocks (world stocks were up 30 percent)[1] but also absolutely—10-year US Treasuries *fell* 9.5 percent.[2] Not what you'd expect from über-safety.

Still, stocks can and do fall much more—in 2008, world stocks were down 40.7 percent![3] But remember, these are all short-term returns. Stocks are generally riskier short-term because the expectation is they'll have better returns long-term. And they have! (See Bunk 2 for more on stocks' long-term superiority.) Overwhelmingly, if you've got a long time to invest (and most investors do—see Bunk 3 on how investors usually underestimate their time horizon to their detriment), stocks are typically a better bet. And if you need portfolio growth and can give stocks a bit of time, they have even been the *safer* bet! It's all about time horizons.

Given Just a Bit of Time

Buying stocks with money you need to pay the rent over the next year is always foolish. But the truth is: Given a bit of time, historically stocks have bigger and, surprisingly, *more uniformly positive* returns than bonds. Figure 1.1 shows three-year rolling real returns (adjusting for inflation) of 10-year Treasuries. Note: There are plenty of down periods—in some cases many of them right in a row. You aren't protected from down periods with Treasuries.

Now compare that to Figure 1.2, which shows the same thing but for the S&P 500. (I use US stocks here because they have longer, better data, and we can measure this over a longer period—but the story is generally the same using world stocks.) You actually have *fewer* negative three-year periods historically. Yes, the negative periods can be bigger, but the positive periods are more numerous and simply huger. Stock returns blow away bond returns, with fewer negative three-year periods!

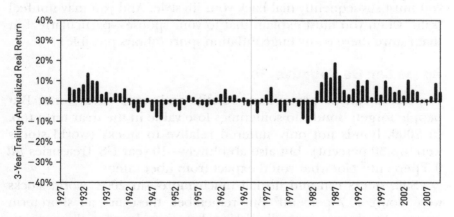

Figure 1.1 US 10-Year Treasuries (Three-Year Rolling Real Returns)— "Safer" Than Stocks?

Source: Global Financial Data, Inc., USA 10-year Government Bond Total Return Index from 12/31/1925 to 12/31/2009.

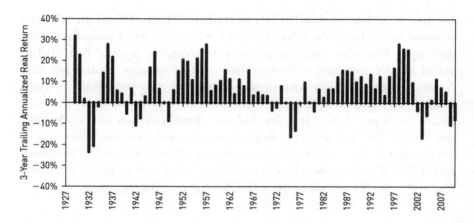

Figure 1.2   US Stocks (Three-Year Rolling Real Returns)—Compare to Bonds

Source: Global Financial Data, Inc., S&P 500 total return from 12/31/1925 to 12/31/2009.

Inflation's Bite

Folks also forget about inflation. If, over your long-term investment time horizon, we have a period (or two) of materially increasing inflation, two things can happen at once. First, long-term interest rates typically rise as inflation does. Bond yields and price have an inverse relationship—so when rates rise, the price and value of your long-term bonds fall proportionally.

Second, and as surely, your bonds get paid back in cheaper, inflated dollars—double whammy! With the amount of recent global money creation (as I write this in 2010) and the huge global deficits, it would be foolish indeed not to consider this a material possible risk. During such inflationary periods, stocks have tended to have lower returns relative to history but positive returns nonetheless (with short-term volatility, of course)—yet returns that generally have beaten inflation and maintained real purchasing power, and then some.

I'm frequently accused of being a perma-bull. I'm not—I've gotten bearish three times in my career thus far and I wrote about it publicly then. (For a history thereof and my other views over the long-term past, see Aaron Anderson's *The Making of a Market Guru: Forbes Presents 25 Years of Ken Fisher,* John Wiley & Sons, 2010.)

But I do have a bias to being bullish if I can't find any decent reasons to be bearish. Why? Look at those graphs! Capital markets are super complex. No one person or group of people can understand all the intricate inter-workings of the massive global market. As such, there are no certainties in investing, only probabilities. And history says you should want to be bullish way more than bearish. Bears can't get that. They see the big down periods for stocks and say, "Eek!" But for some reason, they just can't see the plain truth: Stocks are more consistently positive than bonds historically—given just a bit of time. Therefore, over the longer term, they have been less risky. Stocks are safer than bonds? Sure looks that way.

BUNK ② WELL-RESTED INVESTORS ARE BETTER INVESTORS

Can you sleep at night? For some reason, many investing professionals and pundits have a creepy fascination with what happens in your bedroom. Cooked into their recommendations is often the elusive "sleep at night" factor (which, believe it or not, isn't a primary benchmark determinant—see Bunk 4).

Many people just can't stomach volatility—wild wiggles make 'em crazy! Give them ulcers and keep them up at night. For those folks, before we consider dooming them to what's likely a lifetime of lackluster returns, I'd put a few hard questions to them.

Are You So Sure Stocks Are the Problem?

First, do you know bonds can and do have down years? (You do if you read Bunk 1!) Of course, everyone knows stocks had a dreadful 2008, but most folks (who haven't read this book) don't realize 10-year US Treasuries were hammered in 2009—down 9.5 percent.[1]

Second, are you so sure you hate wild wiggles? Folks think of downside volatility as bad and upside volatility as not volatility at all. But it's all volatility. You like the wild wiggles when they're up wiggles. It's amazing how many folks claiming they hate stocks at the end of a bear market—don't want to hold them ever again— change their tune radically after a couple or three or six years of a bull market and come back to stocks (sometimes just in time to get hammered again). Suddenly, they can't get enough "risk"—want to load up on it. These folks aren't risk-averse; they're myopic— they're heat chasers and crowd followers (and may need a court-appointed financial conservator to protect them from themselves).

A certain amount of stock phobia can be offset by training yourself to ignore the near term and think long term. Of course, many folks can't go there.

It's not easy to do. It requires training. Folks naturally think about near-term survival (see Bunk 7). But if you can train yourself to think longer term, those sleep-at-night factors melt away. Why? Because if you've got a longer time horizon (and if you're reading this book, you most likely do—see Bunk 3), stocks are just likelier to treat you better. And you can learn to sleep, even in difficult volatility (rather the same way as a child you learned to sleep on Christmas Eve, despite knowing all the excitement immediately ahead).

Investing Is a Probabilities Game

Past performance is never indicative of future results—simple fact. But history can tell you if something is reasonable to expect. Investing isn't a certainties game. It is instead, like medicine and many fields of science, a probabilities game. And if you have a 30-year time horizon (as many investors do, even some who are in or near retirement), odds are in your favor with stocks. Since 1927, there have been 54 rolling 30-year periods. Stocks beat bonds in every one, by a huge 4.8-to-1 margin on average. (See Table 2.1.)

Even over 20-year periods, odds are heavily with stocks. Since 1927, stocks have outperformed bonds in 62 of 64 20-year rolling periods (97 percent), by a 3.7-to-1 margin on average. (See Table 2.2.)

Some people are just doggedly bearish. Instead of thinking about what's overwhelmingly more likely based on probabilities, they think, "What if?" What about those times bonds beat stocks? What about a "black swan"? (It's amazing after 2008–2009 how many folks have come to believe that once-in-a-century "black swan"-like disasters happen every few years—including, it seems, the author of the book by that name.) In those rare 20-year periods

Table 2.1 Stocks Versus Bonds (30-Year Rolling Periods)—Stocks Historically Win Big

Average Total Return Over 30-Year Rolling Periods	
US Stocks	2,509%
US Bonds	524%

Source: Global Financial Data, Inc., S&P 500 Total Return Index for US stocks, USA 10-Year Government Bond Total Return Index for US bonds from 12/31/26 to 12/31/09.

when bonds beat stocks, **it was by only a 1.1-to-1 margin** on average (see Table 2.2). Historically, when you bet against the odds and won, you didn't win much—not much bang for your buck. And stocks were still net positive in every period they lagged bonds. Not up huge, but then again, neither was the alternative. Not a lot lost if you had 20 years ahead of you going in.

Even looking into those two periods when bonds beat stocks (Table 2.3), note that one ended in the recent 2007–2009 bear market—a historically super-large bear market. Yet even so, if you'd stuck to your guns and stuck with stocks, in the 20-year period ending 2009, stocks were still up 404 percent. So on average, $100,000 invested in stocks grew to $504,000 versus $533,000 in bonds—the difference of a little return wiggle that could have gone either way. Odds are low in a 20- or 30-year period that bonds outperform—and when they do it's not by much. Odds have to be particularly low after having just come through such a period. But yes, sometimes the unlikely happens. The question is: Do you want to go with a low-probability occurrence for the reward of maybe outperforming 1.1 to 1?

Table 2.2   Stocks Versus Bonds (20-Year Rolling Periods)

Average Total Return Over 20-Year Rolling Periods	
US Stocks	909%
US Bonds	247%
Average Total Return Over 20-Year Rolling Periods When Bonds Outperformed Stocks	
US Stocks	239%
US Bonds	262%

Source: Global Financial Data, Inc., S&P 500 Total Return Index for US stocks, USA 10-Year Government Bond Total Return Index for US bonds from 12/31/26 to 12/31/09.

Table 2.3   When Bonds Beat Stocks—It's Not by Much

20-Year Periods When Bonds Outperformed Stocks	US Stocks	US Bonds
January 1, 1929, to December 31, 1948	74%	91%
January 1, 1989, to December 31, 2008	404%	433%

Source: Global Financial Data, Inc., S&P 500 Total Return Index for US stocks, USA 10-Year Government Bond Total Return Index for US bonds.

If you could go to Vegas and place a bet that 97 percent of the time paid out 3.7 to 1, or one that 3 percent of the time paid 1.1 to 1, you'd go with the 97 percent odds every time. You see that easily, but somehow that doesn't translate for most when it comes to volatility and stocks. Far too many folks rob themselves of likely better long-term results because they get blinded by near-term volatility. Said another way, you may feel like the wild wiggles keep you up at night now, but 10, 20, and 30 years from now, you don't want to lose sleep over having gotten inferior returns—because then you can't get over that. That's real pain.

Still, some folks just can't think about 20- and 30-year time horizons. Too long! Fine. Start training yourself by thinking just a bit longer term. Because even given just a bit of time, stocks start to have better and more consistently positive returns than bonds. (Remember Bunk 1.)

There will always be some folks who simply can't think longer term no matter what. The ulcers and the sleeplessness are just too much for them. That's fine! Folks who can't stomach volatility must lower their return expectations and make up for it through making more money other ways, or frugality, or something else that offsets lower future investment returns. No other way—you can't get stock-like returns without stock-like volatility. And if someone sells you on stock-like returns with materially less than stock-like risk, you must read Bunks 5 and 11 because you may be talking to a con artist. And being 100 percent ripped off will definitely cause you to lose a lot of sleep.

BUNK ③ RETIREES MUST BE CONSERVATIVE

Most investors understand that stocks are a great and appropriate investment vehicle—if they have a long time. So complete this sentence: "If I'm about to retire, I have a ____ time to invest." If you answered "long," congratulations—that's probably correct. If you answered "short" and you're correct, it means you don't have long to live and it is almost certainly a waste of your time to be reading this book. Go do something more important with your short time ahead.

For those still reading: Many folks in their late 50s and 60s—approaching retirement or already in it—have been coached by media and even industry professionals to think about their investing time horizons in a way that, in my view, is all wrong. Most people naturally think their investing time horizon ends when they retire, or when they stop contributing to their retirement funds, or when they start taking cash regularly from their portfolio. They think that's when they should reduce most if not all volatility risk—getting "conservative."

Longer Lives, Longer Time Horizons

In my view, that can frequently mean an unnecessary and sometimes serious reduction of quality of life later on. Why? Folks live longer than ever now, yet many invest, by and large, like they expect to die at age 70. Thanks to better nutrition and mind-blowing technological and medical innovations, folks just live to riper old ages today than even leading-edge thinkers fathomed 40 years ago. Recent IRS actuarial assumptions give today's average 65-year-old a median life expectancy of 85—see Figure 3.1. That means half will live longer. But my guess is even longer. Why? Same reason! Within those 20 years there will be still more medical advancements we can't fully fathom now. And today's retiree is just overall more fit, active, and healthy than even a generation ago when we didn't have so many "senior" sports.

So if you're 65 years old, you don't have a short time horizon. You have a long one! Longer still if you come from a long-living family and are in good health. Longer still if your spouse is younger! And longer still if your spouse is younger with great genes. Folks think reducing risk is smart—they're being safe and "conservative." (Note: There's no set definition of what "conservative" means—but plenty of folks see it as holding a less volatile mix of cash and bonds.)

It's true—having a portfolio full of Treasuries and cash won't be as volatile. (Though Treasury bonds can and do lose value in the near term, as they did in 2009. See Bunk 1.) But volatility risk is just one kind of risk. There's reinvestment risk—the risk that when your

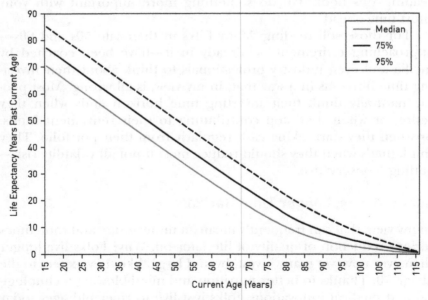

Figure 3.1   Life Expectancy—Keeps Getting Longer
Source: Internal Revenue Service.

bonds mature later on, short-term rates will have dropped, dragging down your expected future returns. Or that long-term rates will rise, reducing the value of bonds you hold that haven't matured yet.

There's also opportunity risk—the risk of missing out on a better investment. Said another way, it's the risk you run out of money because *you failed to plan for a long enough time horizon* and invested too "conservatively." Volatility may make you feel bad in the near term, but if you die before your spouse and fail to plan for her (or his) time horizon, I promise you, you'll seriously reduce her (or his) grieving period.

Aged Poverty Is Cruel!

I call investors who invest for too short a time horizon "wife haters"—because, first of all, ladies have longer life expectancies so they tend to end up with the dough in the end. And second, whether they mean to or not, when folks do this they're likely setting their widows up for aged poverty—or at least being worth markedly less than they would have been if they had planned for the surviving spouse's longer time horizon. And aged poverty is cruel. You don't want to gamble that you and your spouse will be just average and live another 20 years—then find out you're abnormally healthy, live another 30 years, and run out of money after 20. Plus, it's later in life that you'll want the additional comforts money can buy. Seen that way, investing too "conservatively" can be pretty darn risky and not conservative at all.

Most importantly, if you have a long time to invest (and most readers likely do), odds are in your favor when investing with stocks. Table 3.1 shows average returns for 1, 2, 3, and so on through 30 years for US stocks and bonds since 1926. The longer your time horizon, the better the odds stocks, historically, treated you better than cash or bonds—and by a wide margin. Simply, over 20 years, stocks almost never lag, and have averaged 908 percent returns to bonds' 247 percent. Over 30 years, it's no contest.

Most investors with a long time horizon—20 years or more—likely need at least some growth. And don't forget about inflation's impact! (Bunk 30.) Retirees who need their portfolios to stretch and grow to keep pace with inflation (or better) and provide some cash flow are doing themselves a disservice by removing all (or even most) volatility risk from their portfolios. Without risk, you can't get

Table 3.1 S&P 500 Returns Over Time

Time Periods	1 Year	2 Years	3 Years	4 Years	5 Years	10 Years	15 Years	20 Years	30 Years
Stocks have outperformed bonds	63%	67%	69%	69%	72%	82%	91%	97%	100%
Bonds have outperformed stocks	37%	33%	31%	31%	28%	18%	9%	3%	0%
Average stock market return (cumulative)	12%	24%	38%	54%	71%	209%	470%	908%	2,509%
Average 10-year gov't bond (cumulative)	6%	12%	18%	25%	32%	80%	149%	247%	524%

Source: Global Financial Data, Inc., S&P 500 Total Return Index for US stocks, USA 10-year Government Bond Total Return Index for US bonds from 12/31/26 to 12/31/09.

growth. And without growth, your portfolio can be ravaged over time by withdrawals and inflation. To help your portfolio survive the long haul, you likely need to hold some portion of your portfolio in stocks, most of the time. Because, after all, 65-year-olds aren't really old today and have long time horizons. The rest of their lives! And their spouses' too. Who knows? Maybe even a second or third spouse.

BUNK 4 AGE EQUALS ASSET ALLOCATION

There are thousands of books, seminars, and graduate theses on asset allocation. While professionals, academics, and amateurs have myriad different and frequently competing views on asset allocation, various popular prescriptions are driven entirely by age. For example, the popular saying: Take 100 (or 120), subtract your age, and that's the percentage you should have in stocks. Friends: Age is a factor, but by itself is not enough.

Is Age All That Matters?

If age were all that mattered, then two gentlemen aged 75 with similar-sized portfolios should have nearly the same asset allocations—always! If you're a financial-services professional, maybe you like this idea. First, it's less work for you—your client's age becomes the singular driver, and that's easy to figure out. Second, it provides you with cover. Clients can't complain you steered them wrong on allocation because you followed a simplistic equation. Neat!

If you've read Bunk 3, you already sense the age factor alone is wrong. Our two hypothetical 75-year-olds, Jim and Bob, have age and portfolio size in common but little else. Maybe Jim is a widower with one son. Jim doesn't care about maximizing his portfolio for his son. Jim's not mean—his kid is super-successful and rich in his own right and doesn't need the money. But Jim does need it to live on—anything left over is just gravy. Plus, Jim's parents died at age 68 and 72. Jim's not in failing health now, but he's had two heart attacks. His genes and health speak to a short-term time horizon ahead of him, not a long one.

Then there's Bob—his second wife is 60. Bob and his wife are in excellent health—play tennis daily. Plus, Bob's parents both lived to their late 90s. Bob has multiple sources of income—doesn't need cash from his portfolio. He wants it to help support his wife after he dies, but he figures she won't really need it either, so the rest goes to his kids from the first wife—ages 51 and 49—who will likely live another 35 to 45 years, maybe even longer.

Just two examples—neither unusual. There are millions more. Why should people with different goals, income needs, return expectations, family situations, life expectancies, you-name-it, have allocations determined just by their ages alone? Age is a factor, but just one. And the asset-allocation decision is vital—it determines your portfolio's benchmark—or what you're trying to accomplish with your portfolio.

A benchmark is, simply, a market index (like the S&P 500 or the MSCI World Index) or a bond index, or a blend of a stock and bond index. Your benchmark serves as a roadmap for building your portfolio, a risk management tool, and a measuring stick for performance. You don't always need to be exactly like your benchmark, but then you know you are taking deliberate moves away from the benchmark to satisfy some nearer-term goal—like taking a defensive position if you anticipate a bear market, or trying to capture additional upside in some category you have reason to believe is likely to outperform.

Determining Your Benchmark—Three Things

So when folks talk about "asset allocation," they're really also talking about their benchmark. So what determines your benchmark, if not age? Three primary things:

1. Time horizon
2. Return expectations
3. Cash flow needs

Time horizon (as you know from Bunk 3) is how long you need your assets to last. It is *not* some milestone in the future (e.g., retirement date, when you want to start taking cash flow, etc.). This is vital because your investing strategy should encompass the entirety of the life of your assets—*you don't want your assets to die before you do.* Or worse, before your spouse does.

Return expectations cover whether you want to see more or less growth, or maybe none. There are some investors who want *true* capital preservation (see Bunk 6), but that's very rare in my experience. Maybe you've got $50 million, live off $50,000 a year, aren't philanthropic, are in fact a misanthrope, and have no plans for your money. You're the rare person who actually can stuff it in your mattress—you have low return expectations. But most investors can't (or shouldn't) resort to the mattress. And if you're the person who can, you're very unlikely to be reading this book. Most folks need some growth—either to maximize the "terminal" value of their portfolios at the end of their time horizons or to help the portfolio stretch to provide needed cash flow. Or just to help combat inflation! (See Bunk 30.)

Which, then, brings us to *cash flow*—the third consideration. Many investors need their portfolio to cover living expenses, either now or at some future time. How much you need, and when, and for how long factors vitally into what an appropriate benchmark is.

There is a minor fourth consideration, but it usually amounts to small details. Some investors have social "needs" and prefer to not invest in, for example, "sin stocks," like tobacco or gambling—they need a benchmark ex-sin. Or some can't invest in certain stocks because they're on the board of directors for some firm. Or, because of their job, they have big exposure to their firm's stock. (See Bunk 34 on the perils of being over-exposed to one stock, including that of your employer.) They're important details, but usually amount to small tactical maneuvers rather than major strategic shifts.

Not once did I mention age. Age impacts your time horizon, of course. (But most investors fail to think about their time horizons correctly.) And time horizon is important, but so are return expectations and cash flow considerations. They all factor in. Reducing asset allocation decisions to the age of the investor alone leads to some serious errors—the kind that may take a long time to become evident, but when they do, can be difficult or nearly impossible to reverse. Errors like failing to plan for enough growth to cover increasing inflation-adjusted cash flow over the next 25 years, so two decades or so later, you find yourself radically reducing your quality of life. Ouch. Now that's some serious bunk.

BUNK 5 YOU SHOULD EXPECT AVERAGE RETURNS

One reason folks fall prey to investing con artists (more on this in Bunk 11) is they buy into the bewitching idea that consistently high and positive returns, year in, year out, are possible. Not just positive—but positive, high, smooth, and steady—dreamlike. Far too many folks are scammed (or make bad investment decisions that hurt later) because they believe it's reasonable to expect performance of 10 to 12 percent year after year. And why not? They know stocks over the long term have done that on average—give or take a bit depending on what time period you measure.

So just what's the harm in averaging 10 percent a year, anyway? Not a thing—over long time periods. The problem is certain scammers claim to get 10 to 12 percent *each and every year* (which is what Bernard Madoff claimed). Not on average. Regularly! Market is up 35 percent? They get 12 percent. And if markets fall 15 percent, they still get 10 percent. No surprises. No big up years, but no big down years either—ever. Smooth! Some poor folks believe the guy they found is just that good.

Some con artists bag victims by playing straight to greed. Unbelievably, they promise hugely above-average returns with little risk. But more play to humans' innate fear of volatility (and a little bit of greed) by claiming to get smooth, slightly above average but very, very consistent returns. Afterward, some of Madoff's victims claimed they thought they were being *conservative* by not demanding hugely above-average returns! But getting long-term average returns *every year* is a pipe dream—and that is easy to verify yourself through debunkery. Fact is: Average returns aren't normal. Normal yearly returns are extreme.

The average returns are made up of years that mostly vary wildly from the average. Again, *normal individual-year returns tend toward extremity*.

Normal Returns Are Extreme

Table 5.1 shows annual returns for the S&P 500 broken into return ranges and occurrences. Right away, you see "big" returns (annual returns above 20 percent) and negative returns together happen much more often than "average" returns. Individual years with returns close to "average" don't actually happen very often. One point the table doesn't show is stocks have returned anywhere from 10 percent to 12 percent in a year (which scammers want you to think is normal and not a red flag) only five times—1926, 1959, 1968, 1993, and 2004.[1] "Average" returns just aren't the norm. In fact, stocks are up big more than any other outcome—38.1 percent of the time. About two-thirds of all years, stocks are either up big or negative. Again, *normal annual returns are extreme*. It is hard to get people to accept the degree to which that's true.

Table 5.1 Average Returns Aren't Normal—Normal Returns Are Extreme

S&P 500 Annual Return Range			Occurrences Since 1926	Frequency	
	>	40%	5	6.0%	Big returns (38.1% of the time)
30%	to	40%	13	15.5%	
20%	to	30%	14	16.7%	
10%	to	20%	16	19.0%	"Average" returns (33.3% of the time)
0%	to	10%	12	14.3%	
−10%	to	0%	12	14.3%	Negative returns (28.6% of the time)
−20%	to	−10%	6	7.1%	
−30%	to	−20%	3	3.6%	
−40%	to	−30%	2	2.4%	
	<	−40%	1	1.2%	
Total Occurrences			84		
Simple Average			11.74%		
Annualized Average			9.70%		

Source: Global Financial Data Inc., S&P 500 total return from 12/31/25 to 12/31/2009.

It's possible to aim to get smooth, consistent returns. But you likely aren't going to get anything close to the market's long-term averages. If you want smoothness and consistency, you must accept a lower return expectation from bonds and cash-like investments. That's it!

And if you want to *average* about 10 percent a year, that's possible too—but you're going to have individual years with huge volatility around that. And it's still quite difficult to achieve even the market's long-term average. First, most investment managers fail to beat markets over time. Second, investors tend to find ways to harm themselves by chasing heat, switching strategies, or otherwise making decisions based on short-term emotions that impact their long-term performance—and effectively in-and-out the market and categories at exactly the wrong times. (Bunks 7, 17, and 18.)

But tactically, it's quite easy to get average returns in the long run. Just set your portfolio up to be mostly market-like and let it be. You won't beat the market, but you can get what the market doles out, which, over time, is likely to be better than bonds or another similarly liquid asset class—or what most of your friends do—or what most professionals do.

But that means experiencing some uncomfortable down years and big up years. Let me say that again: To my knowledge, no one has ever achieved market-like returns without some market-like downside. If you want to achieve something close to stocks' long-term average, you must accept downside volatility. No way around that. Normal returns are extreme.

BUNK 6 "CAPITAL PRESERVATION AND GROWTH" IS POSSIBLE!

... and I've got a unicorn to sell you.

"Capital preservation and growth" is something the investment industry babbles about a lot and folks crave—but it works as well as a one-calorie dessert. Basically, it's the idea you can get some moderate amount of growth while preserving your capital and not experiencing pesky near-term volatility. Sounds wonderful! Most of the taste but none of the fat or calories! Everybody wants it. And many attempt it. But the result is far from what you'd like it to be. It sounds great but just isn't possible. No more real than Santa Claus. Yet I'm consistently astounded at how many people—professionals even—believe this bunk.

True capital preservation requires absence of volatility risk—no downside, but basically no upside either. Because the one requires the other. I specify *volatility* risk because there are many kinds of risk—volatility is just one. There's interest rate risk—that rates fall so when a bond matures you either must accept a lower yield or reinvest into something higher risk to get a similar yield. There's also opportunity cost—the risk of not having *enough* risk, so you miss out on an alternative with potentially better longer-term performance going forward. Or inflation risk. There are near endless risk types—but folks aiming to preserve capital are usually most concerned with volatility.

For example, you could buy US Treasuries and hold them to maturity—that would be a capital preservation strategy. You wouldn't want to actively trade them—even US Treasuries can and do lose value. (See Bunk 1.) Make no mistake—you can experience near-term volatility even with Treasuries.

Still, buying and holding Treasuries to maturity would preserve capital, but likely yield little. As I write this in 2010, 10-year Treasury rates are under 3 percent. Even a little inflation wiggle could wipe that out. Yet that's still better than what you get in a money market account—likely less than 1 percent in 2010. *That's* capital preservation.

True Capital Preservation as a Goal Is Very Rare

In my experience, capital preservation as a long-term goal is rare. Most people want some growth—whether to simply outpace inflation, improve the odds their portfolios stretch to provide cash flow long term, or maximize their portfolios to leave more to kids, grandkids charities, the save-the-manatees league—whomever or whatever. The degree of growth investors want varies, but *some* growth is a more common goal. Real capital preservation, as the term is usually applied, still means you can lose purchasing power—through the ravages of an uptick in inflation (Bunk 30). Never forget—at a pretty normal 3 percent inflation rate, a buck today would be worth about half that in 20 years. That's why true capital preservation is actually a fairly rare goal.

Over short periods, it's totally different! For example, lots of folks have very short time horizons for certain pools of assets (e.g., when saving for a down payment for a house in a year or two). Then it makes good sense to take little risk. Stocks can and do correct fast even during bull markets. To quickly fall 17 or 18 percent or so and recover is normal—but that can be devastating for short-term money. And if you're saving to buy a house, that *is* short-term money.

But to get growth, even a modest amount, you must accept some volatility risk, which means stepping away from the concept of true capital preservation. Doesn't have to be all stocks! You could have 10 percent of your portfolio in stocks and the rest in Treasuries. That might give you some growth—not much overall. But still, even in that overall fairly nonvolatile portfolio, the stock portion would be volatile and you would have stepped away from pure capital preservation.

"Capital preservation and growth" as a goal is a lie. No nice way to say that. If someone sells it to you, they're either a charlatan or misinformed. If the first, run away. If the second, still run away. Do you want someone managing your money who doesn't understand the very simplest basics of finance theory and economic fundamentals?

Let me completely reverse everything I've just said and say that, yes, capital preservation and growth *as an outcome* is possible. Over long periods, if you've grown your portfolio, you've also inherently preserved capital, looking backward. In all the 20-year periods since 1926, stocks have never been negative at the end.[1] (See Bunk 1, 2, or 3.) Not once. Some periods, stocks have had bigger growth than others, but always *some* growth. But achieving growth and capital preservation that way comes from and is linked directly to the growth goal. It has nothing to do with a capital preservation goal. It's subject to complete stock market volatility in the short term—and it's not what people normally think of when they think of "capital preservation."

If your aim is truly to preserve capital in the short term, you can't get much growth at all. History says the best way to get growth and, as a secondary benefit, preserve your capital is via stocks and thinking very long term.

BUNK 7 TRUST YOUR GUT

Ever had a gut feeling? You just *knew* you should buy XYZ stock but didn't—whatever reason—then it skyrocketed 300 percent. Or you *knew* to sell ABC stock—but ignored your instinct—then it plummeted 80 percent. You have these feelings all the time, and they're usually right—as you recall. But that's also almost certainly your mind being your worst enemy and playing tricks on you.

There's a major school of behavioral psychology now, called *behavioral finance*, dedicated to understanding how our brains evolved—to deal with basic problems of human survival—and why that leads to serious investing errors. Whole books have been and will be written on the topic, and it was the basis for my third question in my 2006 book, *The Only Three Questions That Count*.

Selective Memory and Other Messy Biases

Our brains produce some very basic bunk, making it difficult to deal with counterintuitive problems like publicly traded markets. And one major bit of bunk is the notion you should trust your gut. First, I'd ask if you *really* knew XYZ would rise so much. Or did you have a passing thought and built up your conviction only much later, after the fact? (Usually, it's the latter.) Or do you suffer from *hindsight bias*? You were convinced in your gut that fully 20 different stocks were surefire winners, but in the end, they were all losers except XYZ. But you conveniently forget the ones you were wrong about, and remember the one that lets you crow about being a genius. That happens often—much more often than not—but your brain never catalogs it. (Many investing newsletters make this a regular practice, saying, "If you'd bought these six stocks we recommended, you'd be up a bajillion percent!" They conveniently don't mention the other 874 stocks they touted that did badly.)

Investors tend to put a lot of stock (pun intended) in *gut feelings*—that gripping feeling to react NOW. It helped keep our ancestors alive. It's called "fight or flight." When a wild beast charged, they reacted immediately with flight. Or, if it was small enough, they pulled out a spear and took it home for dinner. It's the instinct to "just do something"—and it worked for our long-distant ancestors.

Clients tell me all the time—and I mean regularly—when I've been wrong that they knew "the whole time" I was wrong. But they rarely did know the whole time. Instead they're likely falling prey to hindsight and convenient memory. What really happened, almost always, was they hoped I was right and feared I was wrong, a perfectly natural instinct. That *fear* I was wrong in their minds morphed into them *knowing* I was wrong. The mind is a cruel trickster when it comes to markets.

In focus groups my firm runs on investors who are serious "hobbyist" investors and CEO types, we can document a tremendous propensity for investors to believe they knew 2007 to 2009 would go down the way it did—as a disaster bear market—and that "anyone could have seen it if they just used common sense and good instincts." Of course, if they really knew, they would have sold out instead of getting hammered. Their memories play tricks on them.

Losses Feel Worse Than Gains Feel Good

It's been measured and proven that US investors feel the pain of loss fully two and a half times as intensely as they enjoy the pleasure of gain.[1] So a 10 percent loss feels about as bad as a 25 percent gain feels good—on average. On paper, that looks ridiculous. Your gut disagrees. And because for our ancestors, avoiding the risk of immediate pain increased longevity, investors' guts tend to tell them to get out of the way if they fear a near-term loss—or a charging wildebeest. There's even a term for it—*myopic loss aversion.* Another way to say that is "aggressive short-sightedness."

In cooler moments, most investors with long-term growth goals agree they should think long term and ignore near-term wiggles. And they plan to. They have ice in their veins! But in the midst of volatility, more primal instincts take over—they want to take action to remove the threat of near-term pain, *even if it costs them future returns.* Why? Because that near-term pain feels so much darn worse than they can imagine those future gains will feel pleasant. Again, investors articulate notions like, "Don't just sit there; do something." It's fight or flight. But sometimes doing nothing is doing something—and the best thing you can do.

Here's an example: 1998 was a terrific year for US and world stocks. If you took a pill that knocked you out from January 1 until December 31—an entire year—it would have seemed glorious! But if you were conscious, it was trying. It started fine—world stocks shot nearly straight up 22 percent by mid-July.[2] But folks feared a financial crisis in Asia that started in 1997 would bleed to the rest of the world—particularly since it led Russia to default on its debt and devalue the ruble (the famous "Russian Ruble crisis"). Debt woes trickled west, pushing huge and super-leveraged US hedge fund Long-Term Capital Management to the brink of default. Folks feared if LTCM failed, it could take down the US financial system—and world stocks went through a stomach-churning correction—down 20 percent in just 11 weeks![3] Yikes!

But corrections move fast because they're grounded in sentiment, not fundamentals—and sentiment changes fast. Folks quickly got over their fears, and world stocks exploded back up 27 percent to finish the year up a big 24.3 percent overall (28.6 percent for US stocks).[4] Investors who ignored their gut and stayed invested were rewarded—hugely. Investors who panicked and sold to stop the pain likely sold at a relative low, and most likely didn't buy back fast—not in time for the fast rebound. Plus, they had to pay transaction fees and maybe taxes. Ouch!

Figure 7.1 shows 1998 global market returns. The solid arrow shows from start to finish, stocks did nicely! But it was no straight shot—stocks rarely climb in steady, smooth steps. The dashed lines show the huge, scary drop and the similarly fast rebound. And as big as the drop was, it felt, for most investors, more than twice as bad. If stocks fell 20 percent, it felt like a 50 percent free fall—or worse—for most folks. That's serious terror. The big surge after was nice, but it felt like what it was—a big, 24 percent move. Nice—but not as nice as the plummet *felt* bad.

And you know that's wrong. The year was up big. That's what matters, not trying to dance around a lightning-fast down-up. But when it happens, our ancestral brains want to take over and do

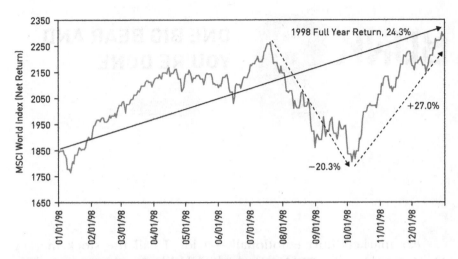

Figure 7.1   A Fine Year for Stocks—1998 Was Up 24.3%

Source: Thomson Reuters, MSCI Inc.,[5] MSCI World Index total return with net dividends from 12/31/97 to 12/31/98.

something. Folks like to think it's possible to time corrections. If it is, no professional has done it consistently over a long time period—ever. So all you'll likely do in trusting your gut and selling out at relative lows is pay more transaction fees and rob yourself of future gains. Sometimes, doing nothing is the most active strategy you can have. Folks think doing nothing is always easy—but it's not! (See Bunk 17.) And that's why it can pay off.

Next time you're tempted to go with your gut, remember: Your Stone Age brain may be good with physical risk, but it is also the same one that governs your investment gut—and it's a truly lousy investment manager.

BUNK 8 ONE BIG BEAR AND YOU'RE DONE

Bear markets hurt emotionally—a lot. I call the stock market The Great Humiliator (TGH). And TGH likes nothing more than scaring as many people out of as many dollars for as long as it can—before it goes up (or down). A bear market is TGH at its absolute deadliest.

TGH robs people of returns any way it can. First, near term, you're down big. Huge unrealized losses. Utter humiliation, fear, and agony. Also, TGH knows people hate losses more than they love gains. Therefore, bear markets are so painful they make folks do crazy things that ultimately hurt them—for most of them, much worse in the long term than if they simply sat on their hands. Things like capitulation-selling at the absolute low. Far too many investors, on their own, do this to their heavy detriment—often in the name of "waiting for clarity." Or, in the depths of bear market agony, many investors suddenly decide they can't handle big stock volatility anymore (or whatever the myriad other reasons) and change their long-term strategy to hold a bunch of cash and bonds, right in time to miss the huge stock market bounce off the bottom. (Read more in Bunk 9.) And maybe a bunch of those investors even swear off stocks for years, then change their minds again late in the next bull market (missing most of the upside), thinking they've gained a new sense of "clarity" that will evaporate (again) in the subsequent bear—which whacks them (again). TGH is cruelly perverse.

Another variation: Some say they'll stay with stocks until they "get back to even" or hit some other arbitrary milestone, and *then* they'll change their strategy—hold cash and bonds because "bonds are safer." (Maybe not—remember Bunk 1.) But if they think stocks are the right asset class to get the growth they need to return to their portfolio high-water mark (or some other arbitrary level) in the near term, then why don't they think stocks can get superior growth longer term? This, too, is perverse. Near term, myopic goals imply a short investment time horizon, for which stocks are almost never appropriate. Longer-term goals imply a longer time horizon, for which stocks are—more often than not—most appropriate. Many investors have trouble thinking this through.

Big Bear Markets Mean a Big Bull Bounce

Facts are: If you have a long time horizon (if you're reading this book, you likely do—see Bunk 3) and goals requiring equity-like growth, a bear market doesn't change that at all—or much of anything relative to what you should do moving forward. What folks fear is being in a hole they can't get out of. They know if stocks drop 25 percent, it doesn't take a 25 percent up-move to breakeven—it takes 33 percent. It takes nearly 43 percent to recover from a 30 percent drop. And if stocks fall huge, as they did from October 2007 to March 2009 (down 58 percent[1]), it takes a 138 percent move just to get to breakeven, not to mention getting any real growth from there. And after all the problems newly envisioned and emerged during the bear market, they have a nearly impossible time fathoming stocks rallying that much—TGH at work again. It never changes.

Is it scary? Sure. Impossible? Nah—something we've seen endlessly through history. Bear markets are normal—happen periodically. Sometimes they're bigger than others. But through history, stocks fall—even huge—then recover and hit new highs again and keep going. If bear markets were unrecoverable, stocks would only fall—but they don't. They rise more than fall, and eventually (and irregularly) keep marching higher over time. And almost always, the bigger the bear market decline, the bigger the subsequent bull market. That isn't always true, but usually is. And even when it isn't, you're better off with whatever subsequent bull market returns you get than if you bailed at the bottom and stagnated in cash—always.

Maybe you think, "It's different this time"—Sir John Templeton's famous "four most dangerous words" in investing. It's almost never different this time in any basic way. Yes, details differ, but the fundamentals driving stocks don't. And human behavior is pretty darn predictable in the way we react to bear market fright. So over long periods, stocks should keep rising overall, with intermittent downside volatility, big and small.

Remember: The future includes as-of-yet unimagined earnings from currently unfathomed products and services born of the boundlessness of human ingenuity, innovation, and desires in years to come. Always been that way. Forever, people have been moaning about stocks being too high and Capitalism done. Fine—but every single time they've been proven wrong. If you're betting with long-term capital, I suggest you bet on the side of it *not* being much, if any, different this time—despite it always feeling different (and the media always giving you countless reasons for why it is now and will be different).

Often the popular conclusion is that social and political trends will overwhelm Capitalism. That isn't a new view. Yet—not always, but almost always in democratic nations globally—Capitalism has ended up more powerful than politicians, social trends, and temporary political will—and wins out in the end. (A concept Steve Forbes depicted very well in his terrific 2009 book, *How Capitalism Will Save Us*, published by Crown Business, 2009.)

Fooled by Averages

One reason many fear bear markets are insurmountable is they're fooled by averages. (A similar problem for those who believe they should "sell in May"—see Bunk 25.) Long term, stocks have averaged about 10 percent per year—give or take a bit (depending on what time period you measure and how you measure it). So if you need 33 percent, 45 percent, or 140 percent to get back to even, that seems like it would take a really, really long time. Except—and people can't seem to get this—the stock market's long-term average *includes bear markets*. Let me say that again—stocks have been down huge during past bear markets, yet still they averaged about 10 percent a year. Why? Normal stock returns aren't average—they're extreme, both up and down, normally! (See Bunk 5.) Folks can somehow accept that stocks can be down a lot—so why can't they remember they're often up a lot too?

This is basic debunkery—looking beneath the averages to what comprises them. Always do that. Bull markets are longer and

Table 8.1 Bull Market Returns—Inherently Above Average

Trough	Peak	Duration (Months)*	Annualized Returns	Cumulative Returns
06/01/32	03/06/37	57	35%	324%
04/28/42	05/29/46	49	26%	158%
06/13/49	08/02/56	85	20%	267%
10/22/57	12/12/61	50	16%	86%
06/26/62	02/09/66	43	18%	80%
10/07/66	11/29/68	26	20%	48%
05/26/70	01/11/73	32	23%	74%
10/03/74	11/28/80	74	14%	126%
08/12/82	08/25/87	60	27%	229%
12/04/87	07/16/90	31	21%	65%
10/11/90	03/24/00	113	19%	417%
10/09/02	10/09/07	60	15%	101%
Bull Market Average		**57**	**21%**	**164%**

*For duration, a month equals 30.5 days.
Source: Global Financial Data, Inc., S&P 500 price return.

stronger than people think. Another way to say that: Bull market returns are inherently above average. Have to be—to make up for the big down years. Table 8.1 shows returns for all bull markets since 1926. On average, bull market returns annualize 21 percent! And though duration varies wildly, they last much longer than many think.

Plus, the bigger a bear market, the bigger and swifter the returns can be—and usually are—off the bottom. (See Bunk 9.) People think, "Well, I went through that big bear market and am down big. Now I must hold mostly cash and bonds to protect myself from future potential risk." Wrong—looking backward tells you nothing about what happens next. Investors should look forward, always, and consider what their long-term goals are, free from TGH's bear market freak-out fears. Don't be fooled by averages. Bear markets can be big, but bull markets are longer and stronger and likely will be as prevalent in our future as in our past.

BUNK 9 MAKE SURE IT'S A BULL BEFORE DIVING IN

Suppose it's a bear market. The big, the bad, and the ugly one! Maybe you've stayed invested throughout—that sure hurts near term. Plus, bear market volatility is huge and scary. Should you bail, wait out the end, then get back in when the signs are clearer? (Another question: Are you that good a market timer?)

Or maybe you're out and know you need to get back in. But when? All that whipsawing is beyond terrifying. Better to just wait until it's certain the bear market is over, a new bull has begun, and all is clear, right?

No—as counterintuitive as it seems, risk is actually least just when sentiment is most black—right as a bear market hits its lowest depths. Clarity is one of the most expensive things to purchase in capital markets and is almost always an illusion.

No one can perfectly time a bear market bottom. Someone telling you otherwise is deluding himself (or herself) or trying to mislead you (see Bunk 11). Or got lucky once. As painful as the wild wiggles of a late bear market are in the near term, you don't want to miss the start of a new bull market. New bull market returns are super swift and massive—quickly erasing almost all late-stage downside volatility. If you suffer the last 15 to 20 percent of a bear market, it is still, almost certainly, small compared to the subsequent initial up-leg of the next bull market.

Think of a bear market like a depressed spring. The more you push down, the bigger the bounce. It works just like that. Figure 9.1 shows this effect—a hypothetical bear market bottom/new bull. Initially, deteriorating fundamentals drive the bear. Folks think bear markets start with a bang—they usually don't. They grind lower

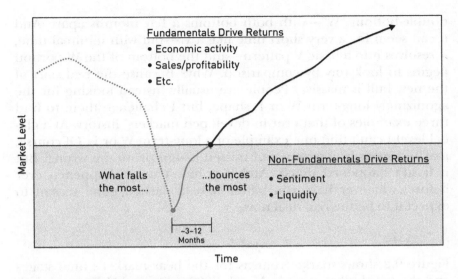

Figure 9.1 Hypothetical V-Bounce

Note: For illustrative purposes only. Not drawn to scale. Not to be interpreted as a forecast.

slowly. It's the end when the bang comes. At a point, diminishing liquidity (like we saw in the fall of 2008 during the financial crisis) and sentiment take over from fundamentals—and, in fact, panic ensues. But panic is usually nothing but sentiment and the temporary lack of liquidity that goes with the sentiment shift and is often confused with something fundamental.

Right then, stocks can drop huge and fast. But as a new bull market starts, the reverse can happen just as fast—stocks zoom higher on sentiment as things aren't quite as bad as freaked-out folks feared and liquidity returns with it. The big initial boom happens not because things are good or improving, but because they end up being not quite as much of a disaster as assumed in the panic. Stocks take off like a bullet—the shape of the new bull market about matching the speed and shape of the end of the bear. I call this the "V-bounce" effect.

(Another common V characteristic: In the late stages of a bear, when sentiment is driving big volatility, those categories that fall most tend to bounce most in the early part of the new bull. Read more on that in Bunk 19 in Part 2.)

It's not just theory—we see the V through history. Sometimes, bear markets end in what chart watchers or technicians call a double-bottom "W"—with both bottoms a few months apart. And it can seem for a very short time like a W—but with minimal time, it resolves into a basic V pattern—and the bottom of the W portion begins to look tiny by comparison. Why? Because the real start of the new bull is massive. People are usually instead looking for the agonizingly long-term W or L shape, but I challenge them to find three examples of that ever in developed markets' history. At a global level I can't find one example of a long-term W or L. Of course, maybe I measured wrong and missed it—go prove me wrong. But it hasn't happened much. And if it hasn't much happened ever before, whatever it is, you better have a darned good reason to expect it to be the real deal now.

A Classic V

Figure 9.2 shows market returns for the bear market's final stages and the new bull starting in March 2009—a typical V. For a period, the trajectory of the new bull nearly perfectly mirrors the late stage of the bear.

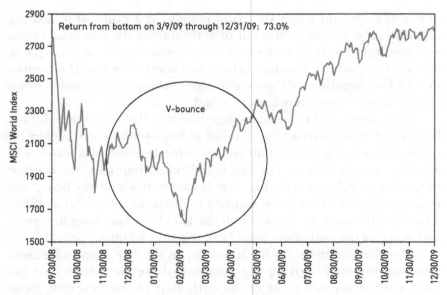

Figure 9.2   World Stocks—V-Bounce Effect 2009

Source: Thomson Reuters, MSCI, Inc.,[1] MSCI World Index total return with net dividends from 09/30/2008 to 12/31/2009.

A normal V. In one sense, abnormal, because US and global stocks had a historically massive bounce off the bottom—68 percent and 73 percent respectively from March 9 through year end—an unusually huge start to this bull.[2] But the preceding bear market was huge too. The initial ascent of a new bull usually just about matches the speed, shape, and descent of the last stages of the prior bear—just what you see in Figure 9.2. Look at the very end of the bear and the beginning of the bull—almost a perfect V.

Being invested for the first initial thrust of a bull market can help eat away a big portion of bear market losses—and fast. The ancestral part of our brains says, "Yikes! We fell a lot! Let's protect ourselves so we can't fall more!" If we act on that, it can make us feel better immediately. But it can rob us of the huge returns we normally get off the bottom of a bear market with the V bounce.

Table 9.1 shows how massive those early returns can be—averaging 21.8 percent in the first three months, and 44.8 percent in the first 12 months. That's big and fast. And in this case, unlike Bunk 5, the averages aren't so misleading because the first 12 months are consistently big and fast—obviously some bigger and faster than others, but all big and fast nonetheless. A bull market's average first year more than *doubles* an average overall bull market year (which, over

Table 9.1 First 3 and 12 Months of a New Bull Market—A Big Early Bounce

Bull Market Start	Bull Market End	First 3 Months' Return	First 12 Months' Return
06/01/1932	03/06/1937	92.3%	120.9%
04/28/1942	05/29/1946	15.4%	53.7%
06/13/1949	08/02/1956	16.2%	42.0%
10/22/1957	12/12/1961	5.7%	31.0%
06/26/1962	02/09/1966	7.3%	32.7%
10/07/1966	11/29/1968	12.3%	32.9%
05/26/1970	01/11/1973	17.2%	43.7%
10/03/1974	11/28/1980	13.5%	38.0%
08/12/1982	08/25/1987	36.2%	58.3%
12/04/1987	07/16/1990	19.4%	21.4%
10/11/1990	03/24/2000	6.7%	29.1%
10/09/2002	10/09/2007	19.4%	33.7%
03/09/2009	????	39.3%	68.6%
Average		**21.8%**	**44.8%**

Source: Global Financial Data, Inc., S&P 500 price return.

time, doubles stocks' long-term average—see Bunk 8). And almost half those first-year returns usually (but not always) come in the first three months!

And here, too, the market is tricky. Because on the occasions when the first three months aren't so straight up, folks are prone to think it's a sign the big boom will never come. This is just the market head-faking folks in another of its standard tactics. Sometimes when the bottom is choppy on the left side of the V it is also choppy on the right side, discouraging investors. But the V pretty much always works over a year.

Missing those huge early returns while waiting for some illusory sense of "clarity" means missing your chance to erase a big portion of your prior bear market losses. Plus, it also hurts you relative to your benchmark. If you've suffered the bumps and agony of a bear market, those early big returns are a welcome salve. They may not undo all of the bear market, but they certainly put you on the way. And missing them can mean it takes *even longer* to erase bear market losses—maybe forever.

There is no bull market "all clear" signal. If there were, we'd know, and everyone would heed it. Look at Figure 9.2 again (the 2009 bear bottom). The opportunity cost of missing even the first three months can be massive and lasting. Volatility is huge on *both* sides of the V bottom. It's only in retrospect you know which volatility you're suffering through—late bear or early bull. You can't know, so don't miss it. You'll regret it later.

BUNK 10 GROWTH IS BEST FOR ALL TIME. NO, VALUE. NO, SMALL CAPS

Many investors, even professionals, have an investing size and/or style they favor. Large cap. Small cap. Small value. Mid-growth. Maybe they're more specific—only investing in large Tech firms. Small Midwestern banks. Mid-cap Consumer Discretionary, but only if they're value and German.

Money managers and mutual funds often offer "products" adhering to strict size and/or style guidelines. And there's nothing wrong with that. That's how the institutional world functions and has for decades. Except, typically, institutional clients will ensure they have exposure to essentially all the major styles and sizes (growth and value in small, mid, and large cap, domestic and foreign, and all the standard sectors). When institutions do that, they typically either do these slices passively or hire what they consider to be best-of-breed portfolio managers in each category. But many individual investors, even professionals, mistakenly think their favored size and/or style is tops—the best for all time—and will continue being best going forward. And they invest solely or mostly in that particular size/style/category. A major mistake!

Chasing Heat

Interestingly, for most folks, attachment to a category usually coincides with a run in that size/style that has gone on for some years. At the end of the 1990s, plenty of folks were hot on large growth stocks—because large growth had done so well for so long—and particularly those with a Tech tinge. Except, shortly thereafter, large growth and Tech got crushed in the 2000–2003 bear. In the early

2000s, small cap was a favorite again. Then, for most of the 2003–2007 bull market, foreign stocks led the way. Suddenly everyone wanted foreign and you heard endlessly how the US was done. (A repeat of what folks said during the 1980s, only to see the US lead for most of the 1990s.) Then, in 2008, foreign stocks were among the worst categories.[1]

That's not to say a hot category must turn cold next year. No! The point is: Some categories lead for a long time. When they do, they gather adherents who want to think that category is simply and inherently superior—forever. Pure bunk!

Figure 10.1 looks like a crazy mish-mosh quilt with no discernible pattern. It shows major asset classes (large cap US, large cap foreign, large US growth, small value, bonds, etc., etc.[2]) and how they performed each year relative to other categories (the best category each year is on top, the worst on the bottom). So, in 1990, bonds did best (Barclays Aggregate is an investment-grade bond index), and foreign stocks (MSCI EAFE) did worst. The boxes move around. Sometimes one style does best for a while, then gets buried. But no one box dominates.

All major categories (properly constructed) change leadership, irregularly. Nonetheless, folks love citing data supporting their beloved category. For example, it's true that since 1926, small cap stocks have outperformed the market as a whole![3] Evidence small cap is inherently better—or is it? A lot of that outperformance is tied to terribly tiny stocks—ones most investors wouldn't hold because of illiquidity issues and increased risk. Plus, early on, tiny stocks had huge bid-ask spreads that ate up return if you actually bought and sold them, but aren't adjusted for in index returns. In the 1930s and 1940s, when much of that supposed outperformance occurred, bid-ask spreads for the small stocks involved were often 20 percent to 30 percent of the price of the stock! So if you actually bought them, there went the return. Then, too, small cap stocks tend to lead early on coming out of bear markets. If you strip out the biggest small cap booms (1932–1935, 1942–1945, 1974–1976, and 2002–2004), large cap stocks overall beat small caps—and typically for agonizingly long periods. And if you can time markets well enough to pick those times—the early phases of new bull markets usually—there are lots of other ways to beat the market too.

If you believed the hype that small cap or even small cap value stocks are permanently better based on the averages, you likely went through agonizingly long periods when you got whacked by other

1990	1991	1992	1993	1994	1995	1996	1997	1998	1999	2000	2001	2002	2003	2004	2005	2006	2007	2008	2009
Barclays Agg [illegible]	Russell 2000 Growth 51.2%	Russell 2000 Value 29.1%	MSCI EAFE 32.6%	MSCI EAFE 7.8%	S&P/Citi Growth 39.4%	S&P/Citi Growth 25.7%	S&P/Citi Growth 33.5%	S&P/Citi Growth 41.0%	Russell 2000 Growth 43.1%	Russell 2000 Value 22.8%	Russell 2000 Value 14.0%	Barclays Agg [illegible]	Russell 2000 Growth 48.5%	Russell 2000 Value 22.2%	MSCI EAFE 13.5%	MSCI EAFE 26.3%	MSCI EAFE 11.2%	Barclays Agg [illegible]	S&P/Citi Growth 34.6%
S&P/Citi Growth 2.6%	Russell 2000 46.0%	Russell 2000 18.4%	Russell 2000 Value 23.8%	S&P/Citi Growth 3.9%	S&P 500 Index 37.6%	S&P/Citi Value [illegible]	S&P 500 Index 33.4%	S&P 500 Index 28.6%	S&P/Citi Growth 35.9%	Barclays Agg [illegible]	Barclays Agg [illegible]	Russell 2000 Value −11.4%	Russell 2000 47.3%	MSCI EAFE 20.2%	S&P/Citi Value [illegible]	Russell 2000 Value 23.5%	S&P/Citi Growth 10.3%	Russell 2000 Value −28.9%	Russell 2000 Growth 34.5%
S&P 500 Index −3.1%	S&P/Citi Growth 44.1%	S&P/Citi Value 9.5%	Russell 2000 18.9%	S&P 500 Index 1.3%	S&P/Citi Value 37.2%	S&P 500 Index 23.0%	Russell 2000 Value 31.8%	MSCI EAFE 20.0%	MSCI EAFE 27.0%	S&P/Citi Value 6.5%	Russell 2000 2.5%	MSCI EAFE −15.9%	Russell 2000 Value 46.0%	Russell 2000 18.3%	S&P 500 Index 4.9%	S&P/Citi Value 19.7%	Russell 2000 Growth 7.1%	Russell 2000 −33.8%	MSCI EAFE 31.8%
S&P/Citi Value −4.9%	Russell 2000 Value 41.7%	Russell 2000 Growth 7.8%	S&P/Citi Value 16.6%	S&P/Citi Value −0.6%	Russell 2000 Growth 31.0%	Russell 2000 Value 21.4%	S&P/Citi Value 31.5%	S&P/Citi Value [illegible]	Russell 2000 21.3%	Russell 2000 −3.0%	Russell 2000 Growth −9.2%	S&P/Citi Value −16.2%	MSCI EAFE 38.6%	S&P/Citi Value [illegible]	Russell 2000 Value 4.7%	Russell 2000 18.4%	Barclays Agg [illegible]	S&P/Citi Growth −35.5%	Russell 2000 27.2%
Russell 2000 Growth −17.4%	S&P 500 Index 30.5%	S&P 500 Index 7.6%	Russell 2000 Growth 13.4%	Russell 2000 Value −1.5%	Russell 2000 28.5%	Russell 2000 16.5%	Russell 2000 22.4%	Barclays Agg [illegible]	S&P 500 Index 21.0%	S&P 500 Index −9.1%	S&P/Citi Value −9.6%	Russell 2000 −20.5%	S&P/Citi Value 31.6%	Russell 2000 Growth 14.3%	Russell 2000 4.6%	S&P 500 Index 15.8%	S&P 500 Index 5.5%	S&P 500 Index −37.0%	S&P 500 Index 26.5%
Russell 2000 −19.5%	S&P/Citi Value 22.2%	Barclays Agg [illegible]	S&P 500 Index 10.1%	Russell 2000 −1.8%	Russell 2000 Value 25.7%	Russell 2000 Growth 11.3%	Russell 2000 Growth 12.9%	Russell 2000 Growth 1.2%	S&P/Citi Value 4.7%	MSCI EAFE −14.2%	S&P 500 Index −11.9%	S&P 500 Index −22.1%	S&P 500 Index 28.7%	S&P 500 Index 10.9%	Russell 2000 Growth 4.2%	Russell 2000 Growth 13.4%	S&P/Citi Value 1.9%	Russell 2000 Growth −38.5%	S&P/Citi Value [illegible]
Russell 2000 Value −21.8%	Barclays Agg [illegible]	S&P/Citi Growth 4.5%	Barclays Agg [illegible]	Russell 2000 Growth −2.4%	Barclays Agg [illegible]	MSCI EAFE 6.0%	Barclays Agg [illegible]	Russell 2000 −2.5%	Barclays Agg [illegible]	S&P/Citi Growth −22.2%	S&P/Citi Growth −19.5%	S&P/Citi Growth −30.2%	S&P/Citi Growth 26.8%	S&P/Citi Growth 6.3%	Barclays Agg [illegible]	S&P/Citi Growth 11.4%	Russell 2000 −1.6%	S&P/Citi Value [illegible]	Russell 2000 Value 20.6%
MSCI EAFE −23.4%	MSCI EAFE 12.1%	MSCI EAFE −12.2%	S&P/Citi Growth 0.2%	Barclays Agg [illegible]	MSCI EAFE 11.2%	Barclays Agg [illegible]	MSCI EAFE 1.8%	Russell 2000 Value −6.5%	Russell 2000 Value −1.5%	Russell 2000 Growth −22.4%	MSCI EAFE −21.4%	Russell 2000 Growth −30.3%	Barclays Agg [illegible]	Barclays Agg [illegible]	S&P/Citi Growth 2.3%	Barclays Agg [illegible]	Russell 2000 Value −9.8%	MSCI EAFE −43.4%	Barclays Agg [illegible]

Figure 10.1 No One Style Is Best for All Time

Source: Thomson Reuters.[2]

styles. (Another debunkery trick: Always look beyond the averages to what makes them up.) For example, from the mid-1980s through 2000, a very long time, small cap value lagged badly. By 2000, few believed in small value—everyone was hot on big cap and Tech— almost the exact opposite of small value! (I admit, I've always loved small value. It's where I got my career momentum, and my firm still manages billions of dollars in that style. But I don't and haven't believed in decades that it was somehow long-term superior. It's just another category).

Large cap isn't inherently better either—although there is a huge realm of investors who think so. All equity categories, over very long periods, should net similar returns, though taking different paths. Why? Supply and demand. Also, investment bankers.

Supply and Demand (and Investment Bankers)

Stock prices, like everything else we buy in free markets, are driven by supply and demand. Near term, stock supply is relatively fixed. Initial public offerings (IPOs) and new stock issuances take tremendous time, effort, and regulatory input—and they get announced well ahead of time, so over the next 12 to 18 months, you don't get big, unexpected stock supply swings. That's when demand rules, driven largely by fickle sentiment—getting more positive or negative—which can happen super fast. (Remember the big, fast 1998 correction in Bunk 7? That's how fast sentiment can move.)

But longer term, supply pressures simply swamp all else. Stock supply can expand or shrink nearly endlessly over the long term in perfectly unpredictable patterns—increasing through issuances or shrinking through buybacks and cash- or debt-based takeovers. And for supply, you need investment bankers. Investment bankers are much maligned as I write in 2010, but they serve a useful societal purpose in helping firms access capital markets. And you want firms to have access to capital markets so they can grow, innovate, hire more people, and so on—or to buy back their stock when it is too cheap, or take over competitors when *they're* too cheap. (If you don't like those things, you need a different book and maybe a therapist.) And investment bankers, like most everyone else, like turning profits. And they do it, in part, by helping firms issue new shares or new debt (or in some cases by destroying supply of securities through buybacks, mergers, acquisitions, etc.).

So when one category starts getting more interest—like Tech in the late 1990s—investment bankers meet that demand by helping new firms in that hot category go public, creating new supply in that category, which dilutes future returns. As that happens, established firms in that same category see how cheap and easy it is to raise money, and they start issuing new shares—raising capital for research and development, capital investment, mergers and acquisitions, whatever. The investment bankers keep printing new stock for both new and established firms until, ultimately, supply swamps demand and prices fall.

Sometimes they fall slowly, sometimes quickly—but demand falls and investment bankers don't want to issue shares for the cold category as much anymore. They want to issue shares for the next hot (or even warm) category—increasing stock supply there. Meanwhile, excess supply in the now-cold category can get swept up as corporations buy back shares or go bankrupt or get swallowed by other firms in cash takeovers. Supply can expand and contract endlessly and, in the long term, will overcome any major shift in demand.

And because firms will always be motivated to raise capital at different points, and because investment bankers will always be motivated to help firms who need (or want) to raise capital by issuing shares to meet demand (or manage buybacks and takeovers for firms), future supply will always be unpredictable but overpowering in the longer term.

Demand should float from category to category irregularly. There's no inherently fundamental reason why, 10 years from now, investment bankers should want to issue more shares of Tech versus Energy versus a larger category like small cap or large. Each category—if well constructed—should travel its own path but net very similar returns over über-long periods, as the forces of supply ultimately drive long-term returns.

Maybe one style, size, category, or sector leads for a long time—longer than you'd think—but you never want to fall in permanent love with any, because leadership rotates. Always.

BUNK 11   A GOOD CON ARTIST IS HARD TO SPOT

The first part of what I'm about to say you know. The rest you likely don't. In December 2008, news hit of the world's all-time largest financial scam. Bernard Madoff scammed investors out of as much as $65 billion. There was, effectively, nothing left in the coffers when authorities rushed in. All gone! You saw the stories splashed across newspaper headlines and the nightly news.

Though Madoff was the biggest scamming rat by far, news quickly followed about other similar scams. Had Madoff not been first, Texas-born Antiguan knight "Sir" R. Allen Stanford's (alleged) Ponzi scheme would have been the biggest ever. His was merely $8 billion. The SEC charges it was a pyramid scheme—nothing more. Stanford had even been a repeat member of the Forbes 400 with what in reality was an illusory net worth. Unlike Madoff, who confessed, Stanford has denied all allegations, been charged, and awaits trial—but it doesn't look good for him. The evidence against him appears beyond overwhelming.

Through 2009 and into 2010, more news about other, though smaller, scams broke—a seemingly endless stream. But for the victims, it doesn't matter if the con artists scammed a big sum or small. If he stole from you, your loss was, in most cases, total.

Also endlessly, media, investors, and authorities asked, "How did this happen? How *could* this happen?" In Madoff's and Stanford's cases, they were two seemingly upstanding people. Employers with many employees. Known philanthropists! Respected by their communities. In fact, many of their victims were close to them. Friends. Associates. Madoff pillaged his own Jewish community particularly hard. And some of their investors were sophisticated—others were big hedge funds. If sophisticated, super-wealthy investors could fall prey, the fear was no one is ever safe from con artists.

And in one sense, that's right. For some reason, folks think con artists only want big-money victims. Not so. Many of Madoff's victims were smaller investors. Some invested just a few thousand with him—their life savings. Madoff took them all, big and small. A con artist doesn't care if you're super-rich or have just a small pile—all they want is your money and as much of it as they can get.

Heed These Five Signs

But the good news: It can be very, very easy to spot a potential fraudster. In the immediate wake of the Madoff scandal, I wrote *How to Smell a Rat* (John Wiley & Sons, 2009)—detailing five key signs of financial fraud. From all the fraud cases through time I researched, all of them had, if not all five of the signs, at least three—usually more. The signs are:

1. Your adviser also has custody of your assets—this is true in 100 percent of the cases.
2. Stated returns are consistently great—almost too good to be true. Also true in 100 percent of the cases.
3. The investing strategy is murky, flashy, or too complicated for the adviser to explain to you so you can understand it— almost always.
4. The adviser promotes himself (or herself, though rats are usually male) as an "exclusive" club, or otherwise distracts you with flash, bling, and connections—none of which have anything to do with investing.
5. You hired the adviser based on a recommendation or through an intermediary and didn't do any real due diligence yourself. Con artists hate anyone who does any real due diligence and avoid them.

All the signs are important. The appearance of any one is a bit worrisome, though not necessarily an indictment. But the biggest, baddest, reddest flag of all is number 1. It is ever-present in these schemes and if you see number 1 *plus* any of the others, get your money back, now, if you can. Then, either do more of number 5 than you can possibly envision, twice over, or take your money and go.

Custody Is the Number One Sign

But what does it mean for the adviser to have custody? For example, Madoff's clients hired Madoff to manage their money. They gave him full discretion to decide what to buy and sell and when. That's a normal thing for a client to have an adviser do. It's what my firm does for its clients and what many other fine registered investment advisers do for theirs. But Madoff's clients deposited their money with Madoff Securities—a custodian that Madoff had direct control over. They gave him the money, and once he physically had it, it was tactically nothing for him to take the money out the back door and put it in his own personal account—which is exactly what he did.

Then he dummied up statements—for years—even decades maybe. And when clients wanted distributions, he just gave them funds from incoming money from new victims. His was a classic Ponzi scheme—and how most all of these scams operate. It's what Stanford allegedly did. It's what Charles Ponzi himself did when his name became synonymous with stealing-from-Peter-to-give-to-Paul-while-taking-most-of-it-for-yourself.

What did Madoff do with the money? I don't know. It seems he spent a lot of it. He may have invested some, intending to return it to clients—but that went badly. But he couldn't have done any of that if he didn't have access to the money. Maybe he didn't start out intending to steal—as he now claims. I think many Ponzi schemes start that way. You have a money manager with custody who gets into some personal problem requiring money. He's got a bunch of money ready and handy in the form of his clients' accounts—again, he has custody. He thinks, "I'll just take a bit and cover my problem. Then, because I see this great opportunity over here, I'll invest in it and make the money back. Then I'll put the clients' money back fast into their accounts, with no one the wiser and no one harmed." Even if he did that successfully (though my guess is usually it blows up, but you never know), someone was harmed because the adviser had a fiduciary obligation to put his clients' interests above his own. When he had that great "opportunity," he should have let the clients have it, not him.

Here's a parallel and in some ways a much bigger rub. Usually that first attempt to invest stolen client money in a hit-big attempt does blow up. Instead of hitting big, it splatters big. So he does it again, but this time trying an even bigger gamble (with probably bigger risk) to get the money back. He's getting desperate. After several failed attempts, he knows he is in too far to get out. So he, in effect, gives up. Instead, he covers requests for redemptions (clients wanting their money back) by giving them money from new victims—effectively rolling the liability forward. Meanwhile, he must dummy up statements to keep everyone in the dark. It just gets bigger and bigger over time. Eventually, all he's doing is bringing in new clients to pay off old ones to keep from getting caught—and avoid going to jail—a major motivator.

Usually, how it all finally blows up is when the market turns down big—as it did in 2008. Then, people everywhere become fearful and lots of clients want their money back, yet the scam artist can't sign on new victims fast enough, and he doesn't have enough new money coming in to keep the charade going. That's 2008's crop.

In Madoff's case, he was lying about performance to keep his clients docile. But because of the bear market, far too many clients tried to redeem at one time and he couldn't support the scam. That's what usually happens. He was outed. From what I've seen, bear market bottoms tend to out more scam artists than anything else.

The remedy is simple. When you hire an adviser to make decisions for you, don't give them access to the money. Separate custody from decision making. If you do that, you can avoid being the victim of this type of Ponzi scheme. Insist your money be deposited in a wholly unconnected, third-party, large, reputable, nationally known custodian—like Pershing, Bank of America, Morgan Stanley Smith Barney, Charles Schwab, Fidelity, UBS, etc. Then give your adviser—not associated with that entity—written authority to make decisions for the money and trade that account but not take money from it. The custodian holds the assets as a watchdog, and the separation of powers promotes integrity—and you don't get Ponzied.

Even a large regional custodian is ok, as long as it's established and well known. You want to wire money to an account in your name alone (or you and your spouse). Or maybe you write a check! But the check is written to you and your own account number. No commingling assets. That way, your adviser can't have access to the money, and it's close to impossible for him or them (or her—but financial scam artists have overwhelmingly been men) to be in cahoots with the custodian and steal that way. (Many custodians have insurance above and beyond normal Securities Investor Protection Corporation [SIPC] insurance, which also protects you from matters that involve their negligence.)

Fortunately, most advisers are already set up with a separate custodian or custodians. I originally set my business up this way myself, purposefully, to protect clients from any of my employees who might go rogue, but also from myself—to ensure that I could never turn myself into a Madoff no matter what I encounter or do! Now, there are myriad reasons some advisers might choose to hold assets themselves—for example, it might make accounting easier. But in my view, the safety and integrity benefits of having separate custody far outweigh any small conveniences. And the SEC tends to agree. Starting in 2009, they began taking a closer look at "dual-registered" advisers—those who make decisions and also hold the dough. As they should!

Protecting yourself is easy. Not every adviser who holds assets is a Ponzi schemer, but every Ponzi schemer I've ever seen has had direct access to the cookie jar. Don't give it to them.

PART ② WALL STREET "WISDOM"

Bashing quote-unquote "Wall Street" is always popular—sometimes even a national obsession. In 2008 through 2010, it replaced baseball as America's national pastime. It even went global, supplanting soccer (sorry—*football* for our non-US friends).

All that is silly. We always look for a scapegoat after a crisis. "Wall Street" is easy because successful folks there can make a lot of money—and folks with pitchforks usually follow the money. Personally, I think the ability to make a lot of money is a great good thing, and you do too, or you wouldn't be reading this book.

Wall Street (no quotes) does provide a useful service—helping firms access capital they need to grow and earn more future profits. More future profits are good! They increase shareholder value, provide jobs (everyone likes jobs), and make products more innovative, cheaper, faster, smaller, sometimes bigger—all good things.

That doesn't mean the brokerage and financial services industries aren't without problems. I set my firm up about as far away as possible from "Wall Street"—literally and figuratively—on purpose. My firm's headquarters are located high in a redwood forest overlooking the Pacific Ocean. Look out our windows and you see tall trees, not the neighboring building's glass and steel.

Why are we ensconced on a 2,000-foot-high mountaintop? In my view, the financial services industry, which in large part is driven by product-centric sales, is rife with the opportunity for conflicts of interest, which can lead—intentionally or not—to a lot of harmful bunk. In fact, "Wall Street" itself is sometimes set up in a way that can actually help you to fail. And Wall Street "wisdom" frequently isn't so wise.

When financial salespeople sell a product—a stock, bond, fund, option, commodity, whatever—they typically get a commission. Whether that product then goes up or down doesn't necessarily influence how they get paid. And how that product performs over your very long time horizon (which most readers have) definitely doesn't figure in for most financial salespeople. That's not illegal—but it can mean your and the salesperson's objectives are misaligned.

I'm not saying financial salespeople are bad. They're not! Most are good, honorable, hard-working people. (Though there are some bad eggs—every industry has them.) It's not necessarily their fault the industry can perpetuate misinformation. For example, many products are designed specifically to make investors feel "safe" in the near term. (Bunks 12, 13, 14, 15, 16.) You know from reading Part 1 that feelings can be your investing enemy number one—and the "safety" of these products long term is highly debatable if not frequently outright bunk. But if you're a commission-driven salesperson (as many are in the industry), it can be easier to react to folks' near-term anxiety (or greed) than help them focus on the long term. The long term is a long, long way away, but the salesperson's mortgage is due at the end of each month.

"Wall Street" can be full of products but short on discipline—which means folks following even the most straightforward, low-cost, (seemingly) no-brainer strategy can fall prey to short-term freak-out mentality—greatly to their detriment. (Bunks 17, 18.)

Confusing matters further, Wall Street churns out impressive-sounding nonsense, couched in supposedly smart "academic" speak—setting investing thought back decades. (Bunks 12, 13, 14, 19, 20, 21, 22.) Heck, most of the industry (helped by mass media) clings religiously to an archaic, utterly broken benchmark—the benighted Dow! (Bunk 23.) Hopefully, after you finish this section, you won't.

So all hail Wall Street (wherever it exists) for the powerful good it does in helping firms access the much-needed capital necessary to drive the awesome engine that is Capitalism. But beware the conflicts of interest that can pop up in "Wall Street"—see the difference more clearly with debunkery. These next few pages show you how.

BUNK 12 STOP-LOSSES STOP LOSSES!

Stop-loss! Even the name sounds great. Who doesn't want to stop losses? Forever! Sadly, stop-losses don't guarantee against losses—you can lose money with them, and badly. You can also stop future gains, pay more in transaction fees, trigger taxable events, and otherwise make much less money than you would simply leaving these be. It would be more accurate to call them "stop-gains." In the long term and on average they're a provable money loser.

How Do They "Work"?

A stop-loss is some mechanical methodology, like an order placed with a broker, to automatically sell a stock (or bond, exchange-traded fund [ETF], mutual fund, the whole market, whatever) when it falls to a certain dollar amount. You pick any arbitrary amount you like. People usually pick round numbers like "15 percent lower than where I bought it" or 10 percent or 20 percent—no reason; people just like round numbers. They could do 13.46 percent or 17.11 percent but they don't. When the stock hits that amount, it's sold. No big 80 percent drops. No disasters.

Sounds great, right? Except stop-losses don't do what people want them to do. If, on average, they were a major money-winning strategy, every professional money manager would use them. But overwhelmingly they don't. To my knowledge, there's no big-name, long-term, super-successful money manager who's ever made a practice of using them—not even occasionally.

Stop-losses don't work because stock prices aren't *serially correlated*. That means price movements by themselves don't predict future price movements. What happened yesterday doesn't have a lick of impact on what happens today or tomorrow. People like stop-losses because they think a stock falling a certain amount (7 percent, 10 percent, 15 percent, 17.11 percent, whatever) likely keeps falling. No! Think this through: If stock price movements dictated later movements, you could just buy stocks that have gone up a bunch. But you know, instinctively, that doesn't work. Sometimes a stock that's up a lot keeps going up, sometimes it goes down, or sometimes it bounces along sideways. You know that. So why don't people understand that correctly on the downside?

There's a school of trading dedicated to *momentum investing*. These folks believe (contrary to a vast body of scholarly research) that price movement is predictive. They buy winners and cut losers. They look for patterns in charts. But momentum investors don't do better on average than any other school of investors. In fact, they mostly do worse. Name five legendary ones. Or even one!

Pick a Level, Any Level

If, against my recommendation and contrary to the industry standard investing disclosure that "past performance is not indicative of future results," you wanted to do stop-losses, then what level would you pick? And why? Suppose you picked 20 percent, just because you like the number 20. (It's as good a reason as any other reason to pick a stop-loss level.) When a stock drops beyond that amount, it's basically a 50–50 chance it continues dropping or reverses course. You're trading on a coin flip. Coin flips make bad investment advisers. (see Figure 12.1.)

For example, say your stock drops 20 percent, triggering your stop-loss, so you sell. But that was because the entire market corrected that much, and this stock went along for the ride. That wasn't the stock's fault—there was nothing wrong with it! You sold at a relative low, paid a transaction fee, and are in cash—and markets rebound fast. You could be sitting in cash while the market and the stock you sold quickly zoom back up—without you. You bought high, sold low. Oops. That happens all the time.

Or maybe some bad news came out, triggering the drop. You sold the stock and have cash, but now what do you buy? Can you guarantee that what you buy only goes up? Maybe you buy a replacement stock with a 20 percent stop-loss. Then that one drops

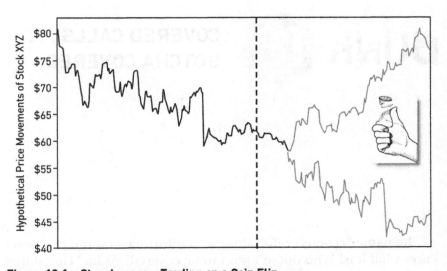

Figure 12.1 Stop-Losses—Trading on a Coin Flip

Note: For illustrative purposes only. Not to be interpreted as a forecast.

20 percent. You can play this game—buying 20 percent losers—all the way to zero. The stop-loss doesn't guarantee that future stock purchases only rise.

Or, suppose the first stock you automatically sold then reversed course and zoomed up 80 percent over the next year. You missed that gain! You sold at a relative low, paid two transaction fees, and missed out on the good part. Maybe you tell yourself you'll buy back once you think the trouble has passed, but I say, "Garbage." If you sold automatically, what fundamentals are you looking at to tell you to buy back in?

Here's another way to see this. Suppose you buy XYZ stock at $50 and it zooms to $100. Then your friend Bob buys it, and it drops to $80—down 20 percent. Should you both sell? Or just you, with your lower cost basis? Or just him?

The only certainty with stop-losses is increased transaction costs (which is, no doubt, why parts of the brokerage world have promoted them). There's no evidence they're better strategies. They're just pricey security blankies for nervous investors. Except blankies don't do any real harm, while stop-losses are pernicious little suckers. Before deploying a stop-loss strategy, lock yourself in a bunker.

BUNK 13 COVERED CALLS . . . GOTCHA COVERED

The name "covered calls" alone is comforting—even if you don't know what it is! Who doesn't want to be covered? As in, "Hey, dude! Don't sweat it; we gotcha covered." Or, "If you're cold, get covered up." Just sounds right.

Technically, covered calls combine a *long* stock position and a *written* call option. Many investors like these because they get a little bit of instant income from the premium received from selling the call. And there's not much risk from the call option. If the stock rises to the strike price before the expiration date, you just hand over the stock. That's why it's *covered*. Sounds safe! Income and seemingly low risk! How cool is that? That's how they are usually sold in the brokerage world.

At the same time, most folks who like covered calls and think they're safe will say with certainty that *naked puts* are risky. Covered is safe, but naked is crazy risky! Naked just sounds bad. "Hey, dude, you're hanging out there naked." Or, "I was warm until I got naked in the snow." But *naked* and *covered* don't mean what you may think or what most investors think. In this case, and counter to what every single covered call operator I've ever seen believes, they mean mathematically exactly the same thing—as I'll show you.

A naked put involves a written put option, so you still get the premium income, but you don't have a position in the underlying security—you're *naked*. I guess only nudists don't fear that. And naked means your loss can be the total strike price, minus whatever premium you collected. But the strike price is normally much more than the premium—so you can have a substantial loss.

Covered Calls Are Just Like Naked Puts?

So a covered call is thought to be safe and smart, and a naked put risky and crazy. Right? Bunk. Despite cosmetic appearances and urban myth, do the math and you'll discover that a covered call and a naked put *are effectively exactly the same thing*. Yet no matter how many times I tell this to covered call fans they never do the math and never figure it out and won't believe it.

Figure 13.1 shows the potential payout of a covered call at the exercise date. As with all options positions, the range of possible exercise profits and losses are known. The x-axis shows the stock price at the exercise date, and the y-axis shows profit or loss from this position. X is the strike price of that option.

The covered call actually pays out a fixed amount for an increasing stock price. Your potential upside is limited because you *must* hand over the stock if the option exercises. Worse, you still have all the downside risk of stock ownership, less only the premium. Capped upside, basically unlimited downside—doesn't sound so great anymore.

In fact, stated that way, it sounds exactly like a naked put. Because it is! No difference. And finance theory says that two securities with identical risk and payouts are, indeed, the same security—as shown in Figure 13.2.

Folks who think covered calls are safe and naked puts risky delude themselves. The perceived safety of a covered call is just that—perception. So if they are identical, with identical potential

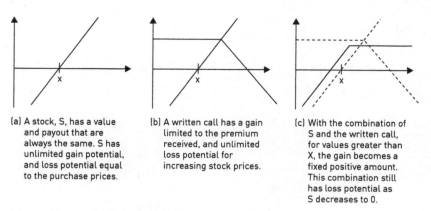

(a) A stock, S, has a value and payout that are always the same. S has unlimited gain potential, and loss potential equal to the purchase prices.

(b) A written call has a gain limited to the premium received, and unlimited loss potential for increasing stock prices.

(c) With the combination of S and the written call, for values greater than X, the gain becomes a fixed positive amount. This combination still has loss potential as S decreases to 0.

Figure 13.1   Covered Call Possible Payout

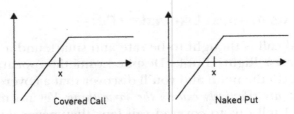

Figure 13.2 Covered Calls and Naked Puts

payouts and risk, why the perception gap? This is a standard cognitive error studied in behavioral finance. Identical information can be perceived differently depending on the framework it's presented in. So investors who do covered calls thinking they are safer than naked puts are simply fooled by framework—nothing more.

So, the next time someone suggests you do a covered call, you can say, "No way! I might as well sell a naked put!" Because you'd be right.

BUNK 14

DOLLAR COST AVERAGING—LOWER RISK, BETTER RETURNS

What is dollar cost averaging (DCA)? It's investing periodically a little at a time. But isn't that what you do with your 401(k)? You sock away a little each month, probably (hopefully) if you are maxing out your 401(k) each year (which most all of you should be doing).

Not entirely. Folks portion out their 401(k) contributions because they usually don't have the cash flow all at once to max it out in one month, so they do it periodically. And the IRS limits how much you can contribute each year, so you're forced to spread contributions out over a long time. DCA is different—when folks have a big boodle to invest, instead of plunging headlong into the market, they often do smaller lumps, spread over time. The theory is DCA protects you from investing it all on a "bad" day. Maybe you accidentally invest at a relative high—just before a big correction. Or worse—at the top of a bull market. We all know we don't want to "buy high." Dollar cost averaging reduces the risk of getting "all in" on a bad day—spreading out your cost basis over time.

And yes—it does do that. But does that actually improve your returns over time? Probably not. But it definitely increases transaction costs—that alone reduces your performance.

DCA—A Fee Bonanza

DCA goes in and out of favor. When markets are strongly rising for a long time, like in the late 1990s, people tend to forget their fear of the "bad" day. DCA usually comes surging back in popularity in bear markets or after, when folks are particularly fearful. During boom times, the only people talking up DCA are usually unscrupulous brokers who want the vastly higher commissions relative to your total assets that come from using DCA's dribbling-it-all-out quality instead of investing in a larger chunk. (There are plenty of fine, honorable brokers—most of them! But in an industry where folks receive commissions for sales, you naturally get some who want to increase commissions however they can.) DCA can be a major boon to brokers looking for fees. You usually pay much more commission per dollar traded on small trades than on large ones. So, when you break your lump sum up into many little pieces, the total commission paid to the broker rises markedly.

But if it's in the interest of managing risk, maybe it's worth it to pay a bit more. Except plenty of studies have shown that DCA doesn't reduce risk nor improve returns. A particularly good and thorough study was done about 15 years ago by Michael Rozeff (former professor of finance at the University of Buffalo). From 1926 until 1990 (before the big 1990s bull market), he compared results from doing a single, lump-sum investment each year to averaging stock purchases over 12 months. A whopping two-thirds of the time, the lump-sum method was more profitable than DCA— just the opposite of what DCA proponents would expect or what the media normally promotes. And, for the entire period, the lump-sum approach got a 1.1 percent higher average annual return— huge when you start compounding returns.[1]

My firm has done our own studies more recently with similar conclusions. We compared the lump-sum investing at the beginning of a 20-year time horizon to DCA—parsing the initial investment out equally for the first 12 months—from 1926 to 2009, with the uninvested portion earning cash-like returns. By our analysis, *lump-sum investing does better 69 percent of the time.* And that doesn't factor in DCA's added transaction costs, which skew results even more in lump-sum's favor. While folks don't want to believe that (particularly not now in the recent shadow of the 2007–2009 monster bear market), it's true.

People often wrongly think the 2000s was a period of flatness, because overall, stocks ended about where they began the decade. Wrong! There was big volatility along the way. And they also wrongly think because that decade ended with stocks no higher than at the beginning, the next decade will be "flat."

Again—wrong. No one anywhere has the ability to forecast stocks that far out—not yet (see why in Bunks 10 and 20). And what just happened isn't predictive of what will happen. But even in a period of flatness, DCA doesn't really help at all. The interest gained from holding cash tends to largely equal the higher transaction costs. DCA really only helps if you *know* there's a falling market ahead. And if you could forecast that accurately, what do you need DCA for?

Simply put: Lump-sum investing, over time, is far more likely to yield better results. Not every year, but enough to make DCA fully irrational. The reason is simple: More often than not, stocks move higher. You benefit more from being invested more of the time than you do trying to avoid near-term wiggles.

Most investors will accept that and acknowledge, long term, it's about time in the market, not timing the market. So why, when getting down to brass tacks, do people suddenly fall prey to DCA? Simple. It goes back to what I've said and will say frequently through these pages. People feel the pain of financial loss over twice as much as they enjoy a similar-sized gain. Investors might be inclined to accept an inferior strategy if it can reduce the possibility of making one big mistake that makes them feel terrible in the near term.

After all, jumping all in on one bad day would cause a lot of regret. As humans, we hate feeling regret. Sometimes, investors do extremely weird and irrational things just to avoid the possibility of the pain of regret—even racking up unnecessary transaction fees and hampering long-term performance. It's not rational, but it happens. But you can avoid falling prey by remembering your emotions are your number one enemy in investing, always.

Even if you do make a very poorly timed lump-sum investment, remember, bull markets over time overwhelm bear market losses. (See Bunk 8.) Bull markets are bigger and last longer than bear markets—and that likely continues. Put simply: DCA doesn't work like folks want it to, and the biggest beneficiary is likely the broker, who just gets more fees. So join me now and say it: "Don't fall prey to DCA." It's like a poem.

BUNK 15

VARIABLE ANNUITIES ARE ALL UPSIDE, NO DOWNSIDE

I've been accused of being hard on variable annuities. So I apologize. I apologize to every high net worth investor for being hard on variable annuities in my public writings instead of über-hard. Instead, it would be better if I had done more to keep people—like you—from buying one. (Hopefully, you haven't bought one.) There's little worse for high net worth investors (and plenty of other investors) than these, particularly equity-indexed annuities. That these are a "safe way" to get market-like growth with less risk is first-order slam-dunk bunk.

First and foremost—annuities are insurance contracts, and only as good as the firm behind them. Investors in 2010 and beyond will remember well: Insurance firms can and do go kaput. If the firm issuing your annuity goes bankrupt, your contract may be null and void and the premiums simply lost.

This is radically different from investing in stocks and bonds. The brokerage firm can go kaput (and they do) but with no impact on your ownership of publicly traded stocks. (Unless you happen to own stock in the bankrupt brokerage, which likely went to $0. But then, that's an issue of never holding more than 5 percent in any one stock so one blow-up doesn't take your entire portfolio down—basic rule covered in Bunk 33.) You own the stocks and bonds—the brokerage (or bank) is just a transparent piggy bank. You can easily journal those securities to another firm for safekeeping—easy to do in the Internet age. But if the firm issuing your annuity blows up, your loss on the contract may be total. Never forget that!

Two Basic Types

There are two basic types of annuities I'll consider here—fixed and variable. *Fixed annuities* are straightforward—you hand over premiums, either periodically or a lump sum, for a guaranteed income stream, now or in the future, for the rest of your life. With these, it's a race against your expected mortality. If you die by the time the insurance firm's actuary calculates you will, the insurance company wins. If you die very much sooner, it really wins. If you live much longer than expected, you win. It's as simple as that. The other risk is the insurance company could go kaput, and with it can go your revenue stream (as stated previously).

Another risk when you pay premiums—they're called "premiums" for a reason—is that they're in essence a fee for some agreed-upon contract. The insurance firm now owns that premium payment, not you. Say you open a large lump-sum fixed annuity with $1 million paid in, and next week, you're tragically hit by a bus. You never collect your annuity payments, and your family gets nothing of the $1 million because the insurance company owns it. Now, maybe they get a death benefit—if you signed up for it and paid for it (called life insurance, which can be bought separately and almost certainly cheaper)—but it's probably much less than the $1 million. Or maybe your spouse gets some income—again, if you signed up for and paid for a "survivor" feature (which is more expensive to you for obvious reasons). But still, in a scenario like that, your family likely is much better off if they had the $1 million and not an insurance contract.

However, fixed annuities typically don't grow in value and are rarely sold to high-net-worth investors as an alternative to stocks or bonds. Instead, *variable annuities* are pitched as a safe-as-mommy way to get growth with no icky market downside. In reality, no such free lunch exists. Most of these are built from standard, everyday mutual fund investments wrapped into an insurance contract dressed up with punitively stiff fees and little upside potential. You would be better off buying the funds directly, in my view.

Big Fees and Tax Trauma

Yes, some annuities can have the benefit of tax-deferred growth of deposited funds. Perversely, very many investors amazingly buy these and *hold them in their IRAs*—of all darned things. (This is the selling of ice to Eskimos—and defeats a major reason to buy the annuity. Funds held in IRAs grow tax-deferred anyway!)

Worse, when you withdraw money from the annuity, it's (usually) considered income, so you pay tax on the gains at ordinary income tax rates—not at the long-term capital gains rate, which is lower for many investors. And death benefit payouts may be fully taxable—unlike traditional life insurance payouts. Simply, tax-wise, annuities can be confusing, and if you do buy one under any circumstances, make sure to employ a tax adviser. (More fees!)

One easy debunkery: A way to know if something is bad for you is to check the broker's or salesperson's fee. Annuity salespeople typically get a huge, huge, how-do-you-say-humongous upfront fee. The bigger the salesperson's commission is on something, typically the worse it is for you, the buyer. He or she is getting that huge commission to sell you something that is bad for you, that you wouldn't otherwise naturally buy, and that if you truly understood the product you would never, ever buy. With variable annuities, the commission is typically 6 to 10 percent of the total assets[1]—and even up to 14 percent for some contracts![2] Said another way, if you buy a $1 million annuity, the broker might get $100,000 or more—*just for that one sale*. Maybe as much as $140,000! And the broker may also get an annual commission for a number of years. Insurance firms have to pay such big fees to brokers because these are very hard to sell. And they're very hard to sell because they are usually very, very bad for you. Think of it this way: You buy one of these and you're putting the salesperson's kid through college. Is that your intent? If so, just give him or her the money and take your investment funds and do what is otherwise best for you. You would be better off.

Some folks may claim, "But my annuity doesn't charge me an upfront sales fee!" Maybe not! But the salesperson *still* gets paid—handsomely— and that money doesn't fall out of the sky.

Speaking of which, variable annuities are also expensive to leave! Most have a "surrender" period. (They need that to keep you in the contract and paying premiums so they can recoup whatever commission was paid upfront to the broker and then make money themselves.) A typical surrender fee starts big and declines over the surrender "period." So the fee might be 7 percent to withdraw the first year, 6 percent the second, 5 percent the third, and so on.[3]

And they're expensive to own. Table 15.1 shows typical annual variable annuity fees. Annually, variable annuity holders pay an

Table 15.1 Typical Annual Fees for Variable Annuities

Fee	Amount
Fund expense	0.94%
Mortality and expense risk charges	1.21%
Administrative fees	0.16%
Distribution	0.09%
Total	**2.40%**

Source: Morningstar, Inc., as of 2008.

average of 2.4 percent, just for the honor of having the annuity. If you have a variable annuity because you want some growth while guarding against downside volatility, that 2.4 percent annually is a massive headwind—you're giving away a lot of upside each year. See it this way: Would you buy a mutual fund that charged 2.4 percent each year? According to Morningstar, average mutual fund expenses run about 1.2 percent.[4] The variable annuity doubles that!

And those fees add up over time. Table 15.2 shows a hypothetical comparison of the impact of 1.2 percent in annual expenses (an average mutual fund fee) versus 2.4 percent, assuming an average annual return of 10 percent (about what stocks have done over long periods).

Over 20 years, the amount lost to fees is no small sum—a difference of over $1.1 million in our hypothetical scenario. And that's in addition to paying any upfront fees and a huge fee to get out (if you're still in the surrender period) when you sober up and come to your senses. And that's assuming you can get similar growth inside an annuity to what you'd get outside. Your investment choices are typically very limited.

Remember, the money most times is basically being invested in mutual funds. If stocks in the long-term future did average 10 percent a year, you'll keep giving up about 24 percent of your annual return (2.4 percent relative to the 10 percent return). Those would have to be pretty special mutual funds to make that work. The way Warren Buffett used to describe it: If stocks do 10 percent a year and you pay an extra 1 percent in fees, you have to be 10 percent smarter than everyone else on average to make up for it. How smart are those mutual fund managers?

Table 15.2 Impact of Fees on Returns ($1 Million Invested) —Taking a Lot Off the Top

Investment Vehicle	Time Horizon	Average Annual Return	Annual Expenses	End Amount
Variable annuity	20 years	10%	2.4%	$4,138,568
Mutual fund	20 years	10%	1.2%	$5,284,362

This example is provided for illustrative purposes only. It is not intended to predict actual expenses or returns of any investment, which will vary.

I've got a longtime buddy who has been married and divorced five times. He knows now he chooses females badly. He has taken to heart the old axiom: "The next time I feel like getting married, I'm going to find a woman I could really hate in the long term and just give her a house." Think that way when a variable annuity salesperson pitches one to you. Just find one whose kid you want to put through college and give the kid the money. Then invest elsewhere.

Variable annuities may sound safe as houses when you're talking to the salesperson, and in some cases, there may be some insurance features to them that are. (As long as the firm is solvent.) But as far as a smart alternative to investment growth is concerned, whatever growth you may happen to get, you're likely giving a huge portion of it away in fees. There are much easier, more efficient, and more liquid ways to get middling returns, all without the risk you might lose it all on a failed insurance firm.

BUNK 16

EQUITY-INDEXED ANNUITIES—BETTER THAN NORMAL ANNUITIES

If you're skipping around in this book and haven't read Bunk 15 yet on variable annuities, go there first, then here. This bunk builds on the other bunk like a bunk bed. Annuity firms know annuities are a tough sale (that's why they pay such big commissions to salespeople!) and folks are figuring out they get lousy growth plus huge fees. So they created a relatively new product—equity-indexed annuities—sold frequently as having more upside potential than a standard variable annuity. Fair enough, but is it true? There are two basic ways these are sold.

The First Pitch

Growth is guaranteed at a minimum rate (like 6 percent) and investors get full upside participation in the stock market. Who doesn't want a guaranteed return floor and full upside?

The Catch

The drawback comes from the confusing nature of linking insurance and investments. (Never forget: An annuity is, first and foremost, an insurance contract.) Normally, with these annuities, it's the *income base* growth that's guaranteed, not the actual *account value*—which fluctuates up and down with the market like any other investment, albeit usually with much higher fees. The income base doesn't really apply unless you decide to surrender ownership of the account in return for regular distributions based on the income base size.

The problem is, many investors who buy these annuities don't intend to surrender the account and take income. They may buy them thinking they're a "safer" alternative to a mutual fund—and yet, the growth guarantee may not apply to the part of the annuity they care about! You must read and understand the convoluted annuity contract. It's hard. They're confusing.

The Second Pitch

Participate in the stock market's upside with no downside risk! Investors are often promised 75 percent to 100 percent of the upside and none of the downside. Guaranteed income base growth may be offered as well.

The Catch

These types of annuities usually have capped returns (hidden in the details), which can substantially lower long-term performance relative to the market.

For example, an annuity promising 100 percent index participation, a 3 percent minimum return guarantee, and a 10 percent annual return cap may sound great. After all, stock market returns have averaged about 10 percent a year over long periods, so you're not giving up much, right? No—remember Bunk 5. Average returns aren't normal. Stock returns are up big and down big more often by far than up middling amounts—the insurance firms know that. After all, they're in business to make money—and they make sure the contracts are solidly in their favor. And there's nothing wrong with insurance firms making money! It's better for the world and society in general if more firms are profitable than not. But don't think insurance firms are giving away returns out of the goodness of their hearts. To them, it's a business transaction—one they design to be profitable to them.

Table 16.1 shows $1 million invested in the S&P 500 for 30 years (through yearend 2009) compared to the same invested in a hypothetical annuity with 100 percent upside capped at 10 percent and a guaranteed annual 3 percent return (similar to many equity-indexed annuities). That 10 percent return cap seriously impaired return, lowering annualized returns from 11.2 percent for the S&P 500 over that period to 7.6 percent[1]—which hurt, big time—a difference of over *$15 million.*

Table 16.1 S&P 500 Versus a Hypothetical Equity-Indexed Annuity—Upside Is Usually Capped

Investment Vehicle	Amount Invested (12/31/1979)	Time Horizon	Annualized Return	End Amount 12/31/2009
S&P 500 Index	$1,000,000	30 years	11.2%	$24,401,353.46
Hypothetical annuity	$1,000,000	30 years	7.6%	$9,110,002.72

This example is for illustrative purposes only. It is not intended to reflect the returns of an actual annuity, and it is not intended to predict return of the S&P 500 Index for any period.
Source: Global Financial Data, Inc., S&P 500 total return from 12/31/1979 to 12/31/2009

Another tactic some (very wretched—which is most of them) annuities use is tying performance to an index that doesn't include dividends, which can make a huge difference over time. For example, from 1926 until 2009, the S&P 500's annualized return *with dividends* reinvested in the index was 9.7 percent. Without dividends, it was just 5.5 percent.[2] Why not include the dividends? That's a normal part of investor total return—just not for many annuity owners.

So why would anyone own one of these? No idea. I've never been able to figure it out. Some folks say they get benefits, like life insurance on the side. Ok, but there are a million better ways to skin that cat—like buying actual life insurance! Term life insurance is exceedingly cheap. When you mix objectives, like "growth, capital preservation, and life insurance," you tend to get an expensive mish-mosh that doesn't really satisfy any of those objectives well.

I could go on and on about the perils of annuities, but won't, because this shouldn't be a 500-page book. Remember this: Read the contract, super closely. Also consider, for all the fees you pay, what the odds are of getting much better results much cheaper elsewhere. (Hint: It's high.)

BUNK 17 PASSIVE INVESTING IS EASY

Passive investing, for the uninitiated, is the idea you mimic an index—either through an index fund, an exchange-traded fund (ETF) that looks like the index, or you buy the stocks in an index in perfect proportion to the index (this latter being possible only if you have a lot of money or there aren't many stocks in the index). Then you simply hold on as the index does whatever it does, forever, come what may, throughout your investing time horizon. The theory is: By simply buying the market passively and holding on, you can do effectively the same as the market—and do better than most people who overwhelmingly lag the market over time by making active decisions that blow up on them.

And there is nothing wrong with that, in theory. If you do this perfectly you'll lag the market by a hair's whisker—by whatever transaction costs or fees you incur, but only by that amount. And that's quite fine. Doing this beats most investors since most investors lag the market.

But then I commonly hear, "Passive investing is easy." It isn't. It's very, very hard.

Passive Is (NOT) Easy

Tactically, it *is* easy! Psychologically, it's tough. Buy an ETF that matches your benchmark—set it and forget it. But in my almost four decades managing money and over a quarter century writing for *Forbes*, I've met few investors who can actually do passive investing. Here's why and how you know.

At a macro view, a fascinating study done by DALBAR, Inc. shows in the 20 years ending 2009, equity mutual fund investors annualized 3.2 percent returns.[1] Over the same time, the S&P 500 annualized 8.2 percent[2]—hugely better—a full 5 percent annual spread. Let me say that again because it's epic. Investors in funds lagged the market—the very same market those funds invested in— by 5 percent a year.

That's a lot of buying funds badly. The main reason is that investors behaviorally can't "set it and forget it" for very long, so they keep inning and outing of the funds and ETFs at all the wrong times whether they're buying active or passive funds. (This is parallel to why women are better investors than men—coming up in Bunk 18.) If passive were so easy, people would do it in volume—and you could see it. But they don't. Even in buying passive funds they typically buy high, don't hold long enough, then bail out at the wrong times.

If Passive Were Easy, People Would Do It

As I've said through these pages, investing tends to be inherently counterintuitive. And there are myriad ways our brains go haywire. Again according to DALBAR, the average holding period for all equity mutual funds is 3.2 years.[3] (You read that right—3.2 percent returns *and* 3.2 years.) To do passive right, you can't sell your funds and change your strategy every 3.2 years—not unless you're the most exquisite of market timers. And if you are, you wouldn't be reading this book! For passive to work, you must, truly, set it and forget it for your entire investing time horizon. And if you're considering a passive equity strategy, your time horizon isn't 3.2 years— it's almost certainly very much longer. (See Bunk 3.)

There are two major forces at work here. One is the desire to in-and-out the market. The other is the desire to shift from this type of index to that. One guy decides at the end of 1995 to be passive to the S&P 500, but at the end of 1999 switches to the tech-heavy and very hot Nasdaq. Why? The S&P 500 annualized 26.4 percent from 1996 to 1999. Nice! But the Nasdaq annualized 40.2 percent.[4] Super hot! He thinks he chose wrong, and decides technology is forever the best—and makes his move just before technology tanks hard and then the market. Yuck. He chose wrong again (he thinks). By 2002 he has switched to a half S&P 500, half 5- to 10-year US

Treasury ETF strategy, just in time for the bull market to begin. By 2006, he's tired of lagging stocks and is back to being all S&P 500—just in time for the next bear market to start late 2007. This is all myopic—and he's even averaging slightly longer than that 3.2-year holding period. But it still isn't nearly long enough to do anything but be destructive—giving great glee to The Great Humiliator (Bunk 8).

Folks who study behavioral finance know human brains aren't hardwired to turn a tough shoulder to any form of big volatility, like 1998's huge correction (Bunk 7) or the massive bear market that ended March 2009. Even normal corrections within normal bull markets create enough volatility to make grown men cry for their mommies. Many professionals (maybe most) can get seriously rattled by big market volatility—even if they rationally know market volatility is normal (Bunk 5). And when stocks are high-flying—like in the late 1990s, or in 2009 when global stocks surged 73 percent from the bottom through year end[5]—many naturally want to think the big returns they got are due to their genius, not the market overall being up a lot. Overconfidence likely torpedoes as many portfolios as fear of volatility does. But it also speaks to most investors being emotionally unable to set it and forget it. People just can't.

That's why, though passive investing is tactically easy, so few investors can actually do it for long enough periods to make it work. It's sort of like getting a bug and going to the doctor who gives you two weeks' worth of pills to take. You take two days' worth and then are annoyed when you don't get better instantly. So you go do something else, and you're mystified that you're still not getting better—and maybe you're getting even sicker! This is pretty much the same thing. Most people emotionally can't keep taking the medicine when it tastes bad.

Other People Are Like That! Not Me . . .

You may say, "Other people are irrational like that. Not me! I am cool and steady." Congratulations! Maybe you are one of the few—ice water in your veins—and can do passive, successfully, for 20 years or more. Folks who stay cool and don't get knocked asunder, falling to the thrall of a hot asset class (or the chill of a cold one), almost certainly do better than most investors. (But if you think that's you, mark these pages and flip back the next time stocks fall 15 percent—a normal-sized correction within a bull market—and see if you are so very cool and steady then.)

Fact is: It's darned hard for almost everyone. It's so easy to succumb to greed, fear, pain, regret, overconfidence, and your Stone Age brain. So get some form of adviser—your spouse, minister, brother, parent, 65-year-old son, investment adviser, Tinker Bell, whoever—but someone who, every time you try to stray from your long-term strategy, reminds you who you are, and that you're not Warren Buffett. (Again, if you were, you wouldn't need to read this book.) And if you need help designing your long-term strategy, get help with that too. (Also, see Bunk 4.) Falling victim to your emotions doesn't make you a bad person—just human. And if you can control yourself, it can make you a better investor. Yet for most humans, passive investing is hard. Real hard!

BUNK 18

DO BETTER WITH MUTUAL FUNDS BY SENDING YOUR SPOUSE ON A SHOPPING SPREE

Whatever you do, don't let your spouse read this chapter or he or she will hate you unless you do what I say. Because he or she will either know you're not doing as well as you could with your mutual fund investments, or demand the right to a shopping spree. Sound nuts or weird? It isn't.

Some folks think I'm anti-mutual funds. I'm not. At all! You know they're a fine vehicle for smaller investors to diversify and get access to professional money management or passive commingled investing more efficiently. But for big investors, they are pretty inefficient and costly. The wealthier you are, the more relatively inefficient they are—and for big investors there are a million better ways to skin that cat. But for smaller pools of assets, the benefits of diversification can outweigh all drawbacks. And mutual funds as a "packaging device" are awfully convenient. Plus, plenty of mutual funds get fine performance.

And you know to pay close attention to the fees with these funds—the higher they are, the more they erode returns. But this is also where folks miss a basic investing truism. I hear from plenty of investors who think their "no-load" mutual funds are just grand. No fees means cheap! Maybe—but sometimes, "cheap" comes at a huge cost. With funds, this is a provable and very slippery slope into potential bunk. Sometimes more is less.

All mutual funds have costs—even "no-load" funds. The *load* refers to the sales charge or commission, which covers the expense of the guy or gal selling you the fund. Some funds have a big upfront fee—5 percent or more! Some charge a *level* load of maybe 1 percent (give or take), annually. And some charge a big fee to exit. And, yes, some funds have no sales charges—hence "no-load." Mind you, even no-load funds have ongoing fees for management and marketing costs. But it's true—if you buy a no-load fund, you won't pay a sales commission. Cheap!

"Cheap" Can Be Relative

Or not. Sure, you won't pay a sales charge, but "cheap" can be relative. In a perverse twist, there's simply no evidence that investors who buy no-load mutual funds get better returns. But there is evidence that the lack of load motivates investors to behave badly—in ways that impair the returns they get with the funds they own. I'm not suggesting you exclusively buy load funds and wholly avoid no-loads, but I am suggesting there is a little-understood problem with no-loads and an easy way around it.

The problem? The absence of a fee means investors may buy and sell mutual funds more frequently—known as "switching." Switching is no performance enhancer—revisit Bunk 17. In fact, quite the contrary. It's usually a performance killer unless you're a very hot hand at timing, which few are—and if you're reading this book, you likely aren't. (And if you're great at timing, you probably aren't timing mutual funds anyway.)

The same things that make passive investing much harder to do than people commonly think—resulting in worse long-term returns—can make no-load investors go chasing willy-nilly after hot funds just in time for them to go cold. Or they get unnerved by volatility and sell at the worst possible time—at a relative low. (See Bunk 7.) They think, "Well, at least I'm not losing money on load fees!" Fine! But that's cold comfort if they end up performing badly relative to what they would have done had they stayed put. For some, the psychological barrier of a fee can give them much-needed discipline—a form of behavioral spine.

From Bunk 17, you know the average holding period for an equity mutual fund is just 3.2 years. That's *average*—many hold them for much shorter periods. And that holding period is for *both* load and no-load equity funds. History shows that load-fund investors hold their funds longer on average than no-load fund investors—dragging up the average. At the very least, funds charging a sales fee create incentive to stay put longer—*and that alone can improve your overall performance.*

How can you know? An excellent and famous landmark study by finance professors Terrance Odean and Brad Barber looked at investing results by gender. Overwhelmingly, women were better long-term investors. Why? Men tend to suffer more overconfidence. (I'm not being sexist—overconfidence is a bad cognitive error and is fundamentally and provably suffered more acutely by men than women on average, though both sexes have it.) Hence, in the study, men made more frequent changes to their portfolios—trading 67 percent more often than the ladies![1] Women made fewer portfolio changes—and got materially better overall returns—outpacing the gents by a whopping 1.4 percent per year on average.[2] If you understand at all the power of compounding interest, you know that's huge. In a sense, a load is the price you pay for greater discipline—a talisman against changes—which can have long-term benefits far outweighing fee avoidance. A 5 percent load can be fully made up for by holding a fund three years longer.

Again, I'm not advocating for or against load or no-load funds, but I do have a suggestion for those who buy mutual funds—another way to force discipline onto yourself: Buy no-load funds but first make a contract with your spouse. Every time you sell a mutual fund, you must deposit 5 percent of the value into your spouse's "folderol account" to be spent on anything and everything your spouse likes—and nothing you particularly like. Spa trips, golf, jewelry, sports cars, $2,000 shoes, his or her own investments so they can spend more later—it doesn't matter what it is—but it's his (or hers) and not yours. It's punitive spending to teach you this lesson: Chasing heat has real consequences. As does freak-out panic selling from market volatility. Both can rob you of future returns.

Now, if you can buy no-load mutual funds and hang tight (so long as the mutual fund is appropriate for you and reasonably well run), do it! But most investors can use a little enforced discipline. And the threat of a wild shopping spree may be what it takes to help you see that no-load mutual funds aren't always so cheap.

BUNK 19

BETA MEASURES RISK

Stocks are risky. Simple fact! But to get return, you must take risk—which many folks feel as volatility. (See Bunk 6.) Volatility is uncomfortable near term for most folks and quite unpredictable—and makes investing even harder than it might be otherwise. Makes many go mental—drives 'em nuts, pure and simple.

Because people are prone to like order, we like to measure. Take beta, for example—the academic concept, widely accepted throughout media and the investing culture, that claims to measure investment risk. Take it outside and leave it there. It's useless. No—less than useless.

Folks (particularly academics who first foisted beta on us) like to think beta measures risk. No—it measures *prior* risk. It *measured* risk—past tense! It doesn't measure anything about the present or future. Beta itself is a simple and accurate calculation. A stock's beta is a number representing its *past* volatility relative to the overall market's *past*, over a specific period. The higher a stock's *past* volatility, the higher its beta. If a stock moved perfectly in line with the overall market (usually in calculating beta, folks use the S&P 500 as the market index—but beta can be calculated against any market index), its beta is 1.0. Lower, and it was less volatile than the market; higher, and more so. Simple enough.

Past Performance Is Never Indicative of Future Results

Academics first presumed, contrary to centuries of common sense and without any sound reasoning, that if a stock *has been* more volatile than the market, it is therefore more risky going forward. The academic world therefore proclaimed beta to measure a stock's risk. While there is no actual evidence of that, ever since, way too many investors believed beta reflects *future* risk, despite hearing and knowing that past performance isn't indicative of future results.

Belief in beta has made folks do all forms of nutty things. Nervous Nellies want only low-beta stocks and low-beta portfolios. Let me give you a simple example of this folly (one I wrote about in my second year as a *Forbes* columnist—"Witch Doctors," June 2, 1986). Take a low-beta stock and have it drop by 90 percent over two years. The beta will go through the roof. Is it now higher or lower risk than before the drop? Well, it can't be higher on any rational basis, but beta says it is. So if you believed beta, you believed once-upon-a-time hot cosmetics maker Avon was relatively low risk with a beta of 0.9 at $120+ in 1973, but high risk *the very next year at $19* after an 85 percent drop—with a beta of 1.3. Intuitively, the risk for Avon as an individual stock must have been higher at $120 in 1973—*before* the monster stock price drop—than at $19 in 1974. Buying after any big drop relative to the market means buying a higher beta, but is one traditional way to look for potential lower-risk bargains going forward.

Another way beta makes folks' brains go haywire: Those who believe more risk means more return (in a sense they're right) have bought into the popular notion that the only way to beat the market is by taking extraordinary risks via high-beta stocks—but then they screw up by using beta as a screening tool. Because beta is a purely backward-looking phenomenon and isn't predictive going forward, buying a group of high-beta stocks doesn't give you a low-risk/high-return approach. This is like driving while looking in the rearview mirror. It's destined to be problematic.

Here's some irony. Academics understand well that stocks are *non-serially correlated*. That's statistical talk saying—in plain English— price action alone tells you simply nothing about the future that's exploitable. Study after study shows that to be so. Yet academics early on bought into the notion that past volatility (which is based solely on price action—which they know is non-serially correlated by definition) is somehow useful. How wrong!

Categories That Fall Most Bounce Most

Think this through another way—and one that can be statistically measured to happen around all bear market bottoms: If you could perfectly time a bear market bottom (which you can't, but this helps illustrate why beta is silly) and invest more heavily in those categories that will perform best over the next 6 and 12 months—would you want to? Of course! But you couldn't if you used beta to manage risk. Let me show you. First: Overall risk going forward, by definition, is actually lowest immediately after the bottom of a major bear market. (Of course, again, we don't know with certainty just when that is.)

You also know from Bunk 9 that bear markets end and bull markets begin in a V. The bigger the end of the bear, the bigger and faster the initial bounce off the bottom—which is just part of what makes timing bear market bottoms so tricky. But then comes another common characteristic of bear market bottoms—one that isn't widely understood, but one my firm demonstrated a long time ago statistically across the span of the history of bear markets.

Those categories that hold up better than the market during the beginning of a bear that then fall the most in back of a bear market (making them high-beta) bounce most in the early stage of the new bull. Figure 19.1 shows this almost perfectly for US stocks—showing sector performance six months before the March 2009 bottom (the dark bars) and six months after (the lighter bars). The sectors that fell most to the bottom then, in fact, had the biggest returns post-bottom. The parallel isn't perfect but is almost perfect any way you cut it (what in statistics is referred to as a *near-monotonic display* and in history is consistent across bear markets).

And because US and non-US stocks can be highly correlated, you see the exact same effect globally in Figure 19.2.

Those categories with the best returns after the bottom had the biggest beta at the bottom. They had more volatility to the bottom and more volatility than the market in the new bull! But the way our brains work, we tend to think: When it's down, it's "volatile," but when it's up, it's "good"! So if you were using beta to manage risk and wanted to avoid "risky" high-beta stocks, you missed the categories that performed best!

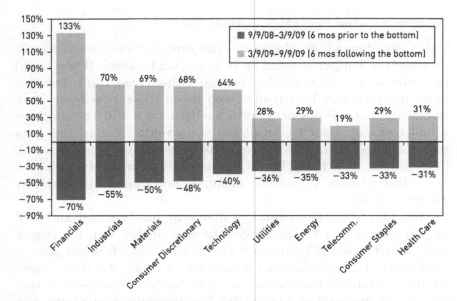

Figure 19.1   What Falls the Most Bounces the Most—US Stocks

Source: Thomson Reuters, S&P 500 price return from 09/09/2008 to 09/09/2009.

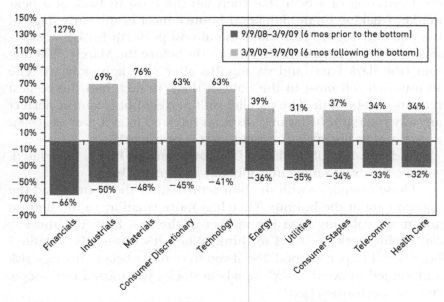

Figure 19.2   What Falls the Most Bounces the Most—World Stocks

Source: Thomson Reuters, MSCI Inc.,[1] MSCI World Index price return from 09/09/2008 to 09/09/2009.

Don't take that to mean a high-beta stock or category is always going to have outsized returns going forward. No! It just means it *was* measured by beta to be riskier than the market at the bottom of a bear market, looking backward. It fell more. It says nothing about whether it will be riskier going forward. Sometimes, in some markets, stocks that lagged the market badly (i.e., had high betas) catch back up and become low beta later. Or high-flying stocks (also high beta) fall back to earth and stagnate. Beta is illustrative of what a stock has been like—not what it will be like. Trying to manage risk or enhance performance through beta alone is a fool's errand. Beta doesn't measure risk; it *measured* risk—and investors should always look forward, not back.

BUNK 20

EQUITY RISK PREMIUMS— FORECASTING FUTURE RETURNS WITH EASE

Wish you could know where stocks will be in 10 years? Me too! I don't think it's possible. Still, people try. There's a notion in academia about the equity risk premium (ERP). The ERP is, literally, the premium you get, expressed as a percentage over some supposed risk-free rate—like the 10-year US Treasury—from holding stocks. Some folks use the T-bill rate. Either way—same basic concept.

And there's nothing wrong with that! It's true—most often investors are rewarded long-term for taking extra volatility risk (done right). Since 1926, the average annualized ERP (using 10-year Treasuries) has been 4.4 percent—Treasuries have annualized 5.3 percent, and the S&P 500 9.7 percent[1]—a huge spread! And theoretically, investors *should* be rewarded for suffering through stock market swings. (Although, they hate the volatility. And the more the volatility, the more they hate it when they rationally should love it since, in the long run, they usually get paid handsomely for it.) If you weren't likely to get higher reward for higher risk, why would anyone want the higher risk—whether measured by volatility or otherwise?

The problem with ERPs is some academics try to model *future* ERPs—predicting *future* stock returns. Bunk. I've never seen any ERP model stand up to historical back-testing. Not one! Yet, every year, we get a new wave of them.

Long-Distant Future Supply

When I say *future*, I mean most ERPs attempt forecasting *far* into the future—usually 7 to 10 years (10 is most common). Yet, you know from Bunk 10 that stock returns in the near term—over the next 12 to 24 months—are driven mostly by shifts in demand. And even those are devilishly difficult to forecast. And further out, supply pressures swamp all. And there is absolutely no way—none—to predict stock market direction 7 or 10 years out unless you can somehow predict future stock supply shifts. Yet I've never seen anyone even attempt that, nor can I fathom a way to do it myself. (Though maybe one day someone can do it—and then a future ERP might be possible.) But not a single ERP model I've ever seen has even addressed the issue of predicting long-term supply flows. And if you can't address future supply, your model is worthless. Because, in the long term with securities, supply is all that matters.

Instead, most ERP models make forward-looking assumptions based on cobbled-together *current* or even *past* conditions. Except, right away you know you can't make 10-year projections based on current or past conditions. Past performance is never, by itself, indicative of future results.

An example of an ERP model might be some nonsense like: Take the current dividend yield, the average earnings per share over the last 10 years, plus the current inflation rate, and subtract the bond yield. Add or subtract a few components. Mix that together with a guesstimate for some percent stocks are supposed to beat bonds by over the next 10 years, based on what Treasuries are yielding now.

Except what does today's dividend yield, inflation yield, earnings, or anything have to say about what will happen 7 or 10 years from now? Or even three years? No one can answer that.

Plus, none of these ERPs stand up to historical back-testing that I've seen. A scientist would say you must test historically—picking multiple past periods and inserting historic data for the ERP assumptions. A model that "worked" would spit out the actual forward 7- or 10-year returns from that past period pretty darn closely. One that didn't would be broken—no exceptions. And none do, or if they do it's merely accidental—they work for a couple of past periods, but not consistently.

Academics who are prone to bearishness—surprise!—produce bearish ERPs, and bearishly biased press promotes them. They say, "The ERP will be below average for the next 10 years, just 1.5 percent!" If the 10-year Treasury is now 3.0 percent, for example, that means stocks will average just 4.5 percent over the next 10 years. Yuck! On the flip side, bullish academics (who are fewer in my observation) produce bullish ERPs—they bake in their own biases. Still, bullish or bearish, all ERP projections are as much bunk as anyone else's long-term forecasts—bias-based guesstimates, nothing more.

We could dissect any number of popular ERP models. And it's a worthwhile exercise to do on your own (straight debunkery)—but the alpha and the omega and the fatty acid reality is they don't address future supply, so creating an ERP is a fruitless fatheaded academic flexercise. (*Flexercise* is technically a *comberation*—see this book's Introduction.)

Meager Assumptions

Another ERP red flag. A huge one! ERP models usually predict 2 percent or 2.5 percent or 3 percent—some small number. Why academics fiddle-faddle over 2 percent versus 3 percent is beyond me. They can easily check history. Looking backward, ERPs are very wildly variable. After all, normal stock returns are extreme—not average. (See Bunk 5.) Table 20.1 shows historic ERPs by decade. The 1960s and 1980s ERPs were darn close to the long-term average ERP of 4.4 percent. Amazing! Other than that, they've been extreme—18.9 percent in the 1950s. And 10.2 percent in the 1990s.

There have been negative ERPs—the 1930s, of course. The ERP was just flat in the 1970s, while stocks overall were positive (though below average). And the 2000s were another. (Without forecasting long-distance stock returns, see how long ERPs were hugely positive following past negative periods. Folks who say that the 2000s being

Table 20.1   Historic Equity Risk Premiums by Decade—Not Predictive

Decade	10-Year Treasuries	S&P 500	ERP
1930s	4.0%	−0.5%	−4.4%
1940s	2.7%	9.0%	6.3%
1950s	0.4%	19.3%	18.9%
1960s	2.8%	7.8%	5.0%
1970s	6.1%	5.9%	−0.2%
1980s	12.8%	17.6%	4.8%
1990s	8.0%	18.2%	10.2%
2000s	6.6%	−0.9%	−7.6%

Source: Global Financial Data, Inc., USA 10-Year Government Bond Total Return Index, S&P 500 total return from 12/31/1929 to 12/31/2009

overall down for stocks means we're in some long-term "new normal" of malaise don't know history. Such a thing has never happened in the past.)

Simply, academic ERPs are usually too bearish, don't address past wide variability, don't stand up to back-testing, and can't address future stock supply shifts. Yet, academics still produce them, the press promotes them, and the investing world laps them up—because they sound quantitative, academic, sophisticated, and rigorous! Wall Street "wisdom" at its finest. Near as I can tell, *sophisticated* has screwed up more investors than bubbles have.

Typically, an academic will pontificate about the multiple complex variables in his ERP and why they combined with his formulaic approach, leading to a vision of the future. (Sophisticated!) Few will say, "My ERP model is a fancy-dancy but useless way to express my basic optimism or pessimism about the next 10 years." Yet, ironically, that's what it really is more often than not.

ERP models almost never predict it right. Maybe academics think overt "optimism" or "pessimism" is unseemly—unprofessorial. But it also runs contrary to empirical evidence. Stocks historically rise more than fall. Stocks historically do pretty well in the long term compared to cash or bonds, but in a widely varying path. That's the truth. That's hard for most folks to get in their bones.

Maybe you can use what you've learned in this book (or maybe read my 2006 book, *The Only Three Questions That Count*) and do a debunkery that uncovers how to do long-term stock supply forecasting. Then you might be able to build a credible, forward-looking ERP! That would give you huge power (at least until the rest of the world figured it out). I'd love to be able to do it, and I'd love for you to be able to do it too. But until then, don't bother with ERPs.

BUNK 21

WHEN THE VIX IS HIGH, IT'S TIME TO BUY

And when it's low, it's time to go. Or is it?

For readers not familiar with this investing Wall Street "wisdom," good for you—your life is infinitely better. The VIX is the ticker symbol for the Chicago Board Options Exchange (CBOE) Volatility Index. It's meant to show the market's expectations of 30-day volatility for the S&P 500. There's nothing wrong with the index; it's forward-looking and well constructed from a range of S&P 500 index options—both puts and calls. And it pretty much does what it's supposed to do—tells you the market's expectation for future volatility.

But that's it! Volatility is volatility. It doesn't tell you where stocks are going to go next—similar to the problem with beta (Bunk 19). But folks who read charts like carnival fortune tellers read tea leaves (and with about as much success) say you can replace "volatility" with "fear." The VIX is sometimes called "the fear index." So a spiking VIX means spiking fear. And because stocks love to climb a wall of worry, increased fear should mean capitulation selling and good times for stocks ahead. And an absence of volatility means less fear—even excess complacency—and possibly a downdraft ahead. Hence, the saying goes, "When the VIX is high, it's time to buy. When the VIX is low, it's time to go."

Coincident Plus Relative Equal Useless

In theory, it's not bad. It is true stocks like to climb a wall of worry. So does it work? Normally, I advise looking at long periods—the more data the better. But VIX fans tend to be short-term trading oriented, trying to capture short-term swings. Again, for most people, a short-term view is wrong. But to be fair to those cute little VIXens, let's look at a short period where the VIX worked beautifully.

Figure 21.1 shows S&P 500 returns (dark line) and the VIX (lighter line) for 1999—a pretty volatile year. And look! Overall, the VIX was pretty high all year, and peaks and troughs on the VIX tended to mirror troughs and peaks on the S&P. Success! Had you bought at relative high points and sold at lows, you'd have timed near-term stock swings pretty darned well.

Except if you'd just bought and held the S&P 500 through 1999, you'd be fine too—up 21.0 percent.[1] And you wouldn't have had all those extra transaction costs or cap gains taxes to pay. Plus, you wouldn't have had to watch the VIX like a hawk—which your spouse likely prefers.

But how would you have done had you bought the VIX peaks and sold the lows? I have no idea. Why? Well, how do you define it? Do you buy at every VIX peak? Or just the major ones? And how do even you know if it's a peak? Look at the graph again—the highs and lows are all relative—you wouldn't know a peak had formed

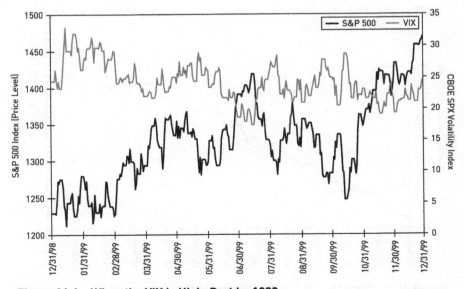

Figure 21.1　When the VIX Is High, Part I—1999

Source: Thomson Reuters, CBOE SPX Volatility Index, S&P 500 price return from 12/31/1998 to 12/31/1999.

until *after* the fact. The VIX peaked higher at the start of the year, then stocks moved choppily sideways. Mid-August there was a peak—but lower than many points earlier in the year—though stocks were pulling back sharply. Weird! And the VIX bottomed just before that pullback—signaling a near-term peak. Cool! Except there were some VIX bottoms late in the year when stocks were generally moving higher. How would you know which peak or trough to act on?

Worse, by the time you can look back and see the VIX peak or trough, you've missed the corresponding S&P 500 bottom or top too (if there was one). There's no lag in stock performance, giving you time to build conviction you are indeed seeing a VIX peak. Coincident, relative indicators might look cool, but they are close to worthless when making forward-looking forecasts.

Useless . . . But Also Inconsistent!

But hang on—that's assuming the VIX always works. It doesn't. Like most all "technical" indicators, for every chart you show me that works, I can probably show you lots more where it falls apart. (See Figure 21.2.)

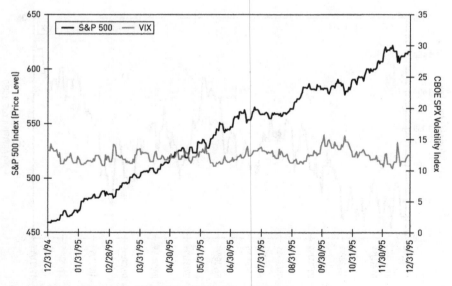

Figure 21.2   When the VIX Is High, Part II—1995

Source: Thomson Reuters, CBOE SPX Volatility Index, S&P 500 price return from 12/31/1994 to 12/31/1995.

1995 was a great year—US stocks up 37.6 percent[2]—almost a perfect, straight shot up! But the VIX was just static—noise. What do you do with it in a year like this? It gives you no guidance. It doesn't even hint to you at the start of the year to *get in now!* VIXens will say the VIX works during heightened volatility. Ok, but 1995 was one heck of a volatile year—it was just all upside volatility! (Folks forget—up or down—it's all volatility.) Overall, the VIX doesn't look very helpful this year. There are peaks and troughs, but they seem disjointed from market action.

In some years, the VIX works great. In others, it's just static. How do you know when the "right" short time period for using the VIX has started? You don't. You couldn't, not until it was over. And then, it only helps if you can build a time machine and go back in time to take action precisely at the right peak or trough. And if you could do that, you would license the time machine and be a multi-billionaire 50 times over and not fuss with stocks.

VIXens claim the tool works when there is "heightened fear"— that's how you know. But how can you measure that? Only hindsight bias lets you look back and say, "Well, I wasn't nearly as fearful then as I am now." Folks never remember fear and pain right—memory fades the pain—it's a survival instinct. (If you don't believe that, ask any woman who's given birth.)

Sure, VIX can sometimes work really well. But you can't fore- cast from it. And when you look at it longer term, there's no way to know when it will work or won't. So when the VIX is high, the VIX is high. That's about it.

BUNK 22 BE CONFIDENT ON CONSUMER CONFIDENCE

Each month, we get a flurry of headlines on consumer confidence. It's up—yay! Things will be good ahead! It's down—oh no! Look out below! The media reports it as if it means something special. It doesn't. That's not to say it isn't nice when people feel better. But—a repeated theme in this book—feelings are not your friends in investing.

Heck, consumer confidence is so popularly followed, it's even part of the closely watched Leading Economic Index (LEI). And though a bit wonky, LEI does a pretty good (though not infallible) job of predicting where the economy is going. But confidence is just one of 10 components in that index. (Folks also like to think LEI is predictive of stock returns, but one of the components is the S&P 500. So those who believe LEI is predictive of future stock returns must believe in part that rising stocks are predictive of future rising stocks. But if that were the case, bull markets would never end. Bear markets neither. Can't be true!)

Confidence Is Coincident

A buddy and I co-authored a scholarly research paper in 2003 on consumer confidence—"Consumer Confidence and Stock Returns"—published in the Fall 2003 *Journal of Portfolio Management*. If you like geek-speak, you can find the paper online. I'll summarize: Consumer confidence indexes are coincident to the stock market at best—and slightly lagging at worst. And you know from Bunk 21 that coincident indicators are worse than useless—people think they are predictive when they're not.

There are two major consumer confidence surveys done by the Conference Board and the University of Michigan, though perhaps the Conference Board's survey is more widely followed these days (and that might change down the road). But they overwhelmingly move together (they're basically surveying the same population), with the occasional wiggle. Both aim to capture consumers' feelings about the economy now and as expected over the next 6 to 12 months—that's the confidence part. There's also the American Association of Individual Investors (AAII) sentiment survey. Now, you know stocks typically lead the economy—up and down. So an investor sentiment survey should—if it's any good—lead consumer confidence. But it doesn't. All three move closely together!

But what do they say about stocks? Figure 22.1 shows S&P 500 total returns and the Conference Board Consumer Confidence Index. They basically move together—coincident. Also note, confidence peaks and troughs are relative. (Like the VIX in Bunk 21! Useless.) You know if there's a peak or a trough only in retrospect. And what's high at one point in time may not be so high at another.

Figure 22.1 Consumer Confidence and Stock Returns—Confidence Isn't Predictive

Source: Thomson Reuters, Conference Board Consumer Confidence Index, S&P 500 total return (monthly) from 12/31/1999 to 12/31/2009.

The Conference Board itself says the index level is less important than percent moves.

What we wrote about in that 2003 paper was when stocks go up, people feel better and more confident about the future. Surveys pick that up. And when stocks fall, people feel grumpier and less confident. A confidence index is reflective of what just happened— not what will happen. It's coincident. In fact, it's even lagging, since the data is released at the end of the *following* month. And it's an average of how people felt over the month—so it's basically reflective of average feelings in the middle of the previous month. Wonky! So, stocks go higher in May. In late June, you find out people were generally more confident on May 15. Why is that useful? You tell me what the stock market did in a month, and I'll tell you with pretty high precision where the confidence indexes are headed and by about how much. But not the reverse.

You cannot tell what stocks will do based on confidence. You can only tell, somewhat, how people felt recently. Stocks impact that on the one hand and confidence indexes reflect that on the other hand.

Not Contrarian Either. Just Useless.

Now, some folks like to get cute and say consumer confidence is a *contra-indicator*—that very high confidence means stocks have risen too much and must fall and low confidence means stocks are too low and must rise. And, like any coincident indicator, that can happen. But, again, like the VIX, extreme peaks are evident only after the fact, making it useless in forecasting. But if that approach worked for the index, it would also work for the stock market—and you know that isn't so. You know that if the market rose for one, three, five, seven, or any given number of months, it tells you nothing about the next however many months.

For example, Figure 22.1 shows confidence hit a low in March 2003 about when the global markets did—and 12 months later stocks boomed 35.1 percent.[1] Being a confidence contrarian worked then—if you had somehow used a magical crystal ball to know that was a confidence trough. In July 2007, there was another near-term confidence peak and 12 months later stocks were down −11.1 percent.[2] And the absolute lowest point in recent history for consumer confidence was February 2009. Markets bottomed in early March and started their historically massive surge. Twelve months after the February confidence extreme low, US stocks were up 53.6 percent.[3] All perfectly matched-up coincident points you couldn't possibly know about until after they'd passed. Useless!

Then what about that 2003–2007 bull? Though trending generally higher, confidence was mostly choppy and sideways. You basically wanted to be invested that entire time (never forget—stocks can rise and keep rising for a long time, longer than most think), and if you were trying to time confidence peaks and troughs, you weren't getting much help. Sure, there was a relative low in October 2005—then stocks rose 16.3 percent over the next 12 months.[4] But a true contrarian indicator (if one exists—I've never seen a reliably good one that is actually useful) shouldn't go sideways during a bull market.

Fact is, confidence surveys aim to predict economic direction over the next 6 to 12 months. But what they do is a great job of telling you how people are feeling right now (with a bit of a time lag), which is almost precisely captured by what stocks just did. The only thing you can be confident about is confidence surveys are useless in forecasting the future for stocks.

BUNK 23 ALL HAIL THE MIGHTY DOW!

I'm consistently surprised at how many investors—even professionals who should know better—obsess over the Dow as if it were indicative of anything. It's all you hear on TV: "The Dow was up XX points. The Dow fell YY points." Who cares? In my entire 38-year professional career, I've never paid attention to the level of the Dow—I learned as a kid it is a useless long-term indicator because it is far too narrow and, worse, it is "price-weighted." Never pay attention to any price-weighted index.

In short, despite an army of proponents, the Dow is an inherently flawed index that doesn't reflect the reality of US markets, let alone global ones. Why does everyone fixate on it so?

What's So Wrong With the Dow?

The "Dow" is, of course, the sainted Dow Jones Industrial Average, which persists out of tradition, mostly. That its publisher owns the *Wall Street Journal* (among other publications) probably doesn't hurt either.

Let's start with some relatively minor problems. First, the index is 30 stocks. Just 30! Those 30 stocks are pretty big, but the index is just 29 percent of the total value of US stocks.[1] And you get some weird concentrations in some sectors. And it's US only! So is the S&P 500, but at least its 500 stocks are 89 percent of the total value of US stocks.[2] And the stocks included in the Dow can be included or booted out of the index for fairly arbitrary reasons by those who select the list. For example, Coca-Cola is included, but Pepsi-Cola—nearly the same size as Coke—isn't. Microsoft is in, but Google and Apple (actually bigger in terms of market value than Mr. Softy as I write) aren't. Why? No idea. Can't be that they don't want close competitors—Merck and Pfizer are both included—a double weight to big pharma.[3] Don't try to puzzle it out—save your brain power for worthier tasks.

Price-Weighted Insanity

Yes, all indexes have their own quirks, but price-weighting is an unforgivable doozy. The only other really famous and widely watched price-weighted index is Japan's Nikkei. (You would do better to track Japan's Tokyo Stock Price Index—the Topix—a vastly better and correctly constructed alternative.)

Price-weighting, despite whatever anyone might tell you, means firms with a higher per-share price impact the overall index's performance more than firms with a lower per-share price. But share price is purely cosmetic. See it this way: As of May 31, 2010, Microsoft's share price ($26) was just one-third 3M's ($79). So 3M had *three times* the impact on the Dow as Microsoft—though Microsoft was (and is still) vastly huger. Microsoft's market cap was a whopping $226 billion, compared to 3M's $57 billion—4:1 in favor of Microsoft. That's nuts! Any rational person can see that Microsoft should impact index performance more than 3M. A firm's share price says nothing about a firm's size or relative importance.

Table 23.1 shows all the Dow constituents, ranked by market cap. Note the disconnect between share price and market cap— the actual size of a firm. (You could also do this with the firm's sales, earnings, book value, or whatever and get similar random craziness.)

Here's the real madness of the Dow: If smaller-cap firms with higher share prices (like 3M, United Technologies, Boeing, or Caterpillar—all firms with market caps below the Dow's weighted-average market cap, but among the highest share prices) do well, but giants (like GE, Pfizer, Bank of America, Intel, AT&T, Cisco, or Microsoft—with among the smallest share prices in the Dow) do poorly, then the Dow does better than the economic return of the companies involved—and by a lot. But that doesn't remotely reflect reality. The reverse is true, too. If those massive firms with smaller share prices do well while the smaller market cap/higher price

Table 23.1   The Madness of the Dow

Stock	Price (as of 05/31/2010)	Market Value ($Millions)
Exxon Mobil	$60.46	$284,044
Microsoft	$25.80	$226,107
Wal-Mart Stores	$50.56	$189,659
Procter & Gamble	$61.09	$175,933
General Electric	$16.35	$174,561
Johnson & Johnson	$58.30	$160,795
IBM	$125.26	$160,627
Bank of America	$15.74	$157,919
JPMorgan Chase & Co.	$39.58	$157,476
Chevron	$73.87	$148,386
AT&T	$24.30	$143,589
Cisco Systems	$23.16	$132,270
Pfizer	$15.23	$122,847
Intel	$21.42	$119,181
Coca-Cola	$51.40	$118,582
Hewlett-Packard	$46.01	$107,898
Merck & Co.	$33.69	$105,054
Verizon Communications	$27.52	$77,792
McDonald's	$66.87	$71,938
Walt Disney	$33.42	$65,455
United Technologies	$67.38	$63,096
Home Depot	$33.86	$56,897
3M	$79.31	$56,553
Kraft Foods	$28.60	$49,864
Boeing	$64.18	$48,715
American Express	$39.87	$47,894
Caterpillar	$60.76	$38,169
E.I. Du Pont De Nemours	$36.17	$32,772
Travelers Cos.	$49.47	$24,504
Alcoa	$11.64	$11,876

Source: Thomson Reuters, as of 05/31/2010.

firms do badly, the Dow does worse than the economic returns of the companies. Crazy!

Better-constructed indexes are size-weighted somehow. The most common and most broadly accepted standard (although there are others) is market-cap weighted. In indexes like the S&P 500, the MSCI World Index, the MSCI All-Country World Index (ACWI), the Nasdaq, Japan's Topix, the UK's FTSE, Germany's DAX, and so on—firms that are, in fact, larger in total market value have a greater impact on index performance—just as they should. Just as a hint, the institutional world (like pension plans, endowments, and foundations) and the professional investing world (like mutual funds, etc.) almost never calculate their performance against anything other than market-cap weighted indexes. You shouldn't either.

Stock Splits and Splitting Headaches

Here is where we go into the Twilight Zone. The longer term the results, the more price-weighted indexes are random. Here's why. Splits! In price-weighted indexes, despite whatever anyone tells you, which stocks do and don't have splits actually matter to subsequent performance. Let me show you.

Stock splits happen all the time—but don't change a firm's value or anything of any real worth. Once a firm had 100 shares outstanding for $100 apiece, now it has 200 shares at $50—no difference. The total value of the company (simply the shares outstanding times the share price) doesn't budge. But in a price-weighted index, splits have very real impact on how individual stocks affect the index in the future after the splits—because all that matters is the stock price for any given day's return! A stock split halves the firm's future impact on the index—or maybe more, if the firm does a 3-for-1 or 4-for-1 split. (Reverse splits are more rare—but they happen too and have the reverse impact.)

About now, Dow proponents are howling indignantly about the "divisor"—a calculation that keeps the series continuous before and after each stock split. And the divisor does that, yes. But it doesn't stop the fact that:

1. A split de-weights a stock within the price-weighted index for no real reason.
2. Those who like the Dow should have taken a course in index construction.

Here's how you know. We'll do it just like the Dow. Pretend we have a two-stock, price-weighted index with ABC and XYZ stocks. We'll call it the Silly Index. Each has a $100 share price and identical market caps. To get the value of Silly, add the two share prices ($200) and divide by total number of constituents (2) for $100.

Straightforward, and just how the Dow does it. Exactly! On day 1, ABC goes up 10 percent to $110, and XYZ falls 10 percent to $90—perfectly offsetting. So we add, divide, and still end up with $100. Fine! So far, so good.

Now, pretend both shares are back to $100 on day 2. That night ABC does a 100-for-1 split. That's crazy (so is the Dow), but for illustrative purposes, it's easier to use big numbers because it amplifies what goes on. A shareholder who had 100 shares of ABC at $100 now has 10,000 shares at $1. Either way, he still has $10,000 worth of ABC—nothing changes for him in an economic sense. Nothing.

Not so for the index. Now, to get the index level, we add ABC ($1) to XYZ ($100), divide by 2, and get $50.50. Oh-oh! That can't be right. Nothing changed but the cosmetic share price, but now the index is worth nearly half of what it was before. That won't do. Time for a "divisor"—just exactly like the Dow does. To get back to the correct level, we divide $50.50 by a number that keeps the index level continuous—in this case the divisor is 0.505. Simple algebra to get the divisor.

But it's also weird. See why: Day 3 starts. ABC is $1, XYZ is $100. ABC rises 10 percent again, and XYZ falls 10 percent—random volatility perhaps, but perfectly offsetting—just like on day 1. So, add the two ($1.10 plus $90), divide by 2, apply the divisor (0.505) and you get $90.20—not $100.

What? That shouldn't happen. This is the same thing that happened on day 1! If economic reality applied, the index would be $100 again, since nothing economic changed. Yet because one firm split, the overall index level falls nearly 10 percent. Why? The higher-priced stock fell—and it has outsized impact on the index. The economic reality of the firms hasn't changed, but the index has. If the firms have the same market value, as they do in the Silly Index, they should have equal impact on index performance. They don't. That's the dirty secret of price-weighting.

That's just one stock split. The economic reality of the index gets skewed with every split. In fact, in any year, if the stocks that split do worse than the stocks that don't split, the index does better than the average stock—and thereafter in future years. If the stocks that split do better than those that don't, the index does worse.

It has always been amazing to me how many folks who claim to be professional investors make long-term forecasts about the Dow or talk about its long-term history as if its history had something to do with some real economic phenomenon—which in the case of any price-weighted index is never true. As I documented in *Forbes* columns more than 20 years ago, in a given year, splits in the Dow can throw its return off relative to what the return would have been had those same stocks not split by as much as 10 percent. And by that I don't mean 10 percent becomes 11 percent or 9 percent; no, I mean 10 percent becoming 20 percent or zero. Huge.

We can know two things about those who make long-term forecasts about the Dow. First, they never took a class in index construction—that's a sure bet. Second, they're blowing smoke completely unless they also have some system that somehow forecasts stock splits—and in my life I've never known anyone who's ever even attempted that. (Plus, they didn't read Bunk 20.)

One final way to know the Dow doesn't remotely reflect reality: Very many investors, both amateur and professional, are fond of saying the market went nowhere from 1965 to 1982—17 infamous years of "no return." When they say that, they mean the *Dow* went nowhere. But that's nonsense. The S&P 500 over the same time period annualized 7.1 percent—below average but still positive.[4] Why the huge difference? The S&P 500 is a better reflection of the reality of the US stock market. It's correctly calculated—not price-weighted but market-cap weighted—the way indexes are supposed to be.

It's very telling that most new indexes—even those published by Dow Jones—are market-cap weighted. No one really does price-weighting anymore or ever will again, for good reason. We're stuck with the Dow and Nikkei from tradition, and that's a bad reason to stick with anything. Forget the Dow. Your life will be better for it.

PART ③ "EVERYONE KNOWS"

Y our mom used to say, "If your friends jumped off the Brooklyn Bridge, would you?" This section covers the bunk that makes otherwise reasonable, rational folks want to follow their buddies off a high bridge into shark-infested, polluted waters.

Investing is tough business. It can seem easier to rely on rules of thumb, common "wisdom," catchy phrases, and other simple rules that "everyone knows." They neaten up investing into easy-to-follow, how-to, you-can-do-its. But "easier" doesn't guarantee "better results." In fact, since the stock market is an efficient discounter of widely known information—including cutesy rules of thumb—following common "wisdom" can usually mean netting much worse or even disastrous results.

In your normal life, "rules of thumb" are fine. Everyone knows: Don't smoke. Don't mix ammonia and bleach. Look both ways before crossing the street. Eat vegetables every day. Floss! No one argues with these—quick, easy-to-remember quips keeping you safe, non-toxic, and vitamin-fortified. It's the investing version of these that can be toxic.

In investing, there are no rules that say, "Always sell when X happens," or "Always buy after you see Y," that work consistently, long term. If only investing were that easy! If there were "rules of thumb" that worked, I wouldn't have written this book, and you certainly wouldn't have bothered buying it. Sure, sometimes some rules work— but that's usually coincidence, not because they're fundamentally correct. Yet, countless investing "do this, not that" shortcut rules exist.

Why? Humans love finding patterns—you know that from Part 1. So much so we find them when none exist—creating rules about when to invest or not based on seasons, months, days of the week, lunar calendars, and possibly astrological signs. All non-fundamental nonsense. (Bunks 24, 25.)

There are some rules that "intuitively" make sense. But the stock market is frequently counterintuitive. Applying our human Stone Age intuition to capital markets can mean getting seriously whacked. (Bunks 26, 27.)

Then, there is the "common wisdom" bred from tradition—which you know from Part 2 is problematic. Humans frequently seek the safety of crowds or the wisdom of "experts." If lots of smart people say something, and have for decades, there's no reason to question it—right? Exactly wrong—debunkery means flipping all that on its head. (Bunks 28, 29, 30, 31, 32.)

A better rule of thumb to follow is: If "everyone knows" something, chances are few people have bothered questioning it—so you should. It doesn't hurt. And it's not that hard. These chapters demonstrate some basic debunkery and the tactics you use for it—checking data, running correlations, even applying some basic finance theory—to check if what "everyone knows" is true. What "everyone knows" could be pure bunk. Costly bunk! And costly bunk can really hurt. A little debunkery saves you.

BUNK 24 — SO GOES JANUARY

"So goes January" is as old as the hills! This popular myth says if the first few days of January are down, the month will be too, and so will the year. There are minor variations of this myth—some claim it's the first day alone that's predictive. Most scoff at that, thinking it's the first 3, 5, 10, 17, or some other random and arbitrary number (unable to see why if one day isn't predictive, then 3, 5, 10, 17, or any other random number won't be either). Some say it's the first week, but then where does the holiday fall into that? And do four days make a week? All of this is nonsense.

Cognitive Errors Galore

There's a whole mess of cognitive errors that happen with this and any other day-, month-, or season-related myth (like "Sell in May," coming up in Bunk 25, or the supposed "Santa Claus" or "summer" rallies). First, almost never do you hear "so goes!" if January starts strong. Folks don't say, "Phew! January was positive. No need to worry about the rest of the year!" No—folks who like this bunk usually use it to prop up bearish biases.

Second, this myth causes folks to *reframe*. If January is down and the year too, the "so goes" crowd claims victory (usually loudly). But if January is down and the year finishes up, the "so goes" crowd never issues a mea culpa.

Instead, they'll claim, "Of course it doesn't work every year. You must look at the long-term average." They change the observation period for occurrences that don't fit their pre-set notions. Years that work the way they think they should are, to them, hard evidence this works. Years that don't aren't, to them, evidence it's hooey. This is a perfect example of the human behavioral quality of confirmation bias: Seeing what you believe and not seeing what you disbelieve—a trait behavioralists have proven in recent decades.

Third, it's a silly human quirk to assign meaning to random groups of 30 or 31 days. There's nothing inherently more or less predictive about January, but because of what behavioralists call "mental accounting," we assign great import to the start of each year. But capital markets care nothing about mental accounting.

It's actually, to me, beyond amazing this bunk endures. Even anecdotally, this one starts falling apart fast. Just think about recent history. The S&P 500 fell 8 percent and world stocks fell 9 percent in January 2009.[1] But the year ended *up* 26.5 percent and 30.0 percent, respectively.[2] If you followed this bunk, you missed that. There are plenty of years January is up, down, or sideways, and the year does something entirely different.

Check the Box

We can use the four-box methodology to debunk this—a good debunkery trick you can use often (and we'll use again for fears of a too-weak/too-strong dollar in Bunk 27). Table 24.1 shows the number of years since 1926 that stocks were up in January and up for the year, as well as down in January and for the year—the way many believe the stock market works. But it also shows when January is up and the year down, and the reverse.

Since 1926, we've had a positive January and then a positive year 45 times—nearly 54 percent of the time. That shouldn't surprise, since in an overall positive year, more months should be up than down. Plus stocks are up more than down over history—roughly two-thirds of the time. Since 1926, January has been up 63.1 percent

Table 24.1 So Goes January? (S&P 500)

		January Return		
		Up	Down	Total
Full Year	Up	45 (53.6%)	15 (17.9%)	60 (71.4%)
Return	Down	8 (9.5%)	16 (19.0%)	24 (29.6%)
	Total	53 (63.1%)	31 (36.9%)	

Source: Global Financial Data, Inc., S&P 500 total return from 12/31/1925 to 12/31/2009.

of the time, and 71.4 percent of the years have been up. (Tell that 71 percent number to folks who mope about secular bear markets and other such silliness.) With no guarantee about the future, historically, stocks have really "wanted" to be up more than down. With so many positives relative to negatives—about two to one—you get more up years than down years and more up Januarys than down ones.

Just 8 times—9.5 percent—January was up and then the year was down. Rare! So if up-up years happen most, and an up January rarely leads to a down year, does that mean January is predictive? Nope. A down January is basically a coin flip—historically you get about the same number of up and down years following a down January—17.9 percent to 19.0 percent—the difference of one occurrence. Seen another way, a flip-flop year—January up in a down year and down in an up year—has happened more often (27.4 percent) than a down January and down year (19.0 percent).

I'll say repeatedly in these pages: One easy way to do debunkery is ignoring any rule that says, "When this happens, that's automatically bad (or good)." No one thing is ever a definitive sign to either bail on stocks or be bullish. If it were that easy, someone, somewhere, would have discovered the trick and be the richest guy in the world. And because it is so easy to do now, we'd all be doing it. Baloney and bunkonometry! Plus, global capital markets are far too complex for one indicator to be so powerful. So ignore January. So goes January is how January goes, and then it's gone—and nothing more.

BUNK 25   SELL IN MAY

Everybody's heard, "Sell in May and go away." Hopefully, most ignore it. It's supposed to mean summer is a bad time for stocks, so you can safely sell in May, let stocks drift lower, and buy back in the fall. It's also very wrong and financially bad advice.

Amazingly, every May, particularly if stocks are down, this gets echoed endlessly in headlines. (It's very similar to "so goes January" from Bunk 24—folks who are bearishly biased seem to love this.) I hear from some clients and *Forbes* readers if stocks have a tough week or two during the summer months, "Everybody knows to 'sell in May!'"

But what does "sell in May" really mean? Sell when in May? May 1? The 31? The 12? April 30? And if everyone knows to sell in May (if we ever figure out exactly when), if you're smart, don't you sell in April before everyone else starts selling? And if you could figure that out, why not sell even earlier to beat that early crowd? When does it end? (People who like automatic sell rules like these never think through that logic.)

Sell in May . . . When? And Then What?

There's more. If I sell in May, when the heck do I buy back? People say it has to do with the summer being bad—so do I buy back on September 1? The autumnal equinox? When? "Sell in May" has myriad permutations, but none hold water. Check history. Vary the date however you want—it doesn't work.

Table 25.1 shows average S&P 500 returns by month. Since 1926, stocks have averaged 0.38 percent in May. Not huge, but not negative. They've averaged 1.19 percent in June and 1.83 percent

Table 25.1 Average Stock Returns by Month—Why Would You Sell in May?

Month	Average S&P 500 Return
January	1.49%
February	0.06%
March	0.72%
April	1.67%
May	**0.38%**
June	1.19%
July	1.83%
August	1.30%
September	-0.75%
October	0.43%
November	1.07%
December	1.74%

Source: Global Financial Data, Inc., S&P 500 total return from 12/31/1925 to 12/31/2009.

in July. July has been historically best—smack dab in midsummer, which some say is so dreadful (and others say it's when you start a "summer rally"—another piece of statistical nonsense). August has averaged fine too. So many stats. So little meaning! Welcome to this little bunkhouse.

Now, some will say "sell in May" doesn't mean May, but that the *summer months* overall are bad for stocks. Fine—June, July, and August together average 4.51 percent.[1] Together, they beat the average of any other three consecutive months! (How the heck did this myth get started?) And it's likely much better than what you could get from a 90-day T-bill, and definitely better than cash, never mind adding in transaction costs and taxes from inning-and-outing. Then some will say, "No, it's the summer *half* that's worse—May to October." Sheesh! This simple saying has a lot of small print. Since 1926, May 1 through October 31 has averaged 4.26 percent, while November 1 through April 30 averaged 7.07 percent.[2] Yes! The "winter" half *is* better. Big deal. (Again, the summer "half" is still positive and still much better than the average returns of cash or six-month T-bills.) We can slice and dice this anyway we want. March through August averages 7.16%, but September through February just 4.38%.[3] So why not "sell in September?" (Probably because it doesn't rhyme with the "and go away" bit.) These are all just statistical quirks.

Plus, these are all *averages*. There's a lot of wild variability cooked into them—big ups and big downs (Bunk 5). Look at September in Table 25.1 again—the only negative average. Should you sell in September? Not because of history alone. Take out the two worst Septembers (down 29.6 percent in 1931 and down 13.8 percent in 1937—both in the Great Depression),[4] and the remaining Septembers don't look so bad. How much faith do you want to put into those two terrible Septembers out of 84 Septembers somehow being representative? Or into any average return from any group of months? Averages often mislead. (Basic debunkery: Look beneath the averages to what comprises them.) And just because something has had a negative average doesn't mean it will be more negative than not going forward. There's nothing inherently more risky about September—except maybe kids are going back to school and you have to be careful driving. And inning-and-outing around one month or a group of months because they have lower average returns historically is silly, particularly since you can't guarantee the alternatives net you anything better.

That should kill "sell in May" forever. Debunkenasia it! But in addition to "so goes January," there are many other day-of-the-week, month, seasonal, and holiday myths—all equally silly. They often feel appealing and sometimes work out ok, but overall, over time, simply don't work and end up costing those who follow them money. Santa Claus rallies. The January effect. Triple witching. Sell on Monday. Since 1980, every time the New York Giants won a Super Bowl (1986, 1990, and 2007), we had a bear market soon after. The Pittsburgh Steelers are supposed to be bullish—silly coincidences as fundamental as "sell in May."

Ignore "sell in May" and any other saying about selling automatically based on dates, months, pro football teams, or anything else not somehow grounded in sound, fundamental economics or portfolio theory. (Though there is the rumor that Harry Markowitz is a Steelers fan.)

BUNK 26 — LOW P/Es MEAN LOW RISK

P eople tend to think low price-to-earnings (P/E) ratios mean low risk for single stocks and the market as a whole. It's an almost universal, near-religious belief that "everyone knows." But it's just wrong. Using P/Es to forecast risk and return over any reasonable time period is about as useful as using a Ouija board.

I debunked the "high P/Es are risky, low P/Es aren't" myth pretty thoroughly in my 2006 book, *The Only Three Questions That Count*. Taking it apart multiple ways took up about half a big chapter. I won't restate that here, but instead take you through yet another way to know P/Es—high or low—aren't predictive on their own. (I also co-authored a scholarly piece on why P/Es don't forecast risk or return with my buddy Meir Statman that you can find on the Internet if you're academically oriented—"Cognitive Biases in Market Forecasts," *Journal of Portfolio Management*, Fall 2000.)

My criticism here doesn't mean P/Es aren't useful. They can be— but not as forward-looking predictors of market or stock returns. Like all commonly used valuations, their predictive power is long gone since anyone can get them lightning fast on the Internet and markets pretty efficiently discount all widely known information. Use them to compare stock peers, sure. Flip the P/E over into an E/P (the earnings yield) and compare that as a form of an interest rate to going bond yields to know if a firm or sector or the entire market has more incentive to issue new shares of stock or engage in cash-based stock buybacks—that can be useful to know too. Stock buybacks reduce the future supply of stocks and, all else being equal, are bullish. Stock offerings are the reverse. There are many ways to incorporate P/Es into other things that are useful. But don't think a P/E alone says where a stock or the market is headed.

Fear of Heights

A major problem with P/Es is our natural fear of heights. Modern humans hit the world about 250,000 years ago—and we've been dealing with basic problems of survival since. Back then, if you were up high and fell, that was pretty much the end of it. Dead, or crippled—which then was about the same thing. So we developed a very healthy fear of heights. And P/E is expressed as a heights framework—high/low.

Modern capital markets came around only in the last few hundred years. Investing didn't become broadly available to average Joe types until the last few decades with the innovation of 401(k)s, IRAs, and discount trading outfits like Charles Schwab. Now, anyone with income can easily open a brokerage account and start buying stocks, mutual funds, bonds, etc. Even just 50 years ago, that wasn't so. Back then, mostly, only those with accumulated wealth did so, and there were precious few of them as a percentage of society.

Simply: Modern investing has evolved much faster than our brains' ability to deal with it. From our past, we believe height is dangerous. Falling a long way is crippling if not deadly—we believe that cold. We naturally think about high P/Es the same way. Anything high is scary—low is safer, so we think low P/Es are less risky, high P/Es more risky. Not so.

Just for fun, and to go off on a tangent, let me show you another simple way to know our ancestral fear of heights can be misleading. Is it safer to have more space between you and lower elevations or less? Depends! Take flying in planes, another thing our brains weren't ancestrally set up to do. If you're in a small plane at 150 feet in elevation and the engine starts acting up, I bet you would rather be at 2,500 feet—more time to get the engine going or coast to a safe place to land. Falling from 150 feet doesn't make you any less dead than falling from 2,500 feet—splattered either way. But sometimes in some frameworks higher is safer. Higher can be and often is misleading when it comes to safety.

Two Moving Parts to a P/E

A basic problem with P/Es is folks fail to remember there are two simultaneous variables—the P and the E. Then they fail to remember that the P/E is telling you about where you are, not where you're going—and all the market ever cares about is where you're going over the next 6 to 24 months.

P/Es were very high at the end of 2008—the S&P 500 P/E was 60.7.[1] Whoa! Way above average. But if you thought high P/Es were risky, you would have avoided stocks and missed the big 27 percent surge in US stocks and 30 percent in world stocks in 2009.[2] The P/E was high then because earnings were temporarily and hugely depressed because of the recession—very low relative to the P, giving it a very "high" P/E. Fact is, year-end 2008 P/Es were also way above where year-end 2007 P/Es were. But 2007 marked the peak of the market—before the recession and earnings started to decline. So if you thought lower P/Es meant lower risk and higher P/Es meant higher risk, you would have presumed the market was lower risk *at the peak of the market* than at its subsequent low, which has to be wrong and backwards.

Another example: The S&P 500 P/E was 31.9 on December 31, 2002.[3] Sky high—but also a great time to own stocks. US and world stocks returned 29 percent and 33 percent in 2003, respectively.[4] Again, P/Es were high then because earnings had crashed during the immediately past recession. It's very common to see high P/Es during and after recessions—usually a fantastic time to own stocks.

At both those points in time, the P/E was reflecting the here and now and the trailing 12 months past—not where earnings were going. But stocks look forward and typically move ahead of the earnings—they fall before earnings do and go up before earnings rise. The P/E doesn't help you see forward earnings and future P/Es, unless you dig down to see *why* earnings are so low relative to prices and make forecasts about the future—and you can't do that if you don't get that those two variables don't necessarily move in sync.

But the feature of the overall market P/E being high at market bottoms is almost universal—just when stocks are very low risk and about to rise hugely. That doesn't mean high P/Es only coincide with bear market bottoms. Sometimes stock prices overshoot even strong earnings—and go higher still. Why? Rapid earnings growth can lead to an even faster rise in stock prices as investors price in boom times ahead. This leads to higher P/Es. Eventually, too much investor optimism can cause stock prices to get out of whack with economic reality, but don't expect P/Es alone to indicate that the tipping point has been reached. That P/Es are high doesn't mean stock prices must fall (any more than low P/Es mean stocks must rise).

P/Es were pretty elevated all during the mid- to- late- 1990s, and stocks kept roaring ever higher. The S&P 500 P/E was 32.6 at 1998's close—then the S&P rose 21.0 percent in 1999.[5] P/Es were way above average at the close of 1995, 1996, and 1997[6]—then stocks did 23.0 percent, 33.4 percent, and 28.6 percent respectively in 1996, 1997, and 1998.[7]

At the close of 1999—just a few months shy of the 2000 peak—prices were indeed high relative to earnings, finally "too high." But the P/E at the close of 1999 was 30.5[8]—*lower* than previous year-end P/E. Lower! Yet stocks were riskier in 2000 than 1999. And that 30.5 was *lower* than at year-end 2002. I'll say that differently—P/Es were *higher* at the tail end of the major 2000–2003 bear market than they were at the start—but stocks were actually much, much less risky at the end.

What about low P/Es? Do they signal low risk? Another way to ask that: Were P/Es low or high in 1929? Folklore says they were high, but as I documented in my 1987 book, *The Wall Street Waltz* (John Wiley & Sons, pages 68–69), they were actually pretty low, about 13—certainly not the sky-high levels of mythology. And that didn't keep stocks from crashing into a massive bear market. In fact, my sense of history is the low P/E gave folks a false sense of security, lulling them into complacency just before earnings went to hell. The P/E was low because earnings were too high.

A low P/E can mean just what mythology implies—that stock prices are "too low" relative to earnings and might rise. Year-end P/Es for 1981, 1982, 1983, and 1984 were low—and stocks did fine each year following, as most folks would expect.[9] Sometimes a low P/E is parallel to a good deal. But a low P/E might mean earnings have run up too far and are unsustainable at those levels, as was the case with 1928 and 1929.

So it's perfectly normal for stock prices to crash before earnings do—which gives you a low P/E, like year-end 1980 when a low P/E (9.2—very low) preceded falling stock prices in 1981.[10] Low year-end P/Es preceded stocks falling in 1930, 1931, 1939, 1940, 1957, 1976[11]—I could go on and on. Those low P/Es didn't *cause* falling prices. They just reflected a snapshot of stock prices falling before earnings fell.

Put another way: As my grandfather's one-time girlfriend and noted literary phenomenon Gertrude Stein once famously said about her hometown of Oakland (across the bay from my grandfather's hometown of San Francisco), "There's no there there."

There's simply no reliable predictive pattern to P/E alone—any way you slice it in any time frame anyone cares about. It's an incomplete snapshot in time. P/E says nothing about forward-looking risk or return over the next one, three, or five years. You must dig deeper to understand why a P/E is high, low, or middling, and what that means (if anything), and where future earnings are going—which isn't easy. Stocks can rise and fall on low and high P/Es equally. And P/Es can be high and stay high for a long time—all while stocks rise. Same with low P/Es.

Many won't want to believe this because they want to believe what they want to believe—a basic part of what behavioralists define as confirmation bias. They'll want to go with their guts (a cognitive error—Bunk 7). They'll want to look for examples that prove they're right and ignore or explain away those contradicting the bias. But for every point anyone can find in history showing that P/Es work the way their guts believe, there are an almost equal number of examples showing the exact reverse and in the same magnitude. (If you're curious, I show this mathematically in my 2006 book, *The Only Three Questions That Count.*)

Let me stretch this a bit further. As bewitching as the idea is of a single valuation or indicator that will tell you where a stock or the market is going, it doesn't exist. P/E, price-to-book (P/B) ratio, my long-beloved price-to-sales ratio (PSR), dividend yield—it doesn't matter. Your single silver bullet has never been shown to work—at least not yet. And if such a thing surfaced, everyone would quickly discover it, and it too would soon become powerless. Unfortunately, investing is never that simple. If it were, everyone would beat the market. And you know that will never happen.

BUNK 27   A STRONG DOLLAR IS SUPER

How often have you heard the following? "A weak dollar is bad for stocks. But a strong dollar . . . that's awesome!" I'd guess quite a lot.

For much of the 2000s the dollar was on the reverse of a tear—falling most years relative to pound sterling, euro, and most of our other trading partners. In 2009, for the first time in over 30 years the Canadian dollar was worth more than the dollar. Horror! There were periods of reversal—2005 saw the dollar strengthen. The dollar was strong in the back half of 2008 too. But never mind! For the most part, folks have it fixed in their brains: A weak dollar is bad for stocks, and a strong dollar good.

After all, the dollar was weak for much of the decade, and stocks overall had a lousy decade—basically flat. Proof! On the other hand, the dollar was weak in 2003, 2004, 2006, and most of 2007 when stocks boomed. And it was strong in 2001 and 2008 when they fell. But, on the third hand, the dollar was also weak in 2002 as stocks fell, strong in 2005 as stocks rose, and weak again most of 2009 when stocks staged a historically massive comeback.[1] So, on the fourth hand, what's behind all this? What's true?

Dollar Dilemma

Folks fear a weak dollar signals people don't have faith in the US economy, which leads to, or is symptomatic of, slow growth and bad stock returns. Plus, a weak dollar makes imports more expensive. Because the US has long been a net importer (see Bunk 48), that makes most things more expensive and could slow growth. Or, at least, that's a big fear. Conversely, folks believe a strong dollar implies faith in the US of A, and that should mean a strong economy and rising stocks. (It doesn't, but we'll get to that soon.)

Mind you, folks gripe about the weak dollar because it has been overall weak for so long. Interestingly, as I write in 2010, the dollar has been strong. Yet you didn't suddenly hear those who griped about the weak dollar yelling, "Hooray! A strong dollar means everything is ok! Bring me another martini!" And plenty of other folks fear a too-strong dollar, too. A strong dollar makes our exports pricier for foreigners, so they'll want to buy less. In the 1990s, it was very common to hear that the too-strong dollar was soon to be the death of our economy. But people forget that.

There are pros and cons to both a weak and a strong dollar. But there's nothing inherently superior about one over the other. See it this way. Currency isn't an appreciating asset like a stock. It's a commodity. And it's weak only relative to something else. So the dollar is weak because euro or pound sterling or a bunch of currencies are strong. And vice versa!

People don't think this way, but if the dollar is weak, then the non-dollar is strong. Run down this logic further: If a weak dollar is bad for the US, then a strong non-dollar is good for the non-US world. Because the US is just under 25 percent of world GDP,[2] a weak dollar should be, by this theory, *less* bad for the world overall than a strong non-dollar is good. So, on balance, a weak dollar should be good. No . . . great!

Of course that's not true either—actually, it's nonsense if you think it through further. Weak or strong, the dollar doesn't matter overall to the world. But people who believe a weak dollar is bad never ride the logic train long enough to see why their belief is silly.

Over time, because currencies are inherently zero-sum and irregularly cyclical, currency impacts on a global portfolio net out to close to zero. But even if you don't want to believe that, and you aren't a master statistician, you can easily test to see if a weak or strong dollar is good or bad for US or world stocks.

Put the Dollar in a Box

Again we can use a standard debunkery four-box (as we did for "so goes January" in Bunk 24). To do a four-box for currency versus stocks, plot the years the trade-weighted US dollar is up or down against years the S&P 500 is up or down. (The trade-weighted dollar

Table 27.1 US Stocks Versus the Dollar—Dollar Direction Doesn't Matter

		US Dollar		
		Up	Down	Total
S&P 500	Up	15 (38%)	15 (38%)	30 (77%)
	Down	4 (10%)	5 (13%)	9 (23%)
	Total	19 (49%)	20 (51%)	

Source: Global Financial Data, Inc., Trade-Weighted US Dollar Index,[3] S&P 500 total return from 12/31/1970 to 12/31/2009.

is the correct way to do this because what we care about most is how the dollar fares against our trading partners. For example, we don't trade much with Bhutan, so we don't care if the ngultrum is super strong or weak against the dollar.) The four-box in Table 27.1 goes back to 1971, which is after the end of the Bretton Woods era.

First, as ever, you see US stocks are up more than down—much more—a big 77 percent in this period. (Folks can't seem to get that in their bones: Stocks rise much more than they fall.) Second, there's no pattern here. When stocks were up, there were an identical number of occurrences of an up versus a down dollar.

People think a weak dollar is bad for stocks, but where's the proof? Years the trade-weighted dollar fell and stocks fell too happened just 5 times—13 percent of the years. Don't take that to mean a weak dollar is great either. It just means dollar movements aren't predictive (and stocks rise more than they fall).

Some might see this and think the dollar is down (slightly) more than up, therefore the dollar is lousy. Wrong conclusion too. Just so happens, as I write this in 2010, we're in a period where the dollar has been weak, averaged over a few years. The dollar is weak only because the non-dollar is strong. Currencies naturally want to be cyclical, and the dollar will go through a period of relative strength again, just as it did during portions of the 1990s.

Interestingly, in Table 27.2 you see the same pattern—almost exactly with slight variances—with world stocks. Weak or strong, the dollar doesn't impact US or global stock market direction.

Where's the Zigzag?

Think this through another way (and borrowing a bit from Part 5): If a weak dollar is bad, then a strong non-dollar should be good,

Table 27.2 World Stocks Versus the Dollar—Dollar Direction Doesn't Matter

		US Dollar		
		Up	Down	Total
MSCI World	Up	14 (36%)	16 (41%)	30 (77%)
	Down	5 (13%)	4 (10%)	10 (23%)
	Total	19 (49%)	20 (51%)	

Source: Thomson Reuters, MSCI World total returns with net dividends from 12/31/1970 to 12/31/2009; Global Financial Data, Inc., Trade-Weighted US Dollar Index[4] from 12/31/1970 to 12/31/2009.

and world and US stocks should zigzag all over. When the US market is up, most times that should mean the non-US market is down and vice versa. But that's not what happens. There's a very strong correlation between US and non-US stocks (see Bunk 43). And it has nothing to do with relative strength or weakness of the dollar, yen, pound sterling, ringgit, or ngultrum. Stocks are globally correlated—have been for years—longer and more strongly than most probably know. US and foreign stocks never move in opposite directions for very long. So the notion that the dollar being down makes US stocks fall but makes non-US stocks rise is bunk and undermines the entire notion of the dollar (or any other currency) driving stocks.

Why does this matter? Because frequently, in any given year, folks want to say the too-weak (or sometimes, too-strong) dollar spells doom for stocks. Ignore it. Or exploit it as a minor bullish factor because fear of a false future factor is nearly always bullish. Yes, something might spell doom for stocks, but it won't be the dollar on its own. Look beyond this provable bunk for what really does move stocks, and you'll spend your time more profitably.

BUNK 28 DON'T FIGHT THE FED

The saying "don't fight the Fed" is the popular (and misguided) notion "everyone knows" that a few consecutive Fed rate hikes are bearish, whereas falling rates are bullish. The idea is loose monetary policy leads to lots of extra liquidity and is good for stocks—but tightening sucks money from the economy and is bad for stocks. Some folks think "don't fight the Fed" applies to the discount rate, others to the fed funds target rate, still others to short-term rates in general. All wrong!

Instead of "don't fight the Fed," I wish everyone knew that any market adage that says, "Always sell on this one condition, buy on that one," is wing-nut time. (If only investing were that easy!) There is, to my knowledge, no one single indicator that works consistently and is failsafe. And if you just know that no one indicator is close to failsafe, you know this adage is bunk.

A Monetary Phenomenon

But suppose you want evidence. Consider recent history. From 2001 to 2003, the Fed steadily cut rates—while stocks tanked. If you had been obediently not fighting the Fed, you would have been nailed by a big bear market. The same was true, but worse, in the 2007 to 2009 bear market. The Fed dropped rates starting late in 2007—just as the bear market began—all the way until the target fed funds rate was down to 0 to 0.25 percent. And that was during a major bear market. Conversely, the Fed raised rates from 2004 through 2006, during a bull market.

What gives? It's true, dropping rates is one way the Fed can increase money supply. But do they do it drastically when the economy is cooking along? Not if they have their heads screwed on straight. Remember what Milton Friedman said about inflation being "always and everywhere" a monetary phenomenon. Dropping rates a bunch when the economy is zipping is like pouring fuel on a fire—it could cause runaway inflation. The Fed, if behaving appropriately, starts raising rates not because the economy is troubled, but because they think it's necessary and, more importantly, the economy can handle it. This is almost the exact opposite of what the "don't fight-ers" are thinking. They presume somehow the Fed is usually wrong. Sometimes it is. Usually it isn't. Usually when they raise rates, the economy and markets can take it.

Truth is, stocks can rise and fall on rising or falling interest rates. While the Fed is being overall accommodative, they might raise or lower rates within a range. The same when they're overall a bit tighter. A move up or down of 25, 50, even 100 basis points might, in the large scheme of things, not be a big deal. Would you buy or sell every time the Fed makes a policy wiggle? And it's true—a lot of liquidity sloshing around globally often does find its way into stocks, and that can be positive. But the fed funds rate isn't the only thing impacting global liquidity. America's economy is just 24.6 percent of world GDP[1]—central bank policy elsewhere matters, too.

Exit Jitters

In 2010 as I write, on the tail-end of a historic, massive wave of glo-bal monetary stimulus (i.e., falling rates globally combined with quantitative easing *all while* stocks fell in 2008 into early 2009), there's huge fear of a "too-early" stimulus exit. (Of course, there are simultaneous fears the exit will be *too late*. Sometimes you can't win.) What folks fear isn't a little rate wiggle in a bandwidth. They fear a total trend reversal—the start of a legitimate tightening cycle—that central banks raising rates will choke off recovery. The world's gone "don't fight the Fed" crazy.

But a check of history (debunkery!) shows there's little prece-dent to worry about the start of a tightening cycle. Table 28.1 shows US stock performance following the first rate hike in a sustained

Table 28.1   S&P 500 Returns Following the First Rate Hike—Don't Fear a Fed Hike

Start Date	Returns From Start of Tightening		
	12 Months Forward	24 Months Forward	36 Months Forward
07/16/1971	8.4%	6.6%	−18.8%
08/16/1977	5.7%	10.6%	25.2%
10/21/1980	−8.9%	5.5%	25.9%
03/22/1984	14.3%	48.9%	90.3%
12/04/1986	−11.5%	7.4%	38.9%
03/30/1988	13.3%	31.7%	45.4%
02/04/1994	1.9%	35.3%	68.0%
06/30/1999	6.0%	−10.8%	−27.9%
06/30/2004	4.4%	11.3%	31.8%
Average	3.7%	16.3%	31.0%
Median	5.7%	10.6%	31.8%

Source: Thomson Reuters, S&P 500 price return.

Table 28.2   MSCI World Returns Following the First Rate Hike—Don't Fear a Fed Hike

Start Date	Returns From Start of Tightening		
	12 Months Forward	24 Months Forward	36 Months Forward
07/16/1971	15.0%	19.0%	−6.9%
08/16/1977	17.3%	24.2%	39.7%
10/21/1980	−13.3%	−7.9%	12.5%
03/22/1984	8.8%	63.1%	132.8%
12/04/1986	6.9%	36.7%	55.3%
03/30/1988	11.0%	7.2%	11.8%
02/04/1994	−2.9%	18.6%	31.6%
06/30/1999	11.0%	−12.6%	−26.8%
06/30/2004	8.1%	24.2%	50.8%
Average	6.9%	19.2%	33.4%
Median	8.8%	19.0%	31.6%

Source: Thomson Reuters, MSCI, Inc.,[2] MSCI World price return. Returns before 1980 use end-of-month values.

tightening cycle. Not always but overwhelmingly, stock returns are positive 12, 24, even 36 months later. There's nothing that says starting a tightening cycle must spell doom.

But because US and non-US stocks are typically strongly correlated, this one works pretty darn well for world stocks too (see Table 28.2). Following Fed rate hikes, world stocks have largely been fine 12, 24, and 36 months later. Nothing to fear here.

Generally, it makes sense that a sustained tightening cycle begins after a recession is widely apparent. While the Fed certainly makes mistakes, they generally don't want to tighten too soon in an economic recovery. After all, Fed heads are inherently political creatures—they're appointed! They like their jobs and want to keep them—they don't want to botch a recovery, which makes their boss (i.e., the president) look bad. He's the guy who reappoints them.

Tables 28.1 and 28.2 also tell you that, generally, stocks tend to rise for long periods—longer than most think. And they tell you an initial rate hike, or even a tightening cycle, is, by itself, little to fear.

BUNK 29

INTEREST PAYS DIVIDENDS

Raise your hand if this applies to you: "I need my portfolio to kick off some reliable amount of cash flow to partially or wholly fund living expenses in my retirement—whenever that is."

You're not alone. With firms veering away from pensions, many investors have saving for retirement as a major goal. (Another way to say it: For many, Social Security won't be enough, and those who plan on relying on it alone will likely be in a world of hurt.)

Now, raise your hand if you think, once you retire, you need a portfolio full of dividend-paying stocks and interest-bearing bonds to provide that income.

You're also not alone—it's a very common view. But this is one dangerous, poverty-inducing bit of easily debunked bunk.

Or maybe not—maybe you have a $10 million portfolio and require only $50,000 a year. And maybe you don't care if the $50,000 isn't inflation-adjusted. Or, if you don't have $10 million, maybe it doesn't matter to you if your assets dwindle because of reinvestment risk or your high-dividend stocks suddenly stop paying dividends.

But chances are, if you're reading this book, you don't want your assets to stagnate or deplete—which is what can happen if you focus solely on coupons, interest, and dividends. What happens when the bond you bought in 2000 that yielded about 6.7 percent per year matures, and a comparable replacement bond in 2010 likely yields about 3.5 percent?[1] And what happens if that stock paying an 8 percent dividend cuts it to 2 percent in tough times? Or zero? That can happen—and that's probably not what you were banking on. (Pun intended.)

And the $10 million question: What about inflation over the rest of your long life?

It's simply not true that interest and dividends are necessarily a "safe" way to get retirement income. But how else can investors get cash from their portfolios? You don't want to—oh, no—sell stocks, do you?

Homegrown Dividends

Sure. Why not? First, many folks mistakenly assign themselves an inappropriate asset allocation, partly because they think they must be "conservative" (Bunk 3)—but also because they think they need the dividend and interest income for cash. This confuses "income" with "cash flow." Interest and dividends are what's traditionally called "income." Even the IRS looks at interest and dividends as income—and tax you for it. But, after tax, you should be agnostic about the source of your cash flow.

When you pay your mortgage, electric bills, or the restaurant tab—no one cares if the money was from a dividend, a bond coupon, or a stock sale. You shouldn't either. And because tax treatment for long-term capital gains can be cheaper than for interest and dividends, which are taxed at your (likely) higher marginal "earned" income tax rate (based on 2011 law), you can get more bang for your portfolio buck from selling stocks—if done wisely. And that means you can, if appropriate, keep more of your money in an asset class that has a higher probability of yielding better long-term returns. (See Bunks 2 or 3.)

All this presumes you have a long life ahead of you whether retired or not, which most folks of normal retirement age do today (again, Bunk 3). Say you have $1 million saved, and you want $40,000 a year to support your lifestyle. (More than 4 percent distributions and your depletion risk increases.) Maybe you want even distributions into your checking account each month—about $3,333, give or take. It's easy—just keep about twice that in cash in your portfolio at all times, or about $7,000. Having that small amount in cash won't materially impact performance in a rising stock market, and in a falling stock market, you needn't rush around to sell stocks at a relative low.

Instead you can be tactical about what you sell and when. You can sell "down" stocks as a tax loss to offset gains you might realize. You can pare back over-weighted positions. And you may even have, quite by happenstance while seeking total return, some dividend-paying stocks to add some cash, but then that's a decision about whether you think they're the right stocks to hold, and you aren't handcuffed to them just because of the dividend. Like any other investing category, high-dividend paying stocks cycle in and out of favor, so sometimes it makes sense to hold more and sometimes less. As a category, they tend to do well when other so-called "value" stocks are doing well and do badly when so-called "growth" stocks are the fad. (See Bunk 10.)

I call raising cash this way "homegrown dividends." It's how my firm does it for many of its clients. It's a tax-efficient way to generate cash flow and has the additional benefit of keeping you optimally, appropriately invested—aimed at investing for your unique time horizon.

So stop thinking "income" and start thinking "cash flow." Be cash flow agnostic.

BUNK 30

BUY A 5% CD FOR 5% CASH FLOW—EASY!

Many folks I talk to just can't see why they need any stocks at all. They consider themselves frugal. Not greedy. They see themselves as "conservative." Maybe they have $500,000 saved up—which isn't a lot or unusual for folks nearing retirement who've had a lifetime to save and done it reasonably. They want just $25,000 a year to live on—plenty for them. Maybe they'll get a bit more from Social Security. They've decided to take as little risk as possible. They'll buy 5 percent CDs—or maybe some other super-safe instruments yielding 5 percent. Everyone knows CDs are safe! No stocks for them. To them, that's not a risky approach—it's a safe one.

Yet it's one of the riskiest things they can do long term. Set aside the fact that, as readers in 2010 and probably even 2011 will know, finding a 5 percent CD is close to impossible. If someone offers you one, it is surely from a very risky institution that runs the risk of failure. (Worse, remember the high CD rates alleged Ponzi schemer R. Allen Stanford offered—Bunk 11.) In the future, it's impossible to know where interest rates will go. And no one can guarantee that when one CD, bond, note, or bill matures, you can always find one to replace it with a similar or better yield. You might have to buy something yielding less! Happens often.

But this scenario ignores the elephant in the room: inflation. Inflation is punk but it's no bunk, and it can be devastating to a poorly constructed portfolio. No one can predict inflation accurately in the long term, but it is a huge risk in the very long-term future that can't be overlooked.

The Silent Killer

This debunkery is easy—you can do the accounting yourself. The question is: Will money today be worth the same 20 years from now? Even without checking data, you know the answer: No way, José. Inflation is the silent killer. It "gets" far too many retirees who fail to plan for enough growth (usually because they underestimate their time horizons—Bunk 3). And, frequently, by the time damage is done, it can be too late to reverse the damage, even a bit.

How does this happen? People think about inflation wrong. In a world of zero inflation, prices wouldn't all be flat. Half would be rising, a little to a lot, and the other half falling, a little to a lot. Some things rise faster than others for basic macro-economic reasons. Figure 30.1 shows percent price changes for a few common categories of items you've probably bought in your life, relative to the Consumer Price Index (CPI)—a common inflation index.

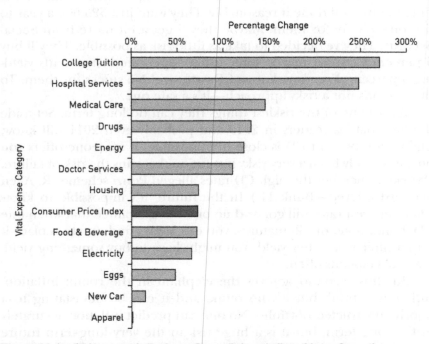

Figure 30.1 20 Years of Inflation—Some Prices Inflate More, Some Less

Source: Thomson Reuters, US Bureau of Labor Statistics, percent change in cost from December 1989 to December 2009.

Amazingly, over the last 20 years, cars, inflation-adjusted, have overall gotten cheaper, as has clothing. Food costs about the same. But eggs have gotten real cheap—omelets look like a heck of a deal—while college tuition has skyrocketed, as have hospital services, medical care, drugs, doctor services, etc.

In retirement, do you anticipate consuming *more* health care services, or less? Those categories experienced more inflation than others. We can bicker about why—but it's likely health care prices will keep rising faster than the average inflation rate.

Suppose you experience just the average inflation rate. CPI has averaged about 3 percent over the last 20 years (through year-end 2009).[1] It might be lower going forward—inflation has been trending down in recent decades. Or it could go higher! But taking a 3 percent average, to keep that $25,000 per year going in real, inflation-adjusted dollars, you'd need about $33,600 a year in 10 years, about $45,000 in 20 years, and $60,000 in 30 years—just to keep the same purchasing power as now. And it's not unreasonable to think many folks, retiring now, might easily live another 30 years. (That's the 65-year-old who lives to be 95—not that exceptional in a world where my grandfather died at 83 but his son, my father, died at 96, and my grandfather's daughter, my aunt, died at 91. Lots of folks in the future will live that long—95 is the new 85.) Then, too, later in life, there are often some additional comforts you might want you're not thinking of now. Or, the things you buy more of are in those categories whose prices rise faster (health care, drugs, energy, etc.).

Either way, your 5 percent CD (if you can get such a thing, and you can find another every time you must reinvest—neither are guaranteed) protects you from near-term stock market volatility, but your purchasing power can get inflation-ravaged. Having just 42 percent of your purchasing power in 20 years may not be what you consider safe or conservative.

To keep your purchasing power, most investors need their portfolios to stretch and grow some. That means your fantasy 5 percent CD won't work. Never forget inflation's impact.

BUNK ③① BABY BOOMERS RETIRE, WORLD ENDS, ETC.

If you, dear reader, aren't a baby boomer—you at least know what one is. And you know the greatest threat mankind has ever faced is . . . gasp . . . retiring boomers!

The story goes: The post–World War II "baby boom" left us with a giant clump of folks who are now in their mid-40s to mid-60s—so a huge wave of boomers will retire all at once, selling stocks to buy safe bonds for retirement—or burying cash in their backyards. And there won't be enough productive younger folks to do all the work to keep those doddering old dependents in geriatric diapers. Hence stocks will fall hard and forever. Or at least for a long, long while.

Boomers Have a Long Time Horizon

Without our stout-hearted boomers propping up stocks as they did when they were younger and accumulating assets, stocks are doomed to fall, right? This is utter nonsense. The market is an exceedingly efficient discounter of well-known information. That the boomers exist has been well known since they started existing. That they would retire one day has been known just as long. Folks have fretted boomer retirement just as long. We can bicker about how fast stocks price in future events, but anything that long is clearly "long enough."

Plus, if you've read Bunks 3 and 4, you know 65-year-olds (i.e., boomers retiring now) should live longer than any previous generation and have a long time horizon—20 years if not more. Much more if they're healthy and/or have a younger spouse. Never mind boomers who are still 10 or 20 years from retiring (most of them statistically)—they might have a 40-year time horizon or much,

much more. Investors who may fear a future inflation uptick and have 20, 30, or 40 more years to invest likely aren't abandoning stocks wholesale.

But forget that. In today's global economy, it's not just your retiring neighbor who buys stocks, but folks globally—including those who live in the 25 percent of global GDP that is emerging markets—which is bigger than America and where per capita income levels are exploding and people are very young on average.

Plus, a stock is a piece of a firm's future earnings. Whether firms globally can continue being profitable has nothing to do with how many people retire and when. If you think boomers won't take some of their accumulated wealth and spoil the grandkids rotten, you're crazy. And that spoiling translates into big future firm earnings.

Glacial Moves Don't Move Stocks

Demographic shifts just can't have the power to drive stocks—up or down—the way so many think they do. Population shifts happen slowly—glacially even—and are well known in advance. Stocks tend not to price in changes that happen slowly over the next 20 to 30 years. They price in what's coming over the next 12 to 18 months—24 months tops—particularly if what's coming was previously unfathomed and a surprise to most.

Markets forever have been simply disbelieving about far distant future problems. Hence there are always a lot of things folks fear way out in the future—and none of them do markets give one whit for in the here-and-now. If you told me with certainty a giant asteroid would collide with Earth, destroying all life as we know it in the year 2020, and if everyone had heard about it, I'd say to you that the market would yawn, forget about it several times, and might start pricing it in about 2018. Markets move based on surprise and urgency and nothing else—because everything else is ignored or priced into the market so efficiently. Global warming? To the stock market that's your grandchildren's problem.

Bankrupting Social Security

For example, another common fear about insidious boomers is that Social Security is slated to go "bankrupt" in 25 years, 30 years, 47.29 years, or some other time, depending on who you ask and why. Fact is, at the rate we're going, the US government will, at a point, pay more in Social Security benefits than it collects in taxes. Hard fact! But bankrupt? That would imply there is some Social Security "fund." There isn't. You pay taxes to the federal government—all types. It goes into a central fund and gets spent.

It's only accounting tomfoolery that creates a Social Security "fund." In any given year, the US government can and does use your Social Security taxes for anything and everything—paying Social Security only accounts for part of the spending. Any estimate about a "bankrupt" Social Security is just that—an estimate of a fund that doesn't really exist at all—although you would almost never know that reading the media.

That's not to say Social Security doesn't have issues. It does. But Social Security goes *poof* with a simple congressional vote, as does the solvency question. Someday those votes will evolve. When? I don't have a clue. That takes a lot of political will, though, and I'm guessing the government won't do something drastic until things get a lot uglier and more in their face. Meanwhile, folks will keep fretting about retirees bankrupting us all. But it doesn't change the fact that any potential Social Security so-called "bankruptcy" is years off and, again, stocks just don't care much about events that far out.

Can't Stop Capital Markets

Stop fearing the boomers. Maybe some sell stocks, but far fewer than you fear. And their massive accumulated wealth doesn't go *poof*—it becomes more wealth over the coming decades as they spend, invest, and/or pass it on to others who spend and invest—helping our economy and adding to firms' earnings and shareholder value. Maybe the selling boomer sells to a few young Brazilian or Peruvian up-and-comers. GDP is growing there at twice US rates.

Fact is, the baby boomer generation as a whole has much more wealth locked up in the private and public businesses they created than they do in stocks and bonds. As they retire, they'll probably sell a lot of that illiquid wealth and reinvest the proceeds back into stocks and bonds, offsetting the trend so many fear.

Folks who think capital markets are some zero-sum game where folks trade stocks like kids trading marbles don't understand Capitalism. Capital markets have been growing and expanding forever. Why? New firms come to market all the time, and existing firms introduce new products and services. Some firms get bought out.

Some firms and products die, but get replaced, usually, by something cooler, faster, smaller, sometimes bigger, and usually better. That's creative destruction for you—and it's the lifeblood of Capitalism. And it means that, forever, some as-yet-unimagined doohickey will always be around the corner—created by someone you likely think wouldn't know how to wipe his own nose—but is helping spawn currently non-existent wealth. That's true whether some large swath of US investors retire to their afternoon bridge games or not.

BUNK 32

CONCENTRATE TO BUILD WEALTH

Another old stock market saw "everyone knows" is: You must concentrate to build wealth, diversify to protect it. And that's true! Concentrating can be great for building wealth. But sometimes it's deadly. Many folks follow some rule of thumb, like, "Never hold more than 5 percent of your portfolio in one stock." Most folks know holding one or just a few stocks is risky. You can certainly get big returns (building wealth), but you can also get whacked (destroying wealth). But whether it's appropriate for you to concentrate or diversify has to do with which road to riches you're on—that makes all the difference.

Taking Stock in Your Employer

In my 2008 book, *The Ten Roads to Riches,* I defined different ways the super-wealthy reliably got that way. Winning the lottery was out—you can't plan on that. But you can plan to become a land baron, manage other people's money, or get a good job and save and invest wisely—three of the ten roads.

Starting your own business is another road—the richest road of all. The world's wealthiest are largely founder-CEOs—folks who routinely flout the 5 percent rule. Like Bill Gates, Jeff Bezos, and Michael Dell—billionaires all, and nearly their entire net worths are and have been their firms—nearly 100 percent in one stock.

And what about Charlie Munger? He's not CEO of Berkshire Hathaway, but he's built himself into a billionaire (worth $1.55 billion[1]) being Warren Buffett's right-hand man. In *The Ten Roads to Riches,* I define that as a very real and very rich road—a "ride-along." Ride-alongs may not get as stratospherically wealthy as super-successful founder-CEOs, but Charlie does ok.

And what about any one of the hundreds of CEOs of big American firms who didn't found those firms (another of the ten roads—becoming CEO of an existing big firm)? Or even very senior managers? CFOs? COOs? Senior VPs? There's a big swath of wealthy people—from founder-CEOs to subsequent CEOs, to the people they rely on most, to their senior managers and executives—who build massive wealth by concentrating in the firm they lead, whether as the Chief Executive or as a small "e" executive. All legitimate roads to wealth.

Is it risky? Heck yes. But a subset of Americans have entrepreneurial spirits unmatched anywhere. If Bill Gates had followed the rule to never be more than 5 percent invested in one stock, he couldn't have founded Microsoft—and I promise the world would be much worse off. I would be much worse off because I never could have had as much success in my career without using Microsoft products.

The difference is founder-CEOs, subsequent big-time CEOs, and the people who put their faith in them as early and influential team members know the risk they take. (Or should know. I'm guessing most do.) Even the most successful people have had major failures. (How many times has Donald Trump, also a billionaire, declared bankruptcy for one of his ventures—and almost overall?) But, as I detail in that 2008 book, if you're following one of these roads to riches—founding a firm, getting in on the ground floor of a new venture, or rising high in the ranks of an existing firm—you can fail big, several times, and still make big wealth. It's difficult—but possible.

Mega wealth requires mega risk. And concentrating heavily is pretty darn risky. Folks traveling these roads know it—it can all disappear one day. They do it anyway. And I'm grateful for those who have done it successfully, and even for those who've done it unsuccessfully, because they learn from that and from those failures come later successes—like Sam Walton's first mis-start. So forget about that 5 percent rule.

The Road More Traveled

And now, I will completely contradict myself and what I just said. (If you aspire to be a founder-CEO, a Charlie Munger-esque right-hand man, or even a top executive, you can tune out.)

The most common road to riches—granted, not massive, billionaire-style riches, but still the most common way wealthy people got their relatively smaller (though still significant) piles of dough—was the "old-fashioned" way. They got a good job, earned a decent or even very high salary, saved, and invested wisely. Or sometimes they invested less wisely and had to make up for that with a higher ongoing income stream or more frugality. Either way, this is the road the most number of "wealthy" folks take—and most folks know when they're on it. On this road, the 5 percent rule is in play and is vital to controlling risk.

And most people know it! They know not to over-concentrate. But for some reason, some folks' brains go haywire when it's their employer's stock—loading up huge. But a stock is a stock is a stock—and the 5 percent rule still applies to stock of a company you work for now or used to work for (unless you're a very senior-level officer—as mentioned earlier). In fact—if you work for the firm, and you're not a super-senior manager and don't have to abide by certain rules for holding periods—you should probably hold *less* than 5 percent in your employer's stock. Otherwise, you're essentially doubling down—your income and your portfolio shouldn't both be dependent on the same source on this particular road.

Regardless of how smart, knowledgeable, or market savvy you are, your presence at work is not insurance against either market-like volatility or the more fundamental risk the firm goes kablooey. In a bear market, most stocks will fall, more or less with the market—yours, too. And your presence isn't a talisman against some other firm-specific trouble.

Nuts and Bolts and Insider Trading

I can't tell you how many times I've heard, "But you should invest in what you know, and I know my firm." Ok, maybe you deeply understand your particular line of business. But unless you are CEO or way up there, there's simply no way you know the nuts and bolts of every part of the firm. Even most CEOs don't know all the nuts and bolts, but instead hire smart people to manage all the nuts and inventory all the bolts and report back (those are the ride-alongs and the senior managers). It can be very tough to know, unless you're involved at a very senior level, if something major is about to go wrong. Or that maybe some senior managers are committing fraud! That's hard to discern too. Or if something major blows up at a competitor, and you get nailed by sympathy selling when the news hits—guilty by association. That happens often. Or, or, or . . . the millions of things that can suddenly torpedo a firm and/or stock. And if you *did* have some knowledge about something material that could impact the firm, positively or negatively, and traded on it, *you'd be committing a felony*—insider trading.

Everyone recalls Enron—imploded on a massive accounting fraud. You heard the sad tales of myriad lower-level Enron employees and middle managers who had nothing to do with the deception. They lost their jobs and saw their retirement accounts decimated because the retirement accounts were invested in Enron stock—doubling down. The same thing happened when Lehman imploded in September 2008. Folks who had all or most of their retirement savings in Lehman stock were ruined. This could not have happened had they had 5 percent or less in their company stock. Bankruptcies happen all the time—even during the best economic times. And not just because of fraud or bizarre government intervention.

Not Gone, Just Down Big

Those are extreme examples. Maybe your firm doesn't go bankrupt. Maybe you work for a fine firm, much admired globally, like GE, and have a big boodle in the stock. But GE fell 62 percent peak to trough from 2000 to 2002—more than the S&P 500.[2] And, as of the end of 2009, it's still 66 percent off its 2000 highs—still badly lagging the S&P 500.[3] That's not to say within that long period there haven't been times GE has performed fine. But a single stock does not a portfolio make.

If it's just one stock that implodes in a diversified portfolio, that's a bummer but not too terrible. You will likely always have some stocks that are down more than the market, some up more. But no matter how much you understand your firm or your line of business, that doesn't change how fast and huge a single stock can drop and stay down for a long time.

Maybe it's not your employer's stock. Maybe it's a stock of a company you like. A sector you favor. The firm your grandfather started. Google or Apple as hot stocks of recent years on a tear. Whatever. None of these protect you from systemic risk when the market overall falls big. And nothing protects you from fraud, bad business decisions, natural disasters, or some other wholly unpredictable event. Only you can protect you by diversifying.

Be entrepreneurial. Start a firm. Follow a charismatic leader and get in on the ground floor. Rise through the ranks. That's a great way to get super-wealthy—through concentration. But if that's not your road, diversify—use the 5 percent rule. This is bunk that's only part-of-the-time bunk—but it's crucial to know the difference.

PART 4 HISTORY LESSONS

Past performance is never a guarantee of future results. So why the heck does this book have a chapter called "History Lessons"? History can't tell you what stocks will do. True—*nothing* can tell you what stocks will do. But history can teach you if something is reasonable to expect.

Far too many people think of investing like a craft. I talked about this in my 2006 book, *The Only Three Questions That Count*. Investors frequently think if they learn and train in the right craft-like methods—apprenticing under a master, rather like blacksmiths used to—they'll eventually become master craftsmen themselves and somehow have an edge over others.

Folks who think this way forget the stock market is an efficient discounter of widely known information—and most all craft-like applications, particularly those taught in masters' programs and at the major banks and brokerages, qualify as "widely known information." Do those crafts—even very well—and by definition you don't have an edge.

Instead, investors should think about investing as a science. In science, you develop a hypothesis, test, confirm, and retest—continuously. It's a non-stop query session. While investors don't have a traditional lab like biologists or chemists, they do have history. History is the investors' lab.

Nearly every day, you can pick up a paper or listen to news and hear folks say, "XYZ is happening, which is terrible, and that will be bad for stocks!" Less frequently (because bad news sells advertising better than good news), you hear, "ABC should happen, which is great for stocks!"

Upon hearing such assertions, your first questions should be, "Has this ever happened before the way they describe it? How often?" Because if factor X has occurred frequently in history but hasn't led very often to the outcome pundits are predicting, they'd better have a good reason why this time is different. (Usually they don't—they just say "scary input A" leads to "scary output B" without providing any evidence why that should be true.)

For example, when budget deficits spike, as they have frequently in history, you hear endless chatter about coming economic and market Armageddon. Yikes! It's an easy story because in our bones we naturally hate deficits and think surpluses are great. Except, why do we think that? Have you ever checked history to see if the fear is warranted? We do that shortly—and the fear is bunk. (Bunk 33.)

There are some basic misconceptions that get easily overturned by checking history—like high unemployment being a stock killer (Bunk 34), gold being a "safe haven" (it isn't—Bunk 35), tax hikes being automatically disastrous for stocks (they aren't—they're a bit of a mixed bag—Bunk 36), high oil prices driving stocks down (Bunk 37), or global pandemics making for sickly markets (Bunk 38). Or that our economy is handcuffed to the whims of fickle consumers! (Bunk 39.)

Not only is history your lab for testing if what you believe is true (Bunks 35, 36, 37, 38, 39), but it can also help you see profitable patterns most refuse to see—even scoff at! (Bunks 40, 41.) And some proper historical perspective can help you see that stocks aren't as "scary" as most think. (Bunk 42.)

No—past performance guarantees nothing. But investing isn't a certainties game—it's a probabilities game! History is one important tool for shaping forward-looking expectations. It should never be your sole guide, but history is a terrific debunkery tool helping you see the world just a bit more clearly. So study up with the next few chapters!

BUNK 33 PRAY FOR BUDGET SURPLUSES

If you've turned your TV on in the last 20 years, you've heard pundits speak in dulcet tones about budget surpluses. According to them (as well as most media, investors—both amateur and professional—and almost everyone else), surpluses are the pinnacle of economic and market righteousness, whereas deficits are terrible. That drone has gotten louder in the last few years, in the US and abroad.

A surplus means the government collects more than it spends, and that's morally and ethically responsible and good (allegedly). And because of all that responsibility, the economy should thrive and stocks rise. Conversely (according to this storyline), a deficit (meaning the government spends more than it takes in) is bad, and you don't want to see any budget deficits if you can help it. And of course, bigger deficits are worse than smaller ones, but they all lead to more debt—which is reprehensible (see Bunk 45).

If Everyone Believes It, Ask If It's True

Most folks believe this—uniformly. And when almost everyone you know believes something so dearly, you know that's a great time to check if it's true. Should you pray for surpluses? And will they bring great stock returns? How can we know? Simple: Through history, we've had big surpluses and big deficits before—many times. Just check when there have been big surpluses, and what stocks did after that—and vice versa. It's easy—there's massive free historical data on our nation's budget and stock returns—and those of other countries too. Straightforward debunkery!

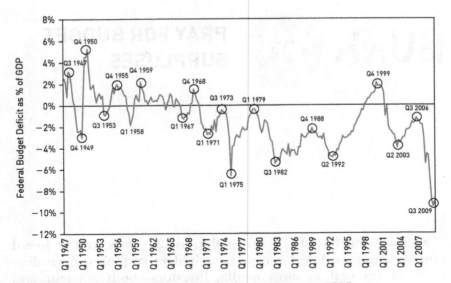

Figure 33.1   US Federal Budget Deficit as a Percentage of GDP

Source: Global Financial Data, Inc., Bureau of Economic Analysis as of 12/13/2009.

Figure 33.1 shows US budget deficits and surpluses as a percentage of GDP going back to 1947. Showing it relative to the size of the economy is the right way to scale the size of the surplus or deficit. Above the horizontal line is a surplus and below a deficit. Peaks and troughs are noted—deficit and surplus peaks. Note we had a big surplus at the end of 1999, and what followed was a big bear market. However, we had a big deficit in 1982 and in 1992, both followed by huge bull markets. And of course, we had a massive deficit all during 2009—while stocks staged a historically massive surge. The surplus didn't help, and the deficits didn't hold stocks down.

Table 33.1 shows that through history, big surpluses didn't lead to great returns, as most think. Surplus and deficit peaks are noted, and subsequent 12-, 24-, and 36-month S&P 500 returns. Following surplus peaks, stocks average –0.2 percent after 12 months and just 7.2 percent *cumulatively* after 3 years. Surpluses don't necessarily help stocks—in fact, they may hurt. Contrast that to deficit peaks—stocks average 22.1 percent 12 months after deficit peaks. Cumulatively after three years, stocks average 35.7 percent—materially better than after surpluses. Ask yourself, honestly, which looks better? The surpluses? Or the deficits?

We can quibble about what's happening when a surplus or deficit is being built up and why. But because a deficit represents the US government spending more than it takes in over a year, it adds to our federal debt, and folks are hardwired to think debt is terrible and more debt even worse (again, Bunk 45). But why? Think about a world with no debt. Most people can't buy a house, purchase a car, or go to college. It's a world where many folks wouldn't start a new business. Why is that good?

But you know that personal debt, used responsibly (as the vast majority of people do) is fine and enhances life and possibly adds to earning potential. Think of all the folks who were groaning in 2008 and after—still in 2010—that banks won't lend, or won't lend enough. They understood that lending is a necessary and healthy economic growth driver. In my experience, those groaning the loudest that banks won't make more loans are also those who complain most that we're over-indebted. (Nearly every politician—globally—comes to mind.) Perverse! Can't have it both ways.

Corporate debt you're generally comfortable with. Firms regularly use debt wisely—to do research and development (everybody likes new, cool, inventive, and life-extending discoveries); build new plants; hire employees (everyone loves higher employment); expand; acquire competitors; and launch new product lines. Sure, some firms get into trouble, always have. Those firms' stocks get hammered and the executives' net worths crater. The CEO gets fired. These days, he (or she) may even get hauled in front of a congressional committee. Maybe the firm goes bankrupt. Using debt irresponsibly has real repercussions that most people and firms fear, expect, and want to avoid. Ignore media headlines designed to evoke emotion—overall, with some exceptions, most people and firms use debt responsibly.

Stupid Government Debt and Velocity

Sadly, our government often uses debt stupidly. When you borrow and spend, you borrow and spend normally. Our federal government borrows and spends on inefficiently run programs of dubious value—happens all the time. You know that. Fortunately, the money the government spends goes to one of three places—another government (foreign, state, local, etc.); an institution (whether for-profit or non-profit); or people. The governments that get the

Table 33.1 S&P 500 Returns Following Deficit and Surplus Peaks—Not What You Think

Surplus Peaks		Subsequent S&P 500 Price Return		
Date		12 Month	24 Month	36 Month
Q3 1947	Annualized	2.6%	1.6%	8.8%
	Cumulative	2.6%	3.2%	28.8%
Q4 1950	Annualized	16.5%	14.1%	6.7%
	Cumulative	16.5%	30.2%	21.6%
Q4 1955	Annualized	2.6%	−6.2%	6.7%
	Cumulative	2.6%	−12.1%	21.4%
Q4 1959	Annualized	−3.0%	9.3%	1.8%
	Cumulative	−3.0%	19.5%	5.4%
Q4 1968	Annualized	−11.4%	−5.8%	−0.6%
	Cumulative	−11.4%	−11.3%	−1.7%
Q3 1973	Annualized	−41.4%	−12.1%	−1.0%
	Cumulative	−41.4%	−22.7%	−2.9%
Q1 1979	Annualized	0.5%	15.7%	3.3%
	Cumulative	0.5%	33.9%	10.2%
Q4 1988	Annualized	27.3%	9.0%	14.5%
	Cumulative	27.3%	18.9%	50.2%
Q4 1999	Annualized	−10.1%	−11.6%	−15.7%
	Cumulative	−10.1%	−21.9%	−40.1%
Q3 2006	Annualized	14.3%	−6.6%	−7.5%
	Cumulative	14.3%	−12.8%	−20.9%
Average	Annualized	−0.2%	0.7%	1.7%
Average	Cumulative	−0.2%	2.5%	7.2%

Source: Global Financial Data, Inc., Bureau of Economic Analysis, S&P 500 price return, as of 12/31/2009.

money a government spends often spend it stupidly again—on $300 hammers and airports with three daily flights to Washington, D.C., and nowhere else—but that money again goes to one of three places (mostly institutions and people).

And the institutions and people who get their hands on any of that money re-spend it normally—on payroll, new computers,

Deficit Peaks		Subsequent S&P 500 Price Return		
Date		12 Month	24 Month	36 Month
Q4 1949	Annualized	21.8%	19.1%	16.6%
	Cumulative	21.8%	41.8%	58.6%
Q4 1953	Annualized	45.0%	35.4%	23.4%
	Cumulative	45.0%	83.3%	88.1%
Q1 1958	Annualized	31.7%	14.7%	15.6%
	Cumulative	31.7%	31.4%	54.5%
Q1 1967	Annualized	0.0%	6.1%	−0.2%
	Cumulative	0.0%	12.5%	−0.6%
Q1 1971	Annualized	6.9%	5.4%	−2.1%
	Cumulative	6.9%	11.2%	−6.3%
Q1 1975	Annualized	23.3%	8.7%	2.3%
	Cumulative	23.3%	18.1%	7.0%
Q3 1982	Annualized	37.9%	17.4%	14.8%
	Cumulative	37.9%	37.9%	51.2%
Q2 1992	Annualized	10.4%	4.3%	10.1%
	Cumulative	10.4%	8.9%	33.5%
Q2 2003	Annualized	17.1%	10.6%	9.2%
	Cumulative	17.1%	22.3%	30.3%
Q3 2009	Annualized	??	??	??
	Cumulative	??	??	??
Average	Annualized	22.1%	13.9%	10.1%
Average	Cumulative	22.1%	30.6%	35.7%

lumber, electricity bills, insurance premiums, groceries, etc. And whoever receives those re-spent dollars spends them again, normally, and so on—and every spend benefits the economy. So, the economy is better off even when the government borrows and spends very stupidly, because the later spends average out to normal.

The rate at which money newly created—through a bank loan, for example—moves through our economy is called *velocity*. In America, when new money is created via a bank lending money to the US government, on average, that money gets spent about six times in the first 12 months. That's six spends that wouldn't happen otherwise. Five of those are normal and often one (the first one) is really stupid. But those five spends help stimulate the economy. And markets know that and love it, which is why, when deficits get huge and even peak, market returns going forward are fine. What you see is all that money flying around with some of it ending up directly in stocks and other parts of it ending up in higher profits for the companies that issue stock.

Which is also why stocks don't do as well after big surpluses. In a surplus situation, the government takes in more than it spends and pays back its loans (reducing its debt), which shrinks the quantity of money relative to what it would be otherwise. And then those spends of the other five folks don't happen and the economy isn't as stimulated. Stocks somehow know that and don't fare as well.

So I don't fear deficits in the US. Nor in other major developed nations. I showed deficit and surplus high points and subsequent stock returns for the UK, Germany, and Japan in my 2006 book, *The Only Three Questions That Count.* The same thing was true—stock returns following deficit high points easily beat those following big surpluses. My guess is it applies pretty universally in all major developed nations.

You may not like government debt, but you shouldn't react negatively to stocks when you see big budget deficits that cause more future debt. History is clear. Instead, react bullishly toward deficits. And if you do heavily fear or dislike government debt and think that might be enough to make you bearish on stocks, you might check out Bunk 45. But when it comes to stocks, what I actually fear is a surplus. You should too. History shows the aftermath of surpluses isn't good for stocks. And that's what counts.

BUNK 34　HIGH UNEMPLOYMENT IS A KILLER

During and after every recession you hear folks say, "Stocks can't rise until unemployment improves!" But stocks do rise. Unemployment lags the stock market—by a lot usually. In my 38-year career, that's been the case, and I can't find a time it wasn't so historically.

This bunk pervades because it's intuitive. Folks believe high unemployment means people spend less. That's bad for profitability since firms aren't selling much and bad for the economy and stocks too—so the story goes. But markets aren't intuitive, they're usually counterintuitive.

You rarely find anyone who says the reverse—that stocks can and should rise while unemployment is high and failing to fall. But it's always been true! And you know, when almost everyone believes something—believes it with a religious fervor and considers you insane for questioning it—that's when you most need to check if it's true. Check history! The data is freely and easily available.

Unemployment Up, Stocks Up Too?

Even if you pause to consider recent history, you start to realize something is wrong. What happened in 2009? Unemployment rose all year—going above 10 percent. Ugh! Yet stocks had a fantastic year—US and world stocks rose 68 percent and 73 percent from the March low, for a 26.5 percent year overall for US stocks, 30 percent for the world.[1] Stocks rose, hugely, while unemployment was rising. That wasn't a one-time fluke. (I even wrote about this 23 years ago in my 1987 book, *The Wall Street Waltz*—see the 2008 edition from

John Wiley & Sons, page 150). Checking history, as far back as we have monthly unemployment data, stocks typically bottom before recessions end. But unemployment typically keeps rising through the end of recessions and often far later. Yes, there are a very few mild exceptions, like the short, shallow 2001 recession—the bear market didn't bottom until after the recession ended. But that was still way before unemployment peaked. Every single time, recessions end and stocks climb before unemployment drops.

Pretend you're a CEO. You feel a downturn coming, so you ratchet down on inventories. You don't want your warehouse full just when your customers decide to shop less. But that's not enough cost cutting, so you also cut staff. No CEO likes doing it, but for the sake of your business, customers, and remaining employees who depend on you, you must get as lean and mean as possible. (People bash CEOs for downsizing—but they usually shouldn't. Is it better if they don't cut staff and the entire firm goes under, causing vastly more unemployed people?)

Now, pop quiz: When do you start hiring? Before you see sales rebounding? No! Utter lunacy! You can't afford to hire, not yet. You wait for a pick-up in sales, which doesn't become clearly apparent until well after the economy starts improving.

But hang on. Just because sales pick up a bit, you still don't rush to hire. Because of cost cutting, you had some productivity gains during the recession (i.e., your remaining staff learned to make do with less). That's powerfully good, because it means you can see a big earnings pop even on a slight pick-up in sales. Which is great for your shareholders.

So your firm is recovering, sales are better, you're getting an earnings boost—maybe returning to profitability—and you're more productive than before. But you're *still* not hiring, not quite yet. You learned in the bad times to not hire and you're sticking with that if you can. You're nervous it can all go *poof* again. Maybe a double-dip recession like they always talk about in the media (but are actually beyond rare—which people would know if they checked history) is around the corner. (It probably isn't, but folks still fear it.)

So instead of hiring full-time employees to whom you must also pay benefits, you start with part-time and contract labor. Cheaper, easier to hire and fire, and you probably don't have to give them benefits. Only after sales are decidedly going in the right direction for some long time, and your employees are completely maxed out and you could be jeopardizing future sales by not hiring, do you start, finally, adding material full-time staff. And even that takes some time because you must recruit and hire—doesn't happen overnight.

Dropping Unemployment Lags the Economy

And that's exactly what you see in Figure 34.1—showing US recessions and unemployment as far back as we have monthly employment data (December 1928). The shaded bars are recession periods, and the line is the unemployment rate. The darker gray bar at the end is my estimate of when the recession that started in December 2007 ended, based on positive US GDP growth and a peak in unemployment benefit claims. (The National Bureau of Economic Research [NBER], which dates recessions, typically doesn't date the end of a recession until many months after it happens.) And the lag has recently gotten longer—probably the result of ubiquitous computer capability allowing firms to manage employment tighter than they

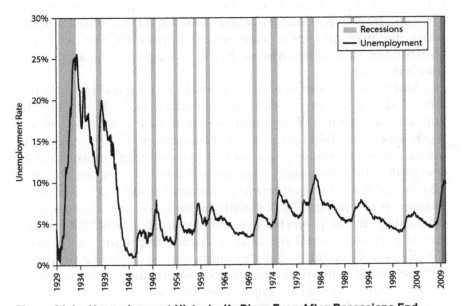

Figure 34.1   Unemployment Historically Rises Even After Recessions End

Source: Global Financial Data, Inc., National Bureau of Economic Research, Bureau of Labor Statistics, as of 02/28/2010.

ever have before. That means this lag phenomenon likely doesn't go away, but probably will get stronger in the future.

Note that for all the media haranguing that the 2007–2009 recession was a new "near Great Depression," or more often, "the Great Recession," fact is: Unemployment never got anywhere near as bad as that and was actually a touch lower than the 1981–1982 recession. But also, in every single recession, unemployment rises the whole time and even after—sometimes for many months. What's going on is CEOs are still being cautious—keeping their firms lean, which contributes to the big earnings pop that's typical at the end of every recession. As they cut, they get better and better at doing it and find more and more places to cut and keep being lean into the expansion.

Not to mention that the unemployment rate is inherently wonky. It doesn't measure what people commonly think it does. It isn't the number of folks who don't have jobs divided by the total labor force. What it measures is those who are currently looking for jobs at a point in time divided by those looking, plus those with jobs. So if folks aren't looking, they aren't counted. As the economy picks up, some who had given up on finding jobs get encouraged and suddenly start looking again, which actually *raises* the unemployment rate—even as payrolls increase! This contributes to unemployment being a lagging indicator, not a predictive one.

And of course, stocks are the ultimate leading indicator, so they almost always rise even before the recession ends. If you wait for confirmation from falling unemployment to buy stocks, you can really miss out. Table 34.1 shows 12-month S&P 500 returns following unemployment peaks and returns starting 6 months *before* the peak. Overwhelmingly, returns are much better for the next 12 months if you buy before unemployment peaks—i.e., *while unemployment is still rising*. That's usually because you can capture some of the big, initial powerful upward thrust of a new bull market. Returns are still good if you time the peak—averaging 14.7 percent for the next 12 months. But 12-month returns average a whopping 30.6 percent if you start 6 months prior to the unemployment peak.

Of course, it's near impossible to time an unemployment peak—I don't know anyone who's done it successfully repeatedly. And I don't know why anyone really would want to try because

Table 34.1 Unemployment and S&P 500 Returns—Stocks Lead, Jobs Lag

Unemployment Peak	S&P 500 Forward 12-Month Return	Six Months Prior to Unemployment Peak	S&P 500 Forward 12-Month Return
05/31/1933	3.0%	11/30/1932	57.7%
06/30/1938	−1.7%	12/31/1937	33.2%
02/28/1947	−4.3%	08/30/1946	−3.4%
10/31/1949	30.5%	04/30/1949	31.3%
09/30/1954	40.9%	03/31/1954	42.3%
07/31/1958	32.4%	01/31/1958	37.9%
05/31/1961	−7.7%	11/30/1960	32.3%
08/31/1971	15.5%	02/26/1971	13.6%
05/30/1975	14.4%	11/29/1974	36.2%
07/31/1980	13.0%	01/31/1980	19.5%
12/31/1982	22.6%	06/30/1982	61.2%
06/30/1992	13.6%	12/31/1991	7.6%
06/30/2003	19.1%	12/31/2002	28.7%
Average	**14.7%**	**Average**	**30.6%**

Source: Global Financial Data, Inc., S&P 500 total return, Bureau of Labor Statistics, as of 12/31/2009.

it's a klutzy statistic. But the point is you shouldn't fear stocks just because the official unemployment rate stays high or fails to fall.

All this fear is because people wrongly assume that since consumers are such a big part of our GDP (approximately 71 percent),[2] high unemployment means spending can't recover, and that dings our economy. But that's a different bit of bunk (Bunk 39).

Unemployment needn't fall for a recession to end. That's just bunk. In fact, it would be very odd if it did. It should in fact keep rising—that's normal and healthy. Repeat: Unemployment should not and will not drop before a recession ends. Growth will begin, and unemployment will keep trending higher. And stocks should move up, big time, before any of that. That's what history and data tell us.

BUNK 35 WITH GOLD, YOU'RE GOLDEN

Another history lesson: Long ago, people drank gold to preserve their youth. Silly them! Poisonous, too. It was recently discovered French King Henry II's famous mistress, the lovely (and two decades older than him) Diane de Poitiers, died from gold poisoning. She would have been better off avoiding the sun and not smoking.

Thankfully, folks don't drink gold now. (Though people do inject themselves with botulinum toxin. Honestly, this quest for youth will kill us.) Yet investors should learn from Diane de Poitiers, lest they harm themselves with too much gold.

Gold fades in and out of favor as a hot investment. Not surprisingly, it tends to spike in popularity after a big run-up—which explains why it was so popular in 2010. (That an investment is popular—talked about and advertised endlessly in the media and seen by many as "the thing"—should be enough to deter you.) Gold is a commodity. An investment class like any other. There's nothing inherently special about this metal making it immune to losses. Gold as a safe harbor is bunk. Sometimes it rises. Sometimes it falls.

Many have some sort of emotional attachment to gold. Perhaps it stems from ancient history, or watching too many Western movies where fortunes were made and lost during the Gold Rush. Or maybe it's from the now-abandoned gold standard for currencies. Since most currencies began to float freely (though some are still pegged—usually to the dollar), gold's usage has been mostly for adornment and limited industrial purposes.

Booms and Busts—But Mostly Busts

But is gold a safe investment? And if it's not safe, does it at least rival stocks? It's easy to check—simply compare its returns to stocks and bonds. Ample free data exists from myriad sources for gold and stocks, from Morningstar, Google Finance, and Yahoo! Finance, to name a few. And there are several ways to compare.

The Bretton Woods agreement was finally dissolved in 1971, separating gold from currencies, but there were lingering controls as the world moved off the gold standard. Gold didn't trade freely—not really—until late 1973. Since then, world stocks returned 2,229 percent, an annualized 9.1 percent.[1] The S&P 500 did better—returning 3,552 percent, an annualized 10.5 percent.[2] Ten-year US Treasuries did ok, returning 1,642 percent for an annualized 8.2 percent.[3] Amazingly, super-safe Treasuries did better than gold—gold returned just 983 percent, 6.8 percent annualized.[4]

Another way to see that is: $10,000 invested in the S&P 500 became $365,200—or *$256,900 more than the same amount invested in gold.* So, gold's long-term returns aren't really so great, but that's still not the whole picture. Gold is also prone to extreme boom-bust periods—normal for most commodities.

Since 1973, there have been six periods I'd call sizable gold booms—shown in Figure 35.1. There are little, smaller bursts in between, but these six are the biggies. The booms last anywhere from 4 to 22 months—but average about 11 months—*and take up 15 percent of the total period.*[5] Compare that to stocks, bonds, even real estate—which all rise more often than they fall. Strip out those six short periods, and gold returns –67.6 percent, an annualized –3.6 percent loss.[6] Miserable. For example, gold lost money from 1982 until 2005—23 years. Can you stomach a money loser that long?

Timing Pros Only, Please

To thrive with gold you must time—both in and out—near perfectly, or be content with long periods of losing results. It goes sideways choppily and down for very long periods, then skyrockets and then again disappoints. So don't ask, "What about gold?" Ask, "How good of a market timer am I?" And ask, "What were the last great timing calls I made?" I know I'm not a good enough timer to time gold. Are you?

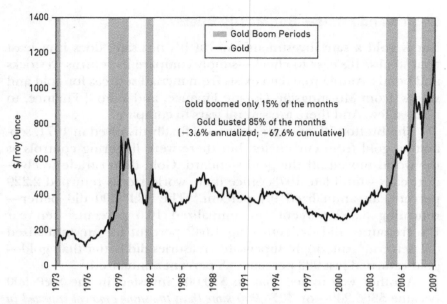

Figure 35.1   Gold Booms and Gold Busts—Are You a Market Timing Pro?

Source: Global Financial Data, Inc., Gold Bullion Price-New York (US$/Ounce) from 11/30/1973 to 12/31/2009.

For example, did you load up on US Tech stocks in the early and mid-1990s? Then, did you short Tech in March 2000? Did you short global stocks in 2001, then buy them back in March 2003 and hold them through 2007? Did you buy oil, another commodity, in January 2007, right before its last steep surge, and sell in July 2008? Did you buy emerging-market stocks in Fall 2008? Or developed-country stocks in early 2009, when sentiment was black? Did you sell euro and buy dollars in April 2008? Then reverse that in March 2009? If you didn't time those right—pretty big, significant swings—what makes you think you can get out of gold at the peak and then back in at the right time for the next gold boom? If you can time gold, which booms only about 15 percent of the time in the long term, you can surely time almost anything else and don't need any advice from me. Go to it.

Amazingly, many normal people who never, ever would think they could time the stock market, bond market, pork bellies, or currencies are content to own gold thinking it is "safe." To them

I say it's just a commodity—volatile like any other. There is nothing golden about gold.

If you're a confident and great timer, great. If not and you do it wrong, you may end up waiting a very long time for that payoff you (wrongfully) hope comes wrapped in a safety blanket. And just maybe you have the constitution to hold onto an asset for a long period—years even—that steadily loses value, waiting. But I doubt it. And consider this: As hot as gold was in 2009, it still lagged stocks—rising 24.8 percent to the S&P 500's 26.5 percent and world stocks' 30.0 percent.[7]

Feel free to buy gold—for earrings, necklaces, and electrical wiring. But for your portfolio, gold has less luster unless you're a super-duper timer.

BUNK 36 STOCKS LOVE LOWER TAXES

Everybody loves lower taxes. Well, maybe not politicians. (But they've got mental problems.) Besides them, it's hard to find anyone who cheers higher taxes. No—almost universally, folks fear higher taxes.

Folks particularly fear capital gains tax increases will nail stocks. As I write in 2010, folks fear the potential sunset of the Bush II–era cap gains tax cuts. Fact is: 10, 20, and 453 years from now, folks will fear higher cap gains taxes dinging stocks and pray for lower taxes. But in history, shocking as this may sound, a simple fact is there are no clear correlations between marginal shifts in tax rates and subsequent stock returns over any reasonably measurable time period. There are several reasons.

Cap Gains—A Tax on Selling?

It seems intuitive higher cap gains taxes should be a major negative, and stocks should love lower taxes. Hence we would expect a tight link between tax rates and subsequent stock returns. After all—cap gains are an actual tax on the sale of stocks! Except, if you think of it that way—everybody knows (except politicians, sometimes) that if you tax something more, you get less of it. (Politicians understand this perfectly if it's something they don't want you to do. People drink too much sugary soda? Tax it! We want to reduce gas usage? Tax it! However, why they can't understand that when they tax income more, folks create less income and the government gets lower income tax revenue is beyond me. But I digress.)

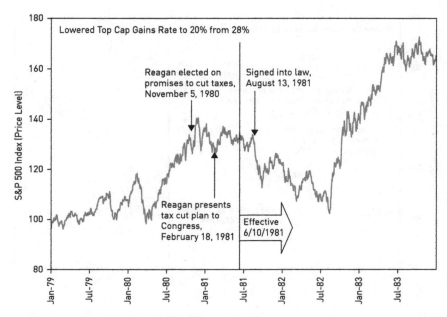

Figure 36.1 Economic Recovery Act of 1981

Source: Global Financial Data, Inc., S&P 500 price return from 12/31/1978 to 12/31/1983.

Cap gains taxes are a tax on *selling* stocks that have appreciated. Not a tax on *holding* stocks. If you make it more expensive to sell stocks, theoretically, people have a greater incentive to hold stocks longer—and less selling pressure should mean higher prices immediately thereafter. A reduction in the capital gains tax rate means a lower tax on selling appreciated stock, which could increase short-term selling pressure on the market after a tax reduction—rather the reverse of what common sense would lead most to believe.

Cap Gains Changes and Impacts

Pray for tax *hikes*? Nah—there's no major evidence to support that either. And while your common sense and/or gut instinct may tell you higher capital gains taxes are bad, we've seen so many times in this book that, when it comes to capital markets, your instincts and common sense are more often than not your enemies and you shouldn't base decisions on them.

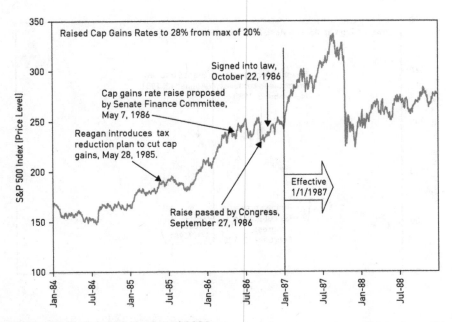

Figure 36.2   Tax Reform Act of 1986
Source: Global Financial Data, Inc., S&P 500 price return from 12/31/1983 to 12/31/1988.

The truth: In the long term, the effects of any given tax change subsequently tend to get entangled with many other forces. And if multiple forces converge, disentangling tax effects from others becomes virtually if not fully impossible in the long term—though in the short term, there may be clues. Since 1981, there have been four major cap gains rate changes shown in Figures 36.1 through 36.4. What happened after each?

- In 1981, the rate was cut from 28 percent to 20 percent. The S&P 500 fell 22 percent over the 12 months after the bill became law.[1] (See Figure 36.1.)
- In 1987, a rate hike from 20 percent back to 28 percent went into effect (Figure 36.2). The S&P 500 soared until stocks fell again in the famous 1987 crash. (But that crash had nothing to do with the 8-month-old tax rate move.)
- In 1997, the rate was cut from 28 percent to 20 percent again. The S&P 500 continued its bull run well into 2000. (See Figure 36.3.)

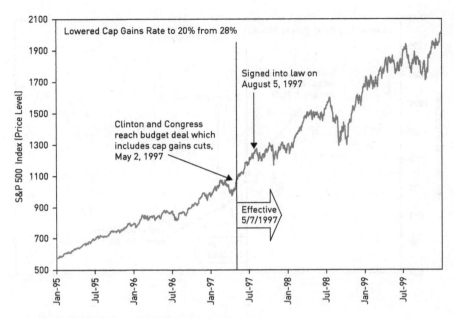

Figure 36.3 Taxpayer Relief Act of 1997
Source: Global Financial Data, Inc., S&P 500 price return from 12/31/1994 to 12/31/1999.

- In 2003, the rate was cut from 20 percent to 15 percent. Stocks fell sharply after it was announced, but began a five-year bull run after it was enacted. (See Figure 36.4.)

So stocks dropped big after a rate cut. They rose hugely after a rate hike. And stocks continued on their merry way after two more tax cuts. What does it mean? Nothing, really.

Though a rate change may have some near-term sentiment implications, market moves seem as often as not to be driven by other bigger forces. Maybe cap gains cuts are a positive, but in America in 1981, other bigger negative forces were in play, so the market fell—just maybe less than it would have otherwise. One way to look at it.

And maybe in 1987 stocks were going to rise big anyway, so the rate hike just held back that force a little bit—and had the capital gains rate not been increased, stocks would have jolted even higher. You can believe that if you want—or that the higher rate in 1987

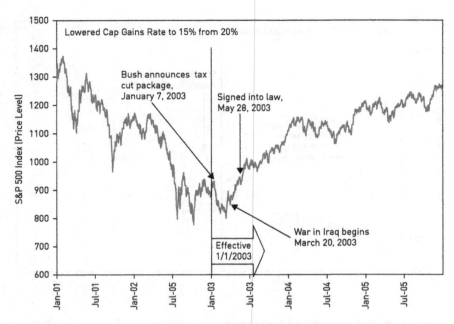

Figure 36.4   Jobs and Growth Tax Relief Reconciliation Act of 2003
Source: Global Financial Data, Inc., S&P 500 price return from 12/31/2000 to 12/31/2005.

was foreseen so folks did their selling before and none afterward, so stocks rocketed then. That's perfectly logical too—believe that if you want. My point is, you'll never really know. But the evidence is contradictory enough for you to not place bets on market direction based on capital gains cuts or hikes—because it's clear there can be overriding impacts. You can't predict market direction based on tax changes. It doesn't work.

So why should cap gains have so little lasting impact? My sense is the stock market is a darn efficient discounter—almost instantly pricing in almost all well-known information. Tax policy moves slowly and is much talked about and covered in the media as it evolves— talked about, debated, deplored, and voted on multiple times before it's signed into law. That can take months or years—maybe longer. Markets have ample time to price in the coming change long before it's ever implemented. Hence my bias is to believe in the case of the 1987 example that any potential tax-motivated selling capacity was sold out of the market long before the law went into effect, so that afterward stocks saw little resistance to rising. Any downward pressure on stocks likely happened before the tax change as folks rushed to beat the date.

It's Only Half the Issue

Plus, about half the total value of US securities are held by entities that pay no taxes—like pension plans and endowments and foundations—or in tax-deferred accounts like IRAs and 401(k)s. Then, the US is currently less than 25 percent of the world's economy and less than half of its total market value[2]—yet the US and non-US markets tend to move in relative tandem (see Bunk 43), so our tax effects get heavily watered down by events abroad. And don't forget, capital markets are incredibly complex. While a change in law might impact US investors a bit in the near term, there can be other, huger drivers impacting the larger world—like a global bear market in 1981 and global bull markets in 1997 and 2003.

As we look in 2010 at the risk of higher capital gains taxes, the fear folks have today must mostly be in stocks before the change is effectuated. People have been fretting this one for years now. Hence, once 2010 is over, whatever tax-motivated selling pressure there was will probably be finished—speaking to a relatively bullish impact after. But that could be wrong and we'll never know because, again, it's likely other forces are more powerful for good or for bad in 2011.

Folks like fretting taxes—it's a national pastime. But there's no evidence proving a tax cut or hike must be good or bad for stocks. You may personally like tax cuts and hate tax hikes. Who can blame you? But your stocks don't much care. And when it comes to stocks, you shouldn't either. Don't try to time the market or be bullish or bearish based on realities or fears about impending tax changes.

BUNK 37 OIL AND STOCKS SEESAW

Some bunk goes in and out of style. This one was red-hot in recent years. But as I write in 2010, you don't hear it as much. It will be back—probably the next time oil prices rise a lot, fast—or rise for a long time.

The fairly universal belief is high oil prices are bad for stocks. When oil is up, stocks go down—they're negatively correlated. And to get higher stock prices, you want lower oil prices. But it's bunk. (Interestingly, this is one you hear more when oil is high. When oil drops a lot in price, folks don't say, "Phew! Everything is great now!") Long term, they mean nothing to each other and one isn't predictive for the other—that's provable.

A Dollar Spent Is a Dollar Spent

The thinking is fairly intuitive (which by now you know to spot right away as a likely bad sign) and goes: We're too oil dependent! Higher oil makes life more expensive—we need oil just to go to the grocery store or work, so we spend more on gas, heating, or air conditioning and less on other stuff. This slows the economy and means lower earnings and profits for firms as money gets sucked away from them and into our gas tanks—and it's all ultimately bad for stocks.

First, borrow for a moment from Part 5 and think globally, and this belief starts seeming silly—even before the data crunching and checking history (which devastates this myth, as you'll soon see). See it this way: A dollar spent in the global economy is a dollar spent in the global economy. If you spend $100 a month, the global economy doesn't care if it's on gas, tennis shoes, tax advice, or pet rocks. If you spend $30 on gas and $70 on everything else—that's $100. But if gas rises, costing you $40, you have just $60 for everything else—except it's still $100 spent. Maybe oil firms profit marginally more (which may be great for their stocks), and other firms less. Or maybe not. Maybe oil prices are being driven higher by transport costs resulting from huge demand for other gadgets. Or maybe those other firms instead gain via innovation, cost cuts, or something else giving them more profits—happens all the time. Capitalism is awesomely adaptive! But ignore that economic reality for a moment.

Long Term—No Correlation

Folks fear higher gas stalls the economy and dings stocks. So when oil goes up, stocks go down—that's the fear. And lower oil means folks have more money to spend (so they think), so that's supposedly better for stocks. But recent history contradicts that. Oil fell in 2001 when stocks dropped and we had a recession. And oil rose in 2003, 2004, 2005, all the way through 2007—right alongside stocks! When stocks started falling in late 2007, oil kept rising. Oil rose while stocks fell all the way through June 2008—just like the myth! Then after June, they both fell through year end, then both rose for most of 2009.

So are oil and stocks—gasp—*positively correlated?* Sure, sometimes. Sometimes they're negatively correlated. Sometimes they're nothing. But over long periods? There is nothing there. And it's easy to check the data yourself—straight debunkery—there's vast, free, easy-to-find prices for both stocks and oil. Figure 37.1 shows monthly returns for both US stocks and oil.

The correlation coefficient (which you can easily get on two data sets in Excel—if that intimidates, ask a teenager to show you how) is a number between $+1$ and -1 that shows how much two variables move together. The higher the number, the more positively correlated they are—zigging together at the same time and to the same degree. A number close to -1 means they're *negatively* correlated—they zigzag the way the myth presumes oil and stocks do. A number close to zero means the two have no relation—one zigs and the other broccolis.

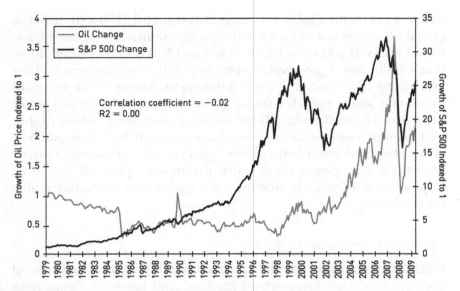

Figure 37.1 Oil Versus Stocks—No Material Correlation

Source: Global Financial Data, Inc., West Texas Intermediate Oil Price (US$/Barrel), S&P 500 total return from 12/31/1979 to 12/31/2009.

Since 1980, the correlation between oil and US stocks is −0.02. Meaningless—the two aren't related in the long term at all. (By the way, you can do the same thing with oil and UK, German, Japanese, and world stocks, and get the same meaningful lack of correlation.) Now look at the R-squared—which is the correlation coefficient, squared. In statistics, that tells us how much of one variable's movement can be explained by the other. Here, it's 0 percent. Said another way, over long periods, anything and everything but oil contributes to the stock market's movement. Anything and everything but! Repeat after me: "Anything and everything but."

Can oil prices impact certain industries and firms more directly? Sure! Energy firms for a start. Particularly if they're drilling for, refining, and/or selling oil or oil products. But overall, oil and stocks aren't correlated—positively or negatively.

Short-Lived Correlation

That's longer term. Over shorter periods, oil and stocks can have short spurts of intense positive or negative correlation. But any two

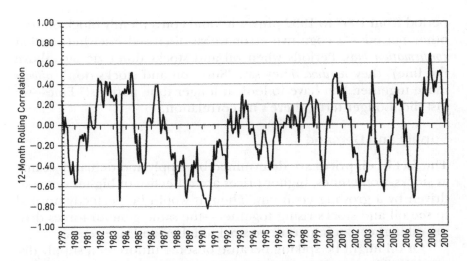

Figure 37.2   Correlation Between Oil Prices and the S&P 500—There Isn't One

Source: Global Financial Data, Inc., West Texas Intermediate Oil Price (US$/Barrel), S&P 500 total return from 12/31/1979 to 12/31/2009.

bizarre variables can inexplicably move together (or oppositely) for short spurts. If you take baseball statistics (or any other totally non-related activity that has regular outputs) and run them against stock prices, you can find periods when they're positively correlated and others negatively. But they're meaningless and fleeting. I assure you, correlating changes in Nigerian rainfall with the Nasdaq 100 will work at some point in time. Means nothing.

Figure 37.2 shows 12-month rolling correlations between oil and stocks—sharp, jagged, short-lived spikes up and down. Above the line means they're positively correlated, below means negatively. There's a long-ish period of varying degrees of negative correlation from 1987 through 1992—but even then it was wildly variable. Other than that, there's no predictability except for the pure randomness.

What's interesting is folks commonly commit a slew of cognitive errors when thinking about oil and stocks. Times when stocks and oil zigzag (below the line) confirm their belief. They say, "Yep! This proves it! They're negatively correlated." Or they seek out periods when oil and stocks were negatively correlated, saying, "See! That period from 1987 to 1992 proves it," and conveniently block out the other periods—a cognitive error we've discussed elsewhere called *confirmation bias*. Periods when oil and stocks don't zigzag (above the line), they *reframe*. They say, "Sure, oil and stocks don't *always* move together. You have to look at longer time periods!" Fine—we just did. Longer term, there's no correlation.

Supply and Demand

The fact is, oil prices are determined by supply and demand—same as stocks. Sometimes, higher prices are reflective of higher demand driven by a growing economy. Then, it would be perfectly normal to see oil and stocks rising together—the same general forces driving oil higher can in part drive stocks higher, and vice versa.

Or oil might be spiking because of some unforeseen supply disruption. That might not necessarily be great for the economy or stocks—and they could zigzag. Or maybe the disruption is short-term in nature, and stocks know it, so they do whatever they were going to do regardless of what oil is doing. Often, oil and stocks move together when the economy is suddenly stronger than expected, which is good for stocks and causes unexpected economic demand that ripples to energy usage. And sometimes the reverse occurs. But knowing where oil is going won't tell you where stocks are headed—provably.

Oil and stocks have completely, wholly, and inherently separate supply drivers. And they have many, many demand drivers—some overlap, many don't. Our economy is intensely complex—there are just no iron-clad "when X is up, sell stocks, and when X is down, buy stocks" rules that work long term.

BUNK 38

SWINE FLU, SARS, EBOLA, AND OTHER VIRAL DISASTERS MAKE MARKETS SICK

In spring 2009, it wasn't yet obvious to all that the major global bear market had bottomed in March. Stocks were on a massive tear—huge upward volatility—but maybe it was just a temporary bounce within a bigger bear market. That can happen and is hard to see with certainty when it does because at bear market bottoms and after, volatility is usually so huge and folks are so terrified, they can't see a new bull market forming. And there is always much to fear.

Plus, there was a new threat forming—pigs. No, not PIIGS—Portugal, Ireland, Italy, Greece, and Spain. We wouldn't worry about the PIIGS debts until 2010. In Spring 2009, it was actual pigs we feared—swine—and a flu strain folks feared would sicken us all, stop the economy, and generally doom the world via pandemic.

I can make light now because, quite obviously, while a very few folks did die tragically and more got sick (all of which is truly sad), the bigger threat to global well-being never materialized. But back in Spring 2009, the media speculated endlessly we were facing a terrible, deadly epidemic, on par with the 1957, 1968, or, worse still, the super-deadly 1918 flu pandemic. And with whole swaths of humanity sick or possibly dying, folks feared a major drag on the economy and the impact on stocks—particularly since we were already mired in a recession. Folks lined up for scarce vaccines, and wearing surgical masks became vogue for airline travelers.

No Fear of Swine (or Any Other) Flu

Even though then we didn't know 2009's swine flu would turn out to be, for most people, a milder form of the normal flu, I knew the flu would likely have zero impact on stocks. How? There are several ways to know. Either the pandemic occurs big or it doesn't. Let's look at both. Usually it doesn't end big and you know intuitively that if that happens it is bullish, not bearish, by the rule that prior fear of a pending false factor is always bullish. And we often go through these scares that end up being, like swine flu, vastly less than feared. Either the threat of the scale of destruction is massively overstated or human ingenuity innovates drugs or a vaccine equal to the threat, or some combination thereof.

Example: 2003 saw us all scared silly of getting severe acute respiratory syndrome—SARS. Remember SARS? The outbreak originated in China. Tourists traveling home found themselves quarantined. Suddenly, folks who hadn't pondered biology since ninth grade were babbling about corona viruses and were sure we were just days from global pandemic. In total, 8,422 people were sickened globally—908 died.[1] Again, sad for all of them—a personal tragedy—but small on a global scale. (Said another way, you had a 1 in 7,375,930 chance of dying of SARS, and odds were about as good as being felled by a lightning strike in 2009.) An 11 percent death rate (of those sickened) is high, but since it turned out SARS didn't transmit easily from person to person and those most at risk were chicken farmers, it was hardly the global whopper first feared. And in 2003, world stocks gained 33.1 percent.[2] The prior fear of a false factor had instilled early pessimism that faded, leading to more optimism, which rippled over to help fuel further the demand for equities.

In 2005 and 2006, we had twin bird flu scares, with similar outcomes—few folks sickened, fewer died, and stocks rose strongly. And in 2009, stocks were gangbusters all while folks were calling their senators to demand vaccines. Folks might say the swine flu, SARS, and the bird flu scares failed to become major pandemics so none of this is proof epidemics can't ding stocks.

Fair enough. So let's consider a biggie! Fact: No modern epidemic can match the 1918 Spanish flu. A rigorously researched and excellent book, *The Great Influenza* (Viking, 2004) by John M. Barry, covers the massive and sudden impact of this deadly virus. Barry also writes about the tireless and innovative work of the early students and graduates of Johns Hopkins School of Medicine in combating that disease. (I'm proud my grampa was one of the very first graduates of that fine medical school and part of that phenomenon—the world leaned heavily on Hopkins and its grads to deal with the crisis.)

Records weren't as reliable then as now, but it's estimated 500 million or more people were infected worldwide. So, in a global population of about 1.6 billion then, about a third fell ill. Of them, 100 million (20 percent) died—more or less. Hard to know precisely because records were spotty even in developed nations, particularly at the pandemic's apex, when doctors and nurses simply lay down next to their patients to die themselves. Municipalities stopped record-keeping. Anyone fortunate enough to avoid sickness didn't dare report for work. But any way you count it, that was a whopper. And it wasn't just America—it was a global whopper.

Reading Barry's book gives you a glimpse of the massive scale. Entire remote villages in Arctic outposts were utterly decimated. Pacific islands, separated by hundreds of miles of oceans, were hit particularly hard, as were parts of Africa—folks in isolated communities lacked the antibodies that protected, somewhat, those in Europe and America.

Most alarming, the flu was deadliest to healthy adults—the working world. A healthy man in his mid-20s might have shown no symptoms in the morning and be dead before dark. Some of those afflicted turned black before dying, eerily reminiscent of the Plague—the Black Death. The world was paralyzed with fear. City streets were empty. Meetings of any kind were canceled. People wore masks if they had to leave their homes and wouldn't speak to others in the faint hope of preventing the disease from spreading. The Spanish flu was a bird flu that mutated to an efficient killing machine. Bird flus are particularly deadly—a fresh mutation ensures that humans lack antibodies to squelch the virus.

Compare how deadly the Spanish flu was with more recent "pandemics." Not even close! Viruses don't have the ability to kill as many anymore—not for lack of trying—they mutate all the time to become better killers and do their best to kill as many as possible. That's their job in nature. But our doctors and fine research brains are getting better, faster, and smarter than those inert killing machines. I'm guessing, as long as our dear governments don't meddle too much in health care, that innovation continues as fast as ever.

Side note: If you wonder what health care would be like in a more socialized system, just consider how many drug and device innovations come out of America (most of them), and how many from places like the UK, France, and Canada (many, many fewer).

So in the face of all that legitimate death, illness, and a workforce that simply stopped, for a long time, showing up to work, how did stocks do? You would intuitively expect them to do terribly, but counterintuitively, they did pretty darn well. In 1918, the height of the pandemic, stocks rose 26 percent.[3] The following year, they were up 21 percent.[4] That tells you health scares don't have the power to drive stocks down the way you might fear. So you don't need to fear this myth.

Can a health scare coincide with a big stock fall, as it did in early 2009 before the massive market surge? Sure! But overall it wasn't the swine flu making stocks fall so far. And certainly, flu fears can cause corrections and pullbacks, as bird flu did in 2005. But any silly thing can cause a correction—that's the nature of a correction. They're based on sentiment, not fundamentals, and typically are over as fast as they start as people realize their fears are silly.

So get your flu shot. I'm for that. But know when the next big health scare comes around—because there will be some periodically—that pandemics don't spell doom for stocks.

BUNK 39 CONSUMERS ARE KING

Since the dawn of time, after every recession, folks have complained the economy can't recover because consumers are too tapped out and won't spend again. And because consumer spending is such a big part of our economy, if they don't spend, we're doomed! Eek! As I write in 2010 there are endless proclamations of US consumers' demise. And though we get the same stories after every recession, pundits treat it like this is the first time they ever dreamed up this notion—and they never learn that the notion is flawed and wrong.

(Interestingly, the flip side is folks often complain US consumers are dangerously profligate and spend too much, and *that* will doom the economy. So, we're doomed when people spend, and doomed when they don't spend? Can't have it both ways! Few folks think through how silly and contradictory these fears are.)

It's true—consumer spending is a whopping 71 percent of US GDP.[1] Clearly, if such a big part falls far and fails to recover, that can hurt for a long, long time. Except consumer spending typically doesn't fall much in recessions—vastly less than commonly imagined. It's two other parts of the economy, business investment and net exports, that, though smaller, are much more volatile and almost always contribute most to an economic decline and recovery—and did this last time around—although it was little noted in the media.

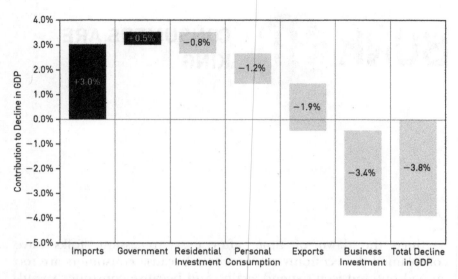

Figure 39.1　Contributors to US GDP Decline Q2 2008 to Q2 2009—Consumption Isn't the Driver

Source: Bureau of Economic Analysis, percentage point contributions to peak-to-trough decline in US GDP (Q2 2008 to Q2 2009).

The Big Decline Wasn't Consumers

Consumer spending doesn't fall that much? Blasphemy! Except it's true. Figure 39.1 shows how much different economic components contributed to the 2007–2009 recession—from when GDP peaked to the trough. (NBER dated the recession's start as December 2007, but GDP didn't peak until Q2 2008 and bottomed in Q2 2009.) Falling imports actually *added* 3.0 percent to GDP. (It's the squirrely way we account for GDP—net exports, or exports minus imports. When imports fall relative to exports they can actually *add* to GDP, even though falling imports is often a sign of a soft economy. See Bunk 48.) Government spending added too—0.5 percent. No big surprise—pretty much everyone knows the government spent more. Residential investment detracted 0.8 percent. (That the decline was relatively so small likely surprises a lot of folks based on what they've read in the papers about the housing implosion.) Exports detracted 1.9 percent, and business investment a big 3.4 percent—by far the biggest drag. By contrast, personal consumption detracted a mere 1.2 percent—not insignificant, but just one small part of the overall decline.

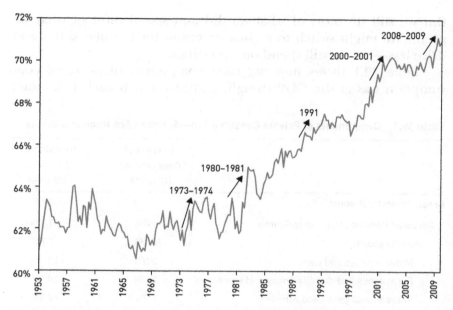

Figure 39.2   Private Consumption as a Percentage of US GDP—Jumps in Recession

Source: Thomson Reuters, Bureau of Economic Analysis.

This isn't unusual. Consumer spending normally isn't as volatile as people think. In fact, consumer spending as a percentage of GDP typically *grows* during recessions—and did this last time—by record amounts. That seems counterintuitive but isn't. If the overall economy falls, and consumer spending falls too but not as much, then it increases relatively. Figure 39.2 shows private consumption as a percentage of GDP through time. Over time, it's been growing, but most notably jumped in the last five recessions. That couldn't happen if consumer spending were as volatile as, say, business investment.

Consumer Spending Is Stable

How can consumer spending be so stable? Simple—think about what we buy. Many may think "spending" and immediately think "cars, dinners out, vacations, jewelry, V-V-V-Viva Las Vegas." But most of what we buy is boring and unsexy—toothpaste, medicine, gas for the car, tax preparation services. Exciting stuff. When times are tough, we economize—making our cars and TVs last another few years. We put off trips or maybe go camping instead of a cruise.

But we still do most of what we did and spend most of what we spent. We might switch to a cheaper brand for the necessities and drive less—but we still spend on necessities.

Table 39.1 shows how big each component of personal consumption was at the GDP trough, and how much each fell. Note:

Table 39.1 Components of Private Consumption—Services Are Huge and Stable

	Percent of Consumption (Q2 2009)	Real Growth Q3 2008 to Q2 2009
Gross Domestic Product		−3.8%
Personal Consumption Expenditures	*100%*	−1.7%
Durable goods	*10.1%*	*−8.8%*
Motor vehicles and parts	3.0%	−15.3%
Furnishings and durable household equipment	2.5%	−10.0%
Recreational goods and vehicles	3.2%	−2.9%
Other durable goods	1.4%	−4.9%
Nondurable goods	*21.8%*	*−2.7%*
Food and beverages purchased for off-premises consumption	7.9%	−2.2%
Clothing and footwear	3.2%	−7.6%
Gasoline and other energy goods	2.8%	1.4%
Other nondurable goods	8.0%	−2.6%
Services	**68.1%**	−0.2%
Household consumption expenditures (for services)	*65.5%*	*−0.2%*
Housing and utilities	18.7%	0.3%
Health care	16.2%	2.1%
Transportation services	3.0%	−4.8%
Recreation services	3.8%	−1.7%
Food services and accommodations	6.1%	−3.7%
Financial services and insurance	8.2%	−1.0%
Other services	9.4%	1.1%
Final consumption expenditures of nonprofit institutions serving households	*2.6%*	*−3.9%*

Source: Bureau of Economic Analysis; percent of consumption based on Q2 2009 GDP "Third Estimate" nominal values.

We spend most (68.1 percent) on services, yet services spending shrank just 0.2 percent. Spending *increased* on the three biggest services components: housing and utilities, health care, and "other services"—which is a catchall for everything not easily categorized with the other components, such as legal services, Internet, school tuition, even haircuts and dry cleaning.

The next biggest chunk of consumer spending is *nondurable goods*—21.8 percent. Nondurables are things intended to last less than three years—like shoes, clothing, food you buy at a grocery store—not entirely but mostly the things you need rather than want. That bit fell 2.7 percent.

The smallest chunk of spending is *durable goods*—mostly the large-ticket items that really do suffer most in a recession among consumer goods. And they shrank most, but are just 10.1 percent of total spending! Though we spend least here, these grab the most headlines. "Auto sales were down some huge number!" Eek squared! But why does that surprise? During a recession, most people can delay buying a car. It's not great for the auto industry, but it's not disastrous for the economy overall—it's too small a part.

That doesn't stop headlines from screaming that consumers won't come roaring back to save the economy. They're right! Consumer spending, overall, just doesn't fall that much in recessions, so it needn't come roaring back to help the economy grow. But oddly, the media is usually silent on business spending, which typically falls more, then bounces big—a huge contributor to early post-recession GDP growth. As I write in 2010, a morose media complains (wrongly) consumer spending hasn't resumed—though it has—and its lack of growth will keep the economy from growing. It won't, on the one hand. On the other hand, the media completely misses that, since US growth resumed in Q3 2009 through Q1 2010, business investment bounced back a massive 19.2 percent.[2]

Are consumers important to the US economy? Of course. But they aren't nearly as fickle as most folks fear. It's a bunking bronco of a myth.

BUNK 40

PRESIDENTIAL TERM CYCLES ARE STOCK MARKET VOODOO

You may have heard some folks claim there's a reliable, gameable stock market pattern in presidential terms—that some years are better than others. You may have also heard that since 1926, every single year ending in "5" (1935, 1945, 1955, etc.) has been positive. Every one! But, you've also likely been warned these are silly indicators—as good as voodoo.

Yes, the year 5 quirk is just that—a statistical quirk. There have been eight occurrences since 1926. Since stocks rise more than fall, you'd normally expect at least two-thirds of those to be positive anyway. It's not unreasonable that in eight coin flips, with a coin weighted to show heads two-thirds of the time, that all eight would be heads. It happens. Not all the time. But it does. But it's still just a quirk.

On the other hand, it's a myth and bunk that the presidential term is just voodoo—there are forceful fundamentals that can make the cycle gameable.

Table 40.1 shows presidents, their parties, and annual S&P 500 returns broken into first through fourth years of their terms. The two pages split the front and back halves of terms. Immediately you see the first two years have worse average returns with greater return variability. It's not that years 1 and 2 are inherently *bad*— there can be great first and second years! There's just more variability and some big negatives dragging down the averages. But the back half is different—average returns are much better with less return variability.

Year 3 averages 17.5 percent without a single negative since 1939, which was barely down 0.9 percent! Year 4 is fine too, with just slightly more negatives, and 2008's big down year doesn't help the average. Still, you get more uniformity and better average returns in year 4. Is this quirk? Or real and fundamental?

Predictable Patterns and Fundamental Drivers

Patterns happen all the time. Doesn't mean you should make bets on them. Unless you can figure whether the pattern is rooted in sound fundamentals, and why, you should chalk it up to *quirk*. But there are two basic fundamental reasons behind this pattern. First, investors feel the pain of loss about twice as intensely as the pleasure of gain. We've been over that in Bunk 7.

Second, the word *politics*, as you know, derives from the Greek "*poli*" meaning many and "*ticks*" meaning small blood-sucking insects. I have no doubt that some poli-tics start as normal human beings. But within three years inside the Beltway, they will have become narcissistic little bloodsuckers with the soul of a tick. Approximately 50 percent of a poli-tic's energy is directed at getting re-elected. The other 50 percent is directed at raising funds for said re-election campaign. This is true for congressmen (and congress-women), senators, even the president, who is Head Tic. If you know a Beltway politician who is truly a human being, you know someone I've never met and I've met hundreds over the decades.

The Head Tic knows tickiology (another *comberation*) very well before getting elected or he (they've always been "he's" in America so far) wouldn't get elected. So he knows his party will lose relative power to the opposition party in the mid-terms—on aver-age 25 House and two or three Senate seats since World War II. (George W. Bush bucked the trend in 2002—one of the few ever in American history—but fell prey in 2006.) He knows that whatever his most onerous legislation (his legacy, if you will)—the toughest, most arduous, and most controversial bills—he must get them through in the first two years when he has more relative power. If he can't get it done then, he could almost never get them through in the back half of his term when his party has less relative power. This is a form of catch-22. America is a centrist country, and the more he tries to push through in his first two years, the more relative

Table 40.1   Presidential Term Anomaly—First Half More Volatile, Back Half Almost All Positive

Who Won	Party	1st Year		2nd Year	
Coolidge	R	1925	N/A	1926	11.1%
Hoover	R	1929	**−8.9%**	1930	**−25.3%**
FDR—1st	D	1933	52.9%	1934	**−2.3%**
FDR—2nd	D	1937	**−35.3%**	1938	33.2%
FDR—3rd	D	1941	**−11.8%**	1942	21.1%
FDR/Truman	D	1945	36.5%	1946	**−8.2%**
Truman	D	1949	18.1%	1950	30.6%
Ike—1st	R	1953	**−1.1%**	1954	52.4%
Ike—2nd	R	1957	**−10.9%**	1958	43.3%
Kennedy/Johnson	D	1961	26.8%	1962	**−8.8%**
Johnson	D	1965	12.4%	1966	**−10.1%**
Nixon	R	1969	**−8.5%**	1970	3.9%
Nixon/Ford	R	1973	**−14.7%**	1974	**−26.5%**
Carter	D	1977	**−7.2%**	1978	6.6%
Reagan—1st	R	1981	**−4.9%**	1982	21.5%
Reagan—2nd	R	1985	31.7%	1986	18.7%
Bush	R	1989	31.7%	1990	**−3.1%**
Clinton—1st	D	1993	10.1%	1994	1.3%
Clinton—2nd	D	1997	33.4%	1998	28.6%
Bush, GW—1st	R	2001	**−11.9%**	2002	**−22.1%**
Bush, GW—2nd	R	2005	4.9%	2006	15.8%
Obama—1st	D	2009	26.5%		
All (Annualized Average)			5.9%		6.5%

Source: Global Financial Data, Inc., S&P 500 total return from 12/31/1925 to 12/31/2009.

power his party loses to the opposition in the mid-terms. This phenomenon has been true for every president.

And legislation, if passed, is nothing more than some form of redistribution of money and/or property rights (sometimes called regulation). The government takes from these rich to give to those poor, or from these rich to give to those other rich, or from these poor

	3rd Year		4th Year	Annualized Average	Margin of Victory
1927	37.1%	1928	43.3%	N/A	54.1%
1931	**-43.9%**	1932	**-8.9%**	**-23.2%**	58.2%
1935	47.2%	1936	32.8%	30.7%	57.4%
1939	**-0.9%**	1940	**-10.1%**	**-6.4%**	60.8%
1943	25.8%	1944	19.7%	12.6%	54.7%
1947	5.2%	1948	5.1%	8.5%	53.4%
1951	24.6%	1952	18.5%	22.8%	49.5%
1955	31.4%	1956	6.6%	20.6%	55.1%
1959	11.9%	1960	0.5%	9.5%	57.4%
1963	22.7%	1964	16.4%	13.4%	49.7%
1967	23.9%	1968	11.0%	8.6%	61.1%
1971	14.3%	1972	19.0%	6.7%	43.4%
1975	37.2%	1976	23.9%	1.6%	60.7%
1979	18.6%	1980	32.5%	11.7%	50.1%
1983	22.6%	1984	6.3%	10.8%	50.7%
1987	5.3%	1988	16.6%	17.7%	58.8%
1991	30.5%	1992	7.6%	15.7%	53.4%
1995	37.6%	1996	23.0%	17.2%	43.0%
1999	21.0%	2000	**-9.1%**	17.2%	49.2%
2003	28.7%	2004	10.9%	**-0.5%**	47.9%
2007	5.5%	2008	**-37.0%**	**-5.2%**	50.7%
				Simple Average	
	17.5%		9.4%	9.5%	

to those rich (if you think that doesn't happen all the time, you're crazy), or from these poor to those poor. Those on the losing end hate the losing more than twice as much as the winners like the winning. And because we do all this in public, those not getting mugged worry they'll get mugged next. So, in general, *political risk aversion* rises when the threat of legislation increases in the first two years. The legislation doesn't even have to pass! It's frequently just the threat and debate that can roil stocks. As political risk aversion rises, total risk aversion rises—a negative for capital markets in general. As risk aversion goes up, overall demand for equities is decreased, hurting stocks. Increased political risk aversion isn't enough by itself to cause a bear market, but it is a negative force on stocks.

Lazy Legislators Mean Happy Markets

But in the back half of a Head Tic's term, that changes. The Head Tic's party has already lost relative power to the opposition. He can't get as much done and he knows it. Plus, he starts thinking about re-election himself, or helping the guy from his party get elected next to reconfirm the legacy of his presidency (or as many used to say, "We elected Ronald Reagan three times but only got him twice").

Suddenly, politicians find lots of creative ways to yap a lot but pass little. Folks fear getting mugged less, and political risk aversion can start falling fast—helping stocks. Amazingly, we never seem to fully fathom this very real macro social phenomenon that is embedded into our political culture.

You can see in history that landmark legislation tends to pass in the first two years. The third year is best, because in year 4, poli-tics start campaigning again, hinting at all the legislation they'll unleash once elected, and stocks like that less. But still, they talk and don't do much usually—because they want to avoid annoying valuable swing voters. And doing annoys—somebody. Getting elected in America, a centrist country, is predicated on getting the swing voters. Democrats don't get there by courting liberal Democrats and Republicans don't get there courting conservative Republicans. Swing voters are everything to politicians. The more you do, the more you annoy swing voters. That's bad for the tics. So fourth years average worse than third years, but are still overall fine and overwhelmingly positive.

Note too you must never look at just the averages, but what comprises them. Yes, first and second years have poorer average returns. But years that aren't negative can be up huge! It's the same fundamental force at work. Legislative risk aversion is typically highest in the first two years, but if that lessens for some reason, that can be a massive positive surprise and boost stocks.

Keep in mind, too, there are myriad factors acting on stocks. Political risk aversion is a powerful force, but just one big one, and other forces can swamp US political silliness. (Plus, though big, the US economy is less than 25 percent of the whole world,[1] and global stocks tend to be positively correlated. But it's important to note there also hasn't been a negative third year of a president's term since 1939 when looking at the global stock market.) For example, 2009 was President Obama's first year and stocks were up huge, tied to a massive global rally following a steep bear market bottom. That was a huge force driving stocks. But tied to that, Democrats newly elected tend to have great first years, which bucks the average but is consistent with what makes up the average. Always dig deeper into the averages. (And read more on this in Bunk 41.) And remember, sometimes seeming voodoo isn't bunk at all.

BUNK 41 MY POLITICAL PARTY IS BEST FOR STOCKS

Too many investors are prone to fall prey to their ideological biases. If you're a strong Republican, you see the world as being better when Republicans are in charge, and vice versa. Folks also think their "team" has been and will be better for stocks. And you can slice and dice the data various ways to support either Democrats or Republicans being better. But inherently, neither party is better or worse. There are timing differences. Thinking otherwise is just an ideological bias at work—a form of cognitive error—and in investing, biases are your natural enemy.

Yes, in long-term history, Democratic presidents have had slightly higher returns on average than Republicans. But think the way a statistician would think. They would routinely throw out the couple of highest and lowest returns by both parties as likely quirky weird phenomena that don't mean anything in and of themselves—and then consider what happens with the rest of all the years. Is there a difference? With statistical consistency? When you do that, throwing out those few outlier quirky returns, Republican and Democratic presidents on average look almost identical (see Bunk 40).

Plus, some of those years when a president did very well or badly, his party controlled Congress and other years the opposition controlled Congress. When you start adjusting returns tied to congressional power versus presidential power things get murkier still.

But by now you know the forces behind what I call the *presidential term anomaly*—fourth years (which are election years) have much better returns than first years (a new president's inaugural year)—depending on how much investors fear poli-tics will redistribute away their money or rights.

Party Can Matter—At Certain Times

That said, the president's party can matter at certain times. One of those times is in election years; another is inaugural years, particularly when parties flip-flop. Election years when presidential power changes D to R, stocks average 13.2 percent (see Table 41.1)—nicely above average. When congressional power changes too—both swinging from blue to red (albeit wholesale party power changes happen less frequently)—returns average a huge 25.5 percent—way above average! That's where the real action is. Why?

The investor class is about two-to-one more Republican than Democrat. And Republican poli-tics are usually seen as being pro-market and pro-business. They say and promise pro-market things as they seek election, and most investors and markets feel reassured by that and do relatively better than they would otherwise—helped by the reassurance. When Republicans get elected, markets tend to do above average *in that election year.*

Conversely, Democrats are seen as big promoters of social policy—they promise fairness and bigger government to oversee all that fairness. Often, those promises are seen as anti-business and anti-free market—that scares most investors and markets, causing them to do worse than they would otherwise. Election years when presidential power changes R to D, markets fall an average 2.8 percent—way below average—like 2008! When Congress changes power R to D, too, stocks fall an average 8.9 percent. Ugly!

Table 41.1 Party Changes and S&P 500 Performance—A Perverse Inverse

	Election Year	Inauguration Year
Presidency changed from Republican to Democrat	−2.8%	21.8%
Presidency changed from Democrat to Republican	13.2%	−6.6%
Both presidency and Congress changed from Republican to Democrat	−8.9%	52.9%
Both presidency and Congress changed from Democrat to Republican	25.5%	−3.0%

Source: Global Financial Data, Inc., S&P 500 total return from 12/31/1925 to 12/31/2009.

A Perverse Inverse

The perverse part comes in the inauguration year—year 1 of a president's term—when all that changes again. A perverse inverse! Inauguration night, after having a few beverages of his choice (I say "his" because they've all been male—so far), the brand-new president immediately begins campaigning for re-election. Maybe there have been a few presidents who waited until the next morning—but I doubt it.

And new presidents know their power base has nowhere to go—they're trapped for the next four years. There is no way conservative Republicans are going to suddenly turn on a Republican president in favor of Democrats any more than liberal Democrats will turn on a Democratic president in favor of Republicans.

So his sole concern in re-election is appealing to valuable independents and the more marginal members of the opposition party. Independents make or break a president. So the president talks to his base loyally but moderates what he actually does, whether he initially intended to do that or not. He backs away from some initiatives and tones down some others that he knows annoy the independents most. This is true for both parties. If he doesn't moderate, he loses popularity fast.

So, in inaugural years, new Democratic and Republican presidents do less than folks hoped (or feared) during the election. The pro-market Republican turns out to be just a politician and not the pro-market champion that markets expected. They're disappointed, so stocks average a loss of –6.6 percent in new Republican presidents' first years. There hasn't actually been a Republican president other than Bush-1, whose first term's first year was positive in the history of the S&P 500. (Look back at Bunk 40.)

But when a Democrat wins power from a Republican, the market is expecting an advocate for French-style socialism. Yikes! But the Democrat is just a politician too. He turns on his captive power base and moderates—doing less than markets feared in the election year. Markets are positively surprised and increasingly relieved—rising a huge average 21.8 percent in new Democrats' inaugural years.

This is exactly what happened with President Obama. Markets were scared to death of him as he took office and then became slowly less afraid, leading to a great inaugural year—US stocks up 26.5 percent[1] (on the heels of a horrid election year—US stocks down −37 percent).[2] Republicans continue to hate Obama as I write, but generally acknowledge he has done less than he pledged to do and less than they originally feared.

In fact, first years of Democrats' first terms are nearly always positive—save Jimmy Carter in 1977 when stocks fell −7.2 percent (see Table 41.2). Perhaps he didn't moderate enough. Some say he was a brilliant man who was a slow learner. And he was a one-term president! Overwhelmingly, despite first years having the worst average returns of any in overall presidents' terms, Democrats' first inaugural years have been just fine market-wise.

Political biases are fine. Most folks have them. Personally, I find politicians of both parties reprehensible, though I find normal citizens who self-identify as either Republican or Democrat perfectly fine. It's like being a fan of a professional sports team. You like your team, hate the opponents. It gives you a sense of community. But political biases are dangerous when investing—blinding you to fundamental forces behind stocks.

There is a time when Republican politics helps markets and others when it hurts markets. Ditto for Democratic party politics. Knowing the difference in terms of how that affects sentiment and demand for stocks and the timing thereof is good. But if you get bullish or bearish just because the party you identify with won or lost, you're reacting with no more real fundamentals, relative to the supply and demand for securities, than if you reacted based off your favorite sports team winning or losing. It's bunk!

Table 41.2   First Years of Democrats' Terms—Almost Consistently Positive

	First Year	S&P 500 Return
FDR—1st	1933	52.9%
Truman	1949	18.1%
Kennedy/Johnson	1961	26.8%
Johnson	1965	12.4%
Carter	1977	−7.2%
Clinton—1st	1993	10.1%
Obama	2009	26.5%

Source: Global Financial Data, Inc., S&P 500 total return.

BUNK 42 STOCK RETURNS ARE TOO HIGH AND MUST FALL

Life would be simpler if there were just one, easy-to-diagnose problem causing us to think wrong about investing. Instead, a whole field of behavioral psychology—behavioral finance—evolved to deal with the myriad ways human brains go haywire when contemplating something as unintuitive and unnatural as investing in capital markets.

One common theme that pops up, though, is fear of heights. It's what makes high P/Es so scary when you look at them in the wrong context (Bunk 26) even though overall P/Es, no matter their level, aren't predictive of future stock returns over any reasonable time frame, despite persistent myth to the contrary. "Too high" can be framed any number of ways that lead your brain to market ruin. And one is how we look at long-term stock returns.

Scary Scaling

You've probably seen Figure 42.1—it's a simple chart of the S&P 500 Total Return Index going back to 1926. This chart scares the pants off some folks, particularly those who think stocks are unreasonably high now (and at any future point in time) and must crash down to earth. Just look at it! It looks like through history, stocks have had pretty steady returns—then, starting about in 1990, stocks took off and had truly unsustainable returns. Too high! Scary! (On this chart, 1929 doesn't even show as a blip—which gives you the first clue to its reality.)

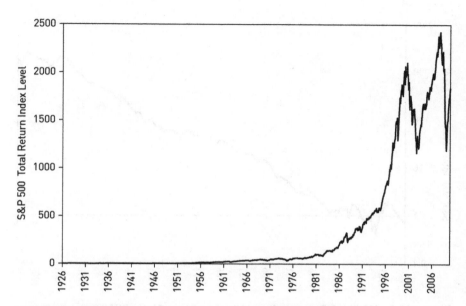

Figure 42.1 US Stock Returns, Linear—Looks Are Deceptive
Source: Global Financial Data, Inc., S&P 500 total return from 12/31/1925 to 12/31/2009, graphed on a linear scale.

Looks deceive. That "scary" run-up is simply the impact of compounding returns over an ultra-long period. Still, many can't shake the notion that stocks have come too far, too fast, and a big crash must be coming—bigger and more lasting than the 2007–2009 bear market, which by historical standards was in fact a monster.

Now consider Figure 42.2. It looks like a reasonable, long-term rate of return—not scary and top-heavy. Except Figures 42.1 and 42.2 *show the exact same data*—S&P 500 total return from 1926 through year-end 2009. The only difference is the scale.

What gives? Figure 42.1 shows returns on a linear scale. Linear scales are fine and used all the time in statistics. Even for stock returns they're fine for shorter periods. The problem with a linear scale for stocks longer term is every point move takes up the same amount of vertical space.

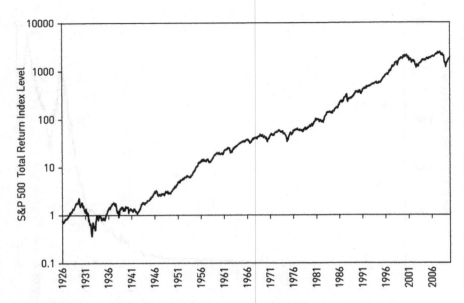

Figure 42.2   US Stock Returns, Logarithmic—Same Stats, Different Perspective

Source: Global Financial Data, Inc., S&P 500 total return from 12/31/1925 to 12/31/2009, graphed on a logarithmic scale.

Envision it this way: An increase from 100 to 200 looks the same as a move from 1,000 to 1,100—both 100 points. But that's not how you experience market growth. A price move from 100 to 200 is a huge 100 percent increase—double! But 1,000 to 1,100 is only a 10 percent rise. So plotting the S&P 500 since 1926 makes more recent gains seem stratospheric because the index level itself is higher. But average annualized returns from 1990 to 2009 were actually smaller than from 1926 to 1989 (7.8 percent and 10.2 percent respectively)[1]—thanks to the two big bear markets during the 2000s. Yet the graph makes those returns look infinitely huger, compared with the totality of earlier decades. Ironic, isn't it?

Figure 42.2 shows market returns on a *logarithmic* scale—a better way to consider long-term market returns. On a logarithmic scale, percent changes look the same even if absolute price changes are vastly different. This is the right way to "see" stock returns in the long term. This way, an increase in index price from 100 to 200 (a 100 percent change) looks the same as a rise from 1,000 to 2,000—also

100 percent. And that's just how you and your portfolio experience market changes.

This is a scaling issue—learning to look at data the right way. Scaling is a classic debunkery tactic. Once you get scale, that inherent fear of heights most people feel goes away. And, you'll see that over long periods, market returns are a lot steadier than you think.

PART 5 IT'S A GREAT BIG WORLD!

Americans are frequently villainized as too materialistic, loud, crass—so some believe. We don't bother speaking French in France. *Quelle horreur!* What those Frenchies (and most others) don't realize is we're much more alike than they know. Almost all investors, from the US to France to Japan to Djibouti, fail to think globally. In fact, investors, as a group, are downright provincial!

Americans may say, "That's fine for those other people, but America is huge! We don't need to think globally. We have all the stocks we need right here in the awesome US of A." The US *is* awesome! Nowhere else I'd rather live. California is problematic. But anywhere else! However, I'd never want to invest solely in the US. You shouldn't either.

But more importantly, neither your portfolio nor your thinking should be constrained by borders—wherever you're from. America is big (and awesome) but is just under 25 percent of total world GDP.[1] Big! But just a quarter of the world. In other words, what happens in America's borders can be heavily influenced by the massive 75 percent of non-US world GDP.

Which means the world is much more correlated than most think. And it's been that way not just in recent history, but for centuries—a point few appreciate. So investors who ignore the world miss powerful opportunities to better manage their portfolios. (Bunks 43, 44.)

That's one benefit—a major one. But there are also major investor misperceptions that linger, just because folks fail to consider the broader world. Folks make investing errors frequently because they see the world perversely—you know that. You know from Part 4 that checking history is a great form of debunkery. But vision can also be cleared up more (and easily) with a little global perspective.

Folks go bonkers over debt—thinking everyone has too much, including the US government. We can bicker about how that debt is used, and why, and what level is too much, but debt fears melt instantly once you consider US debt not only in historical context, but in context of the whole globe—you'll see that in Bunks 45, 46, 47. And of course, because the world loves to demonize the US, many folks fail to realize we have much in common with our non-US friends in terms of economic and fiscal conditions—and it's not been disastrous for them or us. You can use debunkery to see that clearly. (Bunks 45, 48.)

Simply, American financial life—and for that matter everywhere else—is less mysterious if you can do global debunkery. It can help assuage at least one fear about global violence—that it can take down capital markets (Bunk 50)—and alleviate confusion about one very popular and frequently misunderstood economic indicator (Bunk 49).

The beautiful part of global debunkery is it requires no globe-trotting, just standard debunkery tactics—all done easily from the safety of your laptop. And if you can see the world just a bit more clearly than most, you can have a serious advantage over them—and that's no bunk.

BUNK 43 FOREIGN STOCKS JUST FEEL SO . . . FOREIGN

oes even the phrase "foreign investing" give you shivers? Do foreign stocks just seem so . . . foreign? You're not alone. Far too many US investors wholly ignore the non-US world. Or they may consider foreign an inherently "riskier" asset class, holding just 10 percent or 20 percent. Too little!

I've heard even established professionals claim foreign is "riskier." Riskier than what, they don't say. This is easily disproved with free public data and a bit of history. Truth is: Non-US equity and bond investing shouldn't be any more or less risky than US investing. A good, well-diversified equity portfolio will benefit from being fully half in non-US stocks.

Fifty percent foreign? Seem outrageous? It's not. The US is still the largest single nation in terms of total market capitalization—but it's just about 49 percent of the developed world equity markets.[1] Considering the whole world—undeveloped markets too—it's about 43 percent.[2] If you're US only, you miss more than half a world of opportunity plus extra diversification benefits.

Once upon a time, maybe it made some sense for US individual investors to ignore the non-US world. Sometimes, transaction costs for foreign stocks on foreign exchanges were excessive—eating into potential benefit. And we couldn't always count on complete transparency from non-US firms. But in recent decades, as exchanges went electronic, trading globally is now quick and easy—you can buy lots of Chilean stocks as easily as any US stocks. Plus, US investors needn't exchange money anymore—reducing that risk. American depositary receipts (ADRs) let US investors buy stock in many foreign firms on US exchanges in US dollars. And in developed nations and even in many emerging markets (if not most), accounting standards are normalized for publicly traded firms. Whether buying a French or Brazilian ADR or a US stock—accounting and reporting obligations are largely the same.

US and Non-US Stocks—More Correlated Than You Think

If non-US stocks were materially riskier, returns would be wildly variable. But they're not! US and non-US stocks are more correlated than folks think—been that way for millennia. (In my recently updated 1987 book, *The Wall Street Waltz*, I have scads of charts showing strong correlations between the US and foreign markets going back centuries.) We live in a global economy—always have (at least much more so than people have commonly appreciated, as documented in that book)—and many of the same macroeconomic forces acting on US stocks at any one time also impact non-US stocks.

Figure 43.1 shows US and non-US annual stock performance—as measured by the S&P 500 and MSCI's Europe, Australasia, Far East (MSCI EAFE) indexes. Generally, when one is up, the other is too; US might be up or down more than foreign, or vice versa—but they tend not to go in opposite directions. If US stocks want to be down a lot, foreign stocks are down too. It's a question of degree. There can be big divergences, but they're short-lived. Since 1970 (as far back as we currently have exceptionally good data on non-US stocks—the work in my 1987 book was based on much more primitive and less precisely constructed indexes and data), US stocks have annualized 10.0 percent, EAFE 9.4 percent (measured in US dollars).[3] There's just no reason to believe, going forward, one or the other will be inherently better or inherently riskier over long periods. But the two together are overall more stable with less volatility than either by itself. Hence the diversification is worthwhile.

With this great diversification you are fundamentally reducing risk by fully investing globally. Think this through another way. Many complain endlessly that the US is doing wrong things socially and politically, and that will cause America to no longer have the global leadership position it so long held. Well, maybe that's true; maybe it isn't. But if you have those fears, that is even more reason to globally diversify.

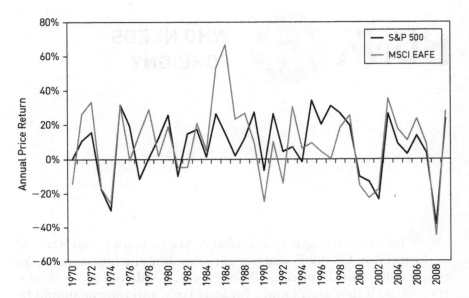

Figure 43.1   S&P 500 and MSCI EAFE Annual Returns—Long Correlated

Source: Thomson Reuters, MSCI Inc.,[4] S&P 500 price return, MSCI EAFE price return from 12/31/1970 to 12/31/2009.

In fact, by not investing as broadly as you can, you could be missing opportunities to manage risk! But thinking you can't benefit from foreign stocks is bunk addressed elsewhere (Bunk 44). There's enough difference year-to-year between US and non-US stocks to reap benefits from diversification. So stop being a stranger to foreign and go fully global.

BUNK 44 WHO NEEDS FOREIGN?

Who needs foreign? You, probably. Maybe you've read Bunk 43 and know non-US stocks as a category shouldn't be inherently more or less risky than US stocks and, long term, should net pretty similar returns. So if they aren't more (or less) risky, and returns should be similar (long term), why bother? Two reasons:

1. Risk management
2. Return opportunities

Yes, in the very long term, US and non-US stocks should have very similar returns (and actually *have had* throughout well-measured history). But for many years at a crack—maybe three to seven, but sometimes more and sometimes less, one category can best the other—just like with all other categories like growth versus value, or big cap versus small cap, or Tech versus Energy. (Bunk 10.)

Figure 44.1 shows the S&P 500 performance divided by the MSCI EAFE Index. When the line is rising, US stocks are overall outperforming non-US (also shaded in gray). When the line is falling (white bars), non-US stocks are outperforming. You intuitively see that the white and gray, rising and falling, almost exactly equal each other. But for years at a crack they don't.

US and Non-US Trade Leadership—Irregularly

Since 1970, US and non-US stocks have traded leadership irregularly for irregular periods. Sometimes US stocks outperform by a lot for a long time—like in the mid to late 1990s when they led EAFE by 193.5 percent.[2]

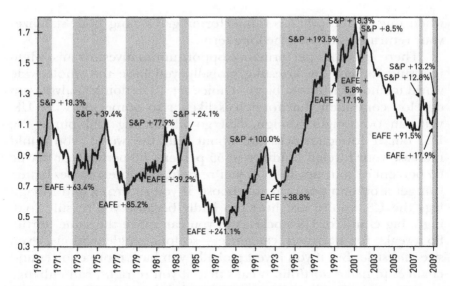

Figure 44.1   S&P 500 Versus MSCI EAFE—Sometimes US Leads, Sometimes US Lags

Source: Thomson Reuters, Global MSCI Inc.,[1] S&P 500 total return, MSCI EAFE total return with net dividends from 12/31/1969 to 12/31/2009.

And sometimes foreign is the winner—like in the 1980s, by a huge 241.1 percent.[3] Sometimes outperformance periods are much shorter.

But over ultra-long periods, you tend to end up in the about same place—remember, since 1970 US stocks have annualized 10.0 percent, and EAFE 9.4 percent.[4] (Bunk 10 covers why.) And don't take this graph to mean they wildly flip-flop! No—they tend to go the same direction overall, but one might be up a bit more or less than the other, or down a bit more or less. (See the graph in Bunk 43 again.)

So you might feel great during the 1990s with an all-US portfolio, but you really missed out for much of the 1980s and big parts of the 2000s. And while you may have an opinion, which is fine, there's no certain way to know which will lead going forward and for how long. So an all-US investor could easily get caught in another long period like the 1980s. Hypothesis: If foreign stocks aren't inherently riskier, and you tend to get similar returns over long periods, with multi-year periods of leadership and laggardness, why miss out when one or the other is outperforming? Owning both stabilizes your return stream over the long term.

There are other performance opportunities investors miss when ignoring foreign. By investing globally, you have the whole wide world to choose from—a bigger choice set. If, in doing analysis, you develop conviction that foreign is likelier to outperform the US, you can overweight foreign. Not go whole hog and purge the US, but if foreign stocks are about half the world, you could increase your foreign holdings to 55 percent, 60 percent, or maybe 65 percent of your portfolio. If you're right and foreign does better, you get a bit of a performance boost! If you're wrong and foreign lags the US, you're not hurt too badly because you're still holding a big chunk of US stocks. And you can make the same portfolio tweaks for narrower categories—sectors, single nations, even size and style. But if you invest globally, you have more choices and chances to make portfolio tweaks that, if you're right, can enhance performance. The best part is you needn't be right all the time—just right more than wrong. That's the performance-enhancing side.

Opportunities to Manage Risk

Investing globally means more risk management opportunities too. The very fundamental nature of modern portfolio theory says diversification—the blending of categories with differing correlations (things that zig when others zag)—lowers total portfolio volatility risk. And the broader you diversify (done right), the more benefit you get.

Why? The broader you invest, the more you diversify away sector, size, style, and single-country risk. Can you still experience downside volatility? Of course! Tons of it! No equity index in the universe (should we have a universal index one day) can diversify away market risk. But can it smooth the bumps a bit and be more of a cushion than a narrower index? Yes—finance theory says so.

Why do US and foreign and all these other categories end up with very similar long-term returns? Read Bunk 10! And don't give away chances to enhance performance and manage risk. It's so easy—just be global.

BUNK 45 BIG DEBT IS NATIONAL DEATH

I don't care your political leaning—left, right, center, libertarian, green, or even French socialist—everyone agrees America has big debt. And most everyone agrees the big debt is terrible and a drag on our economy—possibly forever.

If you're a debt hater like most folks, 2009 likely made you apoplectic as massive stimulus efforts to kick-start the economy added hugely to America's debt. We can quibble about whether the fiscal stimulus was the right response, and whether stimulus programs are well run and the money spent efficiently (they aren't and it wasn't—government spending is always a mess—but when trying to kick-start an economy, there are times when it is better to spend stupidly than not at all). But either way, there's no denying that, at the end of 2009, our net public debt totaled about 53 percent of GDP[1] and was elevated compared to very recent history.

A Long History of Big Debt

But is that so bad? Figure 45.1 shows US net public debt (i.e., debt held by the public and not other branches of the federal government, which is what matters—see Bunk 47) relative to GDP. Debt, though elevated, isn't much higher than anytime from 1991 to 1998—a time of overall economic vibrancy and fine stock returns.

And debt was higher from 1943 to 1955, reaching 109 percent of GDP in the aftermath of World War II. Yes, that was war-related debt. And folks often feel better about war-related debt than peacetime debt—thinking we had to create the war-related debt, but peacetime debt is a choice. But the economy doesn't care about the

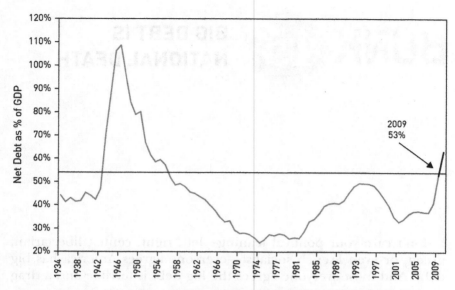

Figure 45.1   US Net Public Debt to GDP Over Time—Back to the '50s
Source: TreasuryDirect, Congressional Budget Office, March 2010 release.

debt's purpose or morality—it just cares there's additional money being borrowed and spent. And the recipients of that borrowed and spent money spend again. And those recipients spend—with each transaction spurring more and more later transactions, all contributing to moving money through the system and bettering the economy. Plus, that earlier period, the late 1940s and early 1950s, isn't remembered as economically troubled—or even as a time of high debt.

Ironically, it was the period before the war—the Great Depression—when debt was lower but the economy miserable. And even the period following the very elevated debt levels of the 1950s weren't times of ruin. Very high levels of debt then didn't irrevocably doom our economy—and shouldn't now.

Bigger Debt Abroad!

Folks who fear US debt fail to do simple debunkery—thinking globally *and* looking at history. For example, the UK has a long history of official GDP and federal debt data—back, amazingly, to 1700—shown in Figure 45.2.

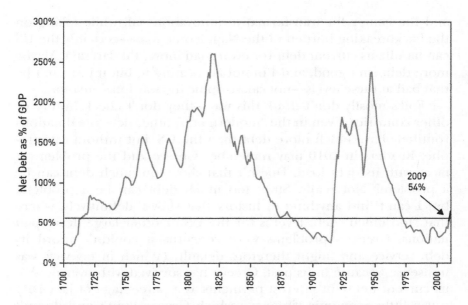

Figure 45.2   UK Net Public Debt to GDP Over Time—Much Higher in the Past
Source: HM Treasury (www.ukpublicspending.co.uk), as of March 2010. Includes budget projections through 2010.

The UK, which, last I checked isn't a smoldering ruin, has had in its history vastly higher net debt levels for very long time periods than anything we've ever contemplated in America—and overall has done fine. From 1725 to 1875 was generally England's golden age—the dominant global economic and military power—similar to America today. This was inclusive of Britain's Industrial Revolution—which began in England in the 1830s and only decades later was exported to continental Europe and then America. England led the world. Yet during the entirety of that 150 years, its net public debt was higher than ours now, and for more than 100 years (from 1750 to 1850) it was above 100 percent, peaking above 250 percent—more than four times more than levels we're approaching now.

Think about it. Then, the UK was a much less developed and much narrower economy in a much less developed overall world where information traveled on slow ships and horseback and via quill pen. (I've studied, and I'm pretty sure they had no laptops back then.) Back then, if they could have four times more debt than the US has now and be a global economic growth powerhouse and the center for transformative innovation—all while taking on the backbreaking burden of the Napoleonic wars—certainly the US can handle its current debt (or even a tad more, I'd daresay). Maybe more debt isn't good, and I'm not advocating it, but it just can't be that bad at these levels—not catastrophic the way folks envision.

Folks mostly don't think this way—they don't check history or other countries. Even in the "modern era," other developed nations routinely have much more debt than the US, but without catastrophe. Readers in 2010 may remember Greece and the problems it faces with its debt load. Doesn't that show too much debt can be a problem? Not really. Sure, too much debt can be a problem, but I can't find anything in history that shows, definitively, where that "too much" debt level is for the US or other large developed nations. Greece's problems were concerns it couldn't afford its debt service and might therefore default. (Which in my view was nonsense because in its past, Greece has survived with over double its current net debt interest payments as a percentage of its GDP.) But a little economic vibrancy—which Greece didn't and doesn't have—makes all that go away!

Interest rates in 2010 are historically low—even for Greece. What Greece needs is a lot less corruption, much less socialism, and much more free-market capitalism—like the US! That leads to more economic growth, which shrinks debt loads relative to GDP and makes the debt more affordable in the future. (If anything, Greece should also serve as a reminder of the perils of an entitlement society, but I digress.)

America's debt level now isn't worrisome, and it could get bigger without being at a level proven to be problematic. Think globally and historically, and it's a lot harder to fret big debt in America now. If you want to see how little it actually costs us to carry our current debt levels and what we've done before, see Bunk 46. We're not at any critical crisis level. That's bunk.

BUNK 46 AMERICA CAN'T HANDLE ITS DEBT

Lots of folks complain America has too much debt (Bunk 45). And we do have plenty—but one reason the debt isn't so problematic is because paying for it isn't as expensive as most folks fear. Our debt interest payments, as I write this in 2010, are quite low—even low compared with recent history.

As 2009 ended, America was spending over $300 billion each year just making net debt interest payments. Yikes! Sounds like a lot, but isn't. This is another case of big, scary numbers taken out of context. We have a massive economy, so items like debt and interest payments can seem unfathomably huge. As with many "big" numbers, a simple debunkery is to consider it in scale—as a percentage of GDP—which is the right way to think about it.

Figure 46.1 shows US net debt interest payments as a percentage of GDP. Amazingly, paying for our debt, even at more elevated levels, is now about 2.2 percent of GDP and perfectly unremarkable compared to past periods.

Our net debt interest payments are lower now than any time between 1979 and 2002—which includes the big 1980s and 1990s bull markets—and not all that far above where they were in the 1950s and 1960s. Interest payments relative to GDP were nearly double what they are now from about 1984 through 1996—perfectly fine times for stocks and the economy overall.

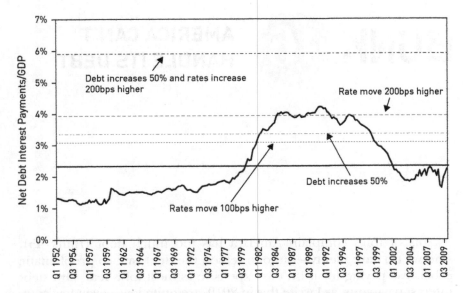

Figure 46.1   US Federal Interest Payments as a Percentage of GDP—At Pre-1980 Levels

Source: Thomson Reuters, Federal Reserve Flow of Funds, US Bureau of Economic Analysis, US Treasury (Q1 1952 to Q4 2009).

Low Interest Rates Lower Costs

How can our interest costs be so low when our debt is so huge? Well, first, our debt isn't as huge relative to the size of our economy as people commonly envision (see Bunk 45). Then, too, interest rates are now historically low—they've been trending lower globally since the early 1980s—that's one big reason. For our interest costs to move to 3 percent of GDP—below where they were from about 1980 to 1999—interest rates would have to move up a full 1 percent on average across the spectrum of our long-term debt. Increase our debt 50 percent relative to GDP with today's interest rates, and we're still under 3.5 percent—not a problematic level. Folks fear our debt is rapidly increasing, but even the most nervous Nellie probably doesn't envision our debt increasing another full 50 percent relative to GDP in the immediate future. To get back up to those debt service levels of 1984 through 1996—terrific times overall for stocks—interest rates must rise a big two percentage points. In other words, our debt costs are cheap and perfectly manageable.

They would have to increase markedly just to get to levels seen in past, economically vibrant times.

Could interest rates increase a lot? Sure—anything can happen. But think globally—our interest rates fell over the last 30 years, almost perfectly in line with global long- and short-term interest rates. So if US rates went back up, logically they would rise in parallel to global rates rising. I could be wrong, but my guess is unless we see a repeat of the gross monetary policy errors that ruled the 1970s, leading to global hyperinflation and ultra-high interest rates, we're more likely to see a period of relatively benign rates for some time. Again, I could be wrong. Yes, rates likely will move higher than the historically low rates we've seen through 2009 and 2010. But that takes some time. Plus, as the economy grows, that shrinks our interest payments as a percentage of GDP.

Big debt isn't some great thing, but interest costs aren't the problem right now that so many fear—not something to go bonkers on immediately ahead. Scale it to see it right, and think globally—simple debunkery.

Blanche DuBois, in the dramatic final scene of *A Streetcar Named Desire*, says, "I have always depended on the kindness of strangers," as she gets taken away to be institutionalized. She's touched in the head, you see. Why else would she rely on strangers?

And that is how many Americans regard America. We're in debt— huge debt—and it's terrible! (It really isn't—see Bunk 45.) But worse— our debt is owned by—eek!—foreigners! Scary foreigners! Worse, mostly the Chinese!

The story goes: The Chinese (and to a lesser extent, other foreigners) prop up our profligate, overspending ways—purely out of kindness. A charity, really. They only do it so we'll keep buying their stuff, giving them the advantage of a trade surplus and us the disadvantage of a trade deficit that will keep piling on and blow up on us later. (No, it won't—see why just ahead in Bunk 48.) The view is: They hold our huge debt like a pistol to our head with their twitchy trigger fingers. And what if they decide, cruelly, to pull the trigger— i.e., stop buying our debt and instead dump it all? In effect saying, "We're done with being nice to you, America! We're not going to, selflessly and for no other reason, buy your dumb debt anymore!" Well, then we'd be sunk. Wouldn't we?

This argument was particularly potent throughout 2009. As the US sold more debt during the wave of global fiscal stimulus aimed at halting the recession, there was endless talk of the world shifting away from the dollar to another reserve currency. Maybe the euro. Or even China's yuan!

Investors Don't Invest Out of Charity

Bunk of the first order. Investors—institutions, nations, even individuals—buy US debt freely and willingly. They don't do it to be nice to us; they do it because it makes vast, self-interested sense for them. Think about your own behavior. Do you invest just to make the issuer happy—or anyone but yourself? Out of charity? (Maybe you do give to charity—but you don't think of that as an investment in the traditional sense at all. It's charity!) No! You invest to satisfy whatever goals you have. You want the best return for whatever amount of risk you're willing to accept.

The Chinese are no different. China is perfectly free, right now, to buy debt from any and almost every other nation—and they do, some. But no other nation remotely matches the size and depth of US debt markets. Plus, China has, to varying degrees, maintained a peg to the US dollar for years (though they loosened it some again in 2010). To do so, they keep large, dollar-denominated reserves. They want their reserves super-safe—hence they buy über-safe US Treasuries. Sure, China could utterly abandon the peg, but they'd likely do so gradually, and officials have said so. Even then, my guess is they'd still maintain large reserves in dollars, as many, many other nations do that don't have a peg.

But all this fear is silly, because the largest holder of US government debt is . . . the US government.

Figure 47.1 shows who owns US Treasuries. About 37 percent is owned by hundreds of US federal government agencies, but mostly the Medicare and Social Security trust funds. You don't worry about debt the US government owes to itself. States, public pension plans, and other local governments hold another 5.7 percent. But you don't worry about California holding US government debt. Rightfully, you worry about California for many other reasons—but not for holding US debt.

Then, American investors—individuals, corporations, charities, banks, mutual funds, hedge funds, a myriad of other entities, people—ones like you—domestic investors—own 27.7 percent. You like owning Treasuries. You see them as safe. (And they are! But not always necessarily in the way folks think—see why in Bunk 1.) You don't usually get a high return on them—haven't since the early 1980s. Over long periods, stocks typically get better results, but you're confident the US government will pay interest and return

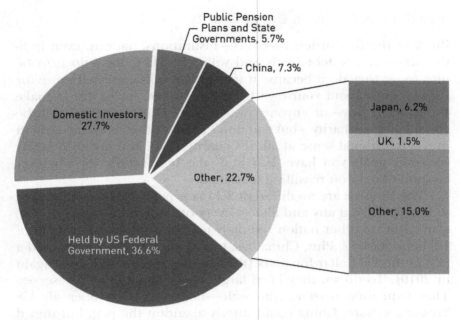

Figure 47.1 Who Owns US Treasury Debt? Uncle Sam Is Biggest!
Source: Thomson Reuters; US Department of the Treasury, as of 12/31/2009.

principal on maturity. My point: With money you want to be super-safe, you probably weren't buying Greek debt in 2010. If you were buying Greek debt, you were thinking of it as high-risk, high-return potential—not US-Treasury safe.

So, 70 percent of US federal debt is held by Americans, American governments, and/or American entities, which benefit Americans. Just 30 percent is held by the non-US world. Of that, 7.3 percent is held by China. Interestingly, Japan holds 6.2 percent—almost the same—but no one complains about them. And you don't hear a lot of phobic fantasizing about Japan dumping its Treasuries. Is there something magical about the Chinese that scares us that isn't magical about the Japanese? That's silly and bunk.

Mathematically, it would make no difference to markets if the Japanese sold while the Chinese bought or vice versa. You know that in your bones. Then, the UK owns about 2 percent—you're perfectly sanguine about that. Britain is our great friend! You don't care about Mexico or Thailand (0.3 percent each), Luxembourg (0.7 percent), Israel (0.1 percent), or India (0.3 percent). All tiny!

Remember—China, Japan, the UK, Thailand, Luxembourg, and India are happy to buy and hold our debt. They can buy other nations' debt. And they do! Just much less. But they like buying our debt and do so to satisfy their own investing and/or policy ends, not from some sense of charity or kindness.

And the countries that hold big positions in our debt change over time. At various times in the last few years, Japan has held more of our debt than China. It goes back and forth. And three years from now, who knows? Could be Eastern European nations own a lot of our debt—or Australia, Brazil, whoever.

Nations will at periods buy more US debt, or buy less, all depending on myriad conditions within their own borders. But whether the world is buying more or less, it cannot compare to the amount of US debt being bought and held within US borders.

If at any point buyers of government debt become unhappy with the interest rates they receive from their various debt holdings, they can sell some to buy others. So today they are happy with their US debt. Maybe tomorrow they'll change their views! If China changes its view and sells US debt heavily, that pushes down the prices of US Treasuries relative to what they were before, and pushes up the yield. That makes US rates relatively more attractive than before, so other investors sell some other country's debt to buy some of the now-more-attractive US debt, offsetting most of the Chinese selling effects. China sells, that impacts US yields, everyone else finds US debt more attractive and buys. The total impact is very small. That's the part that's virtually impossible for most people to get. And that's why, fundamentally, you needn't fear indebtedness to China, Japan, the UK, Brazil, or Bhutan.

Ironically, just 20 years ago we had the same fear of the Japanese. In fact, we pretty much thought about the Japanese then the way we do the Chinese now: "Eek! They're taking over the world and buying up our assets!" Didn't happen. Relax and have more faith in Capitalism. It works.

BUNK 48 TRADE DEFICITS MAKE DEFICIENT MARKETS

Do you know the US has a trade deficit? A huge one?

If not, you must be an aggressive Luddite, eschewing any form of modern interaction for fully the last 30 years. It was $504 billion at the end of 2009.[1] The world's largest! The story goes: Our big trade deficit means we buy more than we sell. That profligacy weighs on our economy and stocks. Then, that big trade deficit hurts the dollar, weakening our currency relative to the world.

Nonsense! The word "deficit" shares a Latin root with "deficient," but when it comes to trade, deficits aren't deficient. Thinking globally frees you from this fear—standard debunkery. Stocks are highly globally correlated, and globally, all trade balances. By definition it must.

No one frets North Dakota having a trade deficit to California. North Dakotans like getting fresh produce in the winter and think the value they get by not subsisting on local barley and sunflower seeds through the long winter is well worth the money sent to sunny California. No one frets municipal debt based on state trade deficits or prefers municipal debt from states with state trade surpluses.

You Are Your Own Trade Deficit

Think it through another way: In one sense, you, personally, are a walking trade deficit. You go to the grocery store and buy milk, tomatoes, and macaroni and cheese. But you don't sell the store anything in return. You just give them money! Egad! You must be bankrupt! You know that's silly and that it's an apples-oranges comparison in terms of your real and overall financial accounting and well-being. But so are national trade deficits, as I'll show you.

You have money because you do something else to earn money. You could grow your own tomatoes and make your own pasta and cheese. But unless you're a professional farmer, you know your time is better spent working at a job you're better at and that takes advantage of your specialization of labor than cheese-crafting. So you take your salary and decide where and how to spend it on stuff you need and want, creating a trade deficit with the grocery store, the home electronics store, the liquor store—and all stores wherever. But you don't think it would be better if, instead of giving the grocery store money, you stayed home and raised chickens to barter. No! You think that is crazy and rationally understand why the current arrangement makes more sense. The great British economist David Ricardo (1772–1823) proved that specialization of labor is not only good for you—which you intuitively know—but it's also good for nations, which isn't always so obvious to everyone. But it's true. Why?

Because, nationally, it's not much different from you earning income elsewhere and spending it how you choose at the grocery store, liquor store, whatever-store. Our huge trade deficit, instead of being harmful, can be seen as evidence of long-term economic vibrancy. We have a huge income so we can afford to import more than we export. That's different from spending more than we make.

Scale It to See It

But maybe you still don't buy it. Fine—$504 billion is big. But an easy debunkery is scaling big, "scary"-sounding absolute numbers to see them correctly. Our brains are naturally scared of big numbers—part of the way our brains evolved. Big is scary, small is less scary. It makes sense when a mammoth is charging you versus a bunny rabbit—a charging mammoth hurts while a charging bunny is just weird. But that intuitive thinking is all wrong for capital markets. After all, the US is a big economy—over $14 trillion! So consider the trade deficit as a percentage of GDP—the proper way to think about it. It's currently about 3.5 percent.[2] Now, is *that* big or small? Depends!

Do you think the UK has a big trade deficit? Folks probably never think about it. If they do, they just assume that the US is

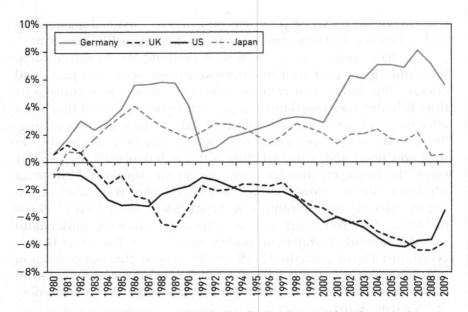

Figure 48.1 Trade Balances—Would You Rather Be the US or Germany?

Source: Thomson Reuters, visible trade balances as a percentage of GDP from 01/01/1980 to 12/31/2009.

bad and everyone else is sainted. But no, the UK now has a bigger trade deficit than the US—about 5.9 percent of GDP.[3] Though bigger now, since 1980, both great Uniteds have had very similar-sized trade deficits as a percentage of GDP on the same trajectory. And they've both shrunk a bit from recent highs. That's not a great thing—it's likely tied to the recent recession. You don't want a smaller trade deficit if it takes a recession to get there.

Figure 48.1 shows balance of trade as a percentage of GDP for the US, UK, Germany, and Japan—currently the largest developed nations. You see the US and UK closely tracking each other with trade deficits nearly the entirety of the last three decades. Japan has had a surplus nearly the entire time, and Germany all of the time, with a big surplus now.

Which Country Would You Rather Be?

Now, which country would you rather be? Since 1980, the US averaged 2.8 percent annual real GDP growth, and its stocks have annualized 10.3 percent.[4] UK GDP has annualized 2.1 percent and stocks 11.0 percent.[5] If a trade surplus is so helpful, then Germany and Japan should have had better growth and market returns. Except Japan had 2.2 percent annual growth—basically lagging the US and in line with the UK.[6] And Japan's stocks annualized 7.0 percent[7]—lagging big-time. German stocks did 9.5 percent[8]—better than Japan, but still lagging the US and UK. And German growth averaged just 1.7 percent![9] A surplus isn't necessarily so good. A deficit just sounds bad, but isn't.

Their big surpluses haven't helped them any more than our big deficits hurt us. In fact, one could argue, because Germany and Japan have heavy government throttles to promote big surpluses, the government intervention in free markets has actually held back their growth, depriving them of the magic of relatively more free markets that exist in the two great Uniteds. At least that's what David Ricardo would have predicted and smiles at from his grave.

Plus, during the entirety of the time the US has had those deficits, we've had periods of strong growth, plus a few recessions. And we've had tremendous market growth, plus some bear markets. Yet the trade deficit keeps going, regardless. If a trade deficit were truly all that bad, our economy and stocks would surely have primarily dropped for the last 30 years. They haven't. Instead they've led the developed world.

What about the charge a trade deficit depresses the dollar? Wrong. Here's how you know. For the last 30 years, we've had periods of dollar strength and dollar weakness—no correlation with the size of the deficit. But for almost that entire period, the pound sterling has been very strong—one of the developed world's strongest currencies. So, to say our big deficit is bad for the dollar, you'd have to also argue that Britain's equal-sized and sometimes bigger deficit as a percentage of GDP is *good* for the pound sterling. But you can't argue that because you can't have it both ways. That would be crazy.

Simply said, if we grow faster than they do, we can afford to buy more from them than we export to them. End of story. And, even now in 2010 as I write, while we're not growing faster than everyone, like the emerging-market nations, we are growing faster than most of the developed world, including Europe and Japan, and the non-emerging, less developed nations. And growth comes from letting the free-market magic transform us in its classically creative-destruction-and-resurrection mode that has fostered the greatest human transformation ever seen since capitalism emerged from mercantilism in the early nineteenth century—when David Ricardo was getting older and no longer feeling his oats but seeing the emergence of his views around the world. Growth allows for trade deficits. Lack of growth allows for stagnation and misery all around.

Few bother to think these things through. They just say, "The trade deficit is big and bad," because deficits sound bad and don't bother to check if it's true. Debunkery helps you see this right. Lose your fear of deficits. Instead say, "I love big trade deficits and want to see bigger deficits, not smaller."

BUNK 49 — GDP MAKES STOCKS GROW

I t's widely and commonly believed good stock returns require strong GDP. And that's true! Sort of. (And not in the long term—see Bunk 10 for why supply sets price in the long term, making all correctly calculated categories' returns almost equal with widely varying paths en route.) But different types of stocks shine in weaker versus stronger economies.

Some stocks are defensive in nature and tend to do better relatively when GDP is weaker—sectors like Consumer Staples, Health Care, and Utilities—though not always and everywhere. When times are tough, folks don't upgrade their TVs and go on cruises so much (or somewhat more prosperous folks who are struggling nonetheless might buy a new TV instead of going on a cruise), but they typically do keep buying toothpaste and electricity and aspirin. (If times are really tough, maybe they need more aspirin! See Bunk 39.) So those kinds of stocks typically do better than the market overall in downturns—though you can certainly find periods historically in a strong economy when they do fine too.

Stocks Move First—Up or Down

But there are two problems with this thinking: First, stocks lead the economy, not the other way around. If you wait for confirmation from the economy before making a move—you can pay big. (See Bunk 9.) For example, the US economy did fine overall in 1981, growing 2.54 percent[1]—though a recession started midyear.[2] Stocks knew it was coming—falling 4.9 percent for the year.[3] GDP was positive, yet stocks fell!

That recession lasted until November 1982, and GDP shrank 1.94 percent that year.[4] But stocks started pricing in the coming recovery, moving higher before the economy—up 21.6 percent in 1982.[5] Negative GDP—yet hugely positive stocks! If you looked just at GDP—expecting it to tell you which way the market was going, you would have missed that.

The same thing happened in 2000 when real US GDP grew 4.14 percent.[6] Way above average! But US stocks peaked and started their first down-leg of a major bear market in March, falling -9.1 percent in 2000—signaling the 2001 recession.[7] Stocks peaked in 2007 and started falling before the 2007–2009 recession began. GDP was actually *positive* in 2008, though flattish—growing 0.44 percent for the year.[8] Not much, but stocks fell a big 37.0 percent.[9] In 2009, stocks turned up in March, but the economy didn't turn positive until Q3. Though growing by year end, US GDP shrank 2.44 percent in 2009, while US stocks boomed 26.5 percent.[10] The positive Q3 GDP reading was first released at the end of October. If you waited for that, you missed a 31.5 percent move in US stocks from the March low.[11] Stocks move first—up or down.

Second problem: Even during a growth cycle, stocks can be below average when growth is above average, and vice versa. In 1992, real GDP growth was nicely above average—3.4 percent—but stocks returned a fairly lackluster 7.6 percent.[12] In 1995, GDP grew 2.5 percent.[13] That is below the average since 1980 and a laggard in the overall booming 1990s. Meanwhile, stocks soared 37.6 percent—way above average.[14]

What gives? Even during periods of strong growth, expectations can get out of whack. Maybe the consensus is for very strong growth—way above average. If growth is above average but below prior expectations, that can disappoint—usually not enough for a bear market, but enough for returns to be muted. Same thing in reverse. Maybe folks are expecting much weaker growth, and if growth is better than expected while still below average, that can boost returns.[15] Ultimately, surprise moves the market in the intermediate term, for good or for bad.

And never forget! Stocks look forward, while GDP measures what *just* happened and is released at a lag. So while economic growth is an overall market driver, don't expect it to be a perfect market indicator or any form of leading indicator. It isn't.

Huge Growth—Wildly Variable Returns

The US is a huge developed nation—the largest economically by a long shot. In smaller developed nations, you can get even more disconnect. And GDP can make folks' brains go even more haywire in emerging markets.

China has had huge growth in recent years—topping 13.3 percent in 2007![16] (See Table 49.1.) And China has had some huge market years—up 87.6 percent in 2003, up 82.9 percent in 2006, and up 66.2 percent in 2007.[17] Except Chinese GDP grew 9.3 percent in 2008 when stocks plummeted 50.8 percent.[18] And Chinese stocks fell huge in 2000, 2001, and 2002—when its economy boomed.

It's normal to see emerging nations (those that are emerging successfully—some emerge, others submerge) have huge GDP growth—even for years in a row. As the nation grows, it has huge per capita GDP gains. As more of its citizenry moves up into an emerging middle class, they start purchasing cars, appliances, electronics, etc., which also fuels growth. It can feed on itself for a while since growth requires more infrastructure build-outs that result in greater wealth and more growth—and the need for more infrastructure, etc. etc.

Plus, though China remains officially "communist," it has loosened its economy tremendously (relatively). A lot of that growth is

Table 49.1 Chinese GDP and Stock Market Returns —Stocks Don't Necessarily Reflect GDP

Year	China Real Annual GDP	MSCI China Returns
2000	8.0%	−30.54%
2001	7.4%	−24.70%
2002	8.0%	−14.05%
2003	9.4%	87.57%
2004	9.6%	1.89%
2005	10.2%	19.77%
2006	11.2%	82.87%
2007	13.3%	66.23%
2008	9.3%	−50.83%
2009	8.5%	62.63%

Source: International Monetary Fund, World Economic Outlook Database; Thomson Reuters, MSCI China Total Return in US dollars.

years of suppressed ingenuity and productivity hitting its economy all at once. Can it continue? Sure. But China could certainly mess it all up—fast. But there's no inherent reason (other than government meddling) China has to slow down. It slowed somewhat in the global recession in 2008 and 2009—if you can call 8.5 percent slow. But nearly a billion Chinese remain at levels Americans would consider worse than poverty. The growth potential there, if the government allows it, could be huge for a long, long time.

But none of that has much to do with the stock market. Thanks to its fast growth, China is now much bigger than even 10 years ago—now about 8.5 percent of global GDP and the third largest single economy (as of year-end 2009) behind the US and Japan.[19] Huge! If it continues at its current growth pace, it will surpass the US before long. But its stock market is relatively tiny—just 2.26 percent of the world[20]—much smaller than you'd think an economy that size should be. (I'm only counting those stocks that non-Chinese can purchase. There are stocks the Chinese government limits to Chinese nationals, but since we're thinking globally, we want to focus on stocks the globe can buy.) Its capital markets are tiny and lack depth and diversity—very common for emerging markets—adding to volatility. Another big key to demand for Chinese stocks moving forward is the unpredictable flow of new supply of Chinese shares (again, see Bunk 10). In the long term, supply flows control pricing. In the short term, demand shifts do.

Emerging markets typically are also less stable politically, which impacts both supply and demand. This isn't the case with South Korea or even Brazil so much anymore, but many emerging markets (even China, though China is no Venezuela—eek) have miserable private property protections. That adds still more variability you don't get in developed nations, which is why emerging nations can have market returns hugely detached from their economies, with huge shifts in both demand and supply for stocks.

The truth is—emerging or developed—GDP is a great read of where the economy *was*. But if you expect GDP to be predictive of market direction, you can get whipsawed big time.

BUNK 50

TERRORISM TERRORIZES STOCKS

The world is dangerous—a fact Americans were brutally reminded of on September 11, 2001. There are few times when you can honestly say, "It's different this time," but for Americans, something fundamental changed that day. We know thugs can reach us if they really want to.

The good news is, while thugs can be deadly, they haven't taken down our vibrant economy or capital markets—and likely never will. How do you know? It would be hard for any future attack to match the pure shock value of September 11. Right now, most Americans would agree it's not a matter of if we're hit again, but when, and what it looks like. So to know the impact of the next major terrorist attack on US soil (or on our friends or interests abroad), think globally and check history.

Markets Globally Are Resilient

Stocks did fall big following the September 11, 2001, attacks. It's not surprising—considering the scale and the utter first-time-surprise effect of that attack. The exchanges closed for days, and when they reopened on September 17, the S&P 500 fell –4.9 percent and kept falling the entire next week.[1] US stocks were down –11.6 percent by September 21.[2] But then they reversed course sharply. That's about the size of a small but normal correction within a bull market. By October 11, stocks were back at September 10 levels, and they largely traded above there for months afterward.[3] But this wasn't a correction within a bull market. Those attacks came two-thirds of the way down through a huge bear market that was already long underway—and it didn't end, arguably, until March 2003. But the back of that bear market wasn't driven by the terror attacks.

How can we know? Look at later, similar attacks. On March 11, 2004, terrorist goons struck the Madrid train system, bombing it into disability. Spanish stocks fell several percent in the days following, but gained over 29 percent for the year.[4] Global stocks also fell that day, but hit pre-attack levels 20 days later and finished the year higher.[5] Then the London Underground was bombed on July 7, 2005. Stocks barely flinched. By the end of the next trading day, the UK's FTSE 100 was higher and would finish the year up 21 percent.[6] Global stocks were up 9.5 percent in 2005.[7]

Another way to think of all these attacks is while there might be a short-lived reaction, even major terror attacks can't derail stocks from their overall near-term trend. In 2001, stocks were in a bear market that continued after the attacks, and in 2004 and 2005, terror bombings couldn't stop a bull market.

How can markets be so dismissive of terrorism, when it's such a new, terrible, and very real threat? In many ways it's because we fear it, think intuitively, and fail to think counterintuitively. Markets are inherently counterintuitive. Fact is, sadly, terrorism is tragic, but not a very new threat nor very significant in the grand scheme of the global economy.

History Shows Stocks Don't Scare

The September 11 attack wasn't the first on US interests or even on US soil. Previously, we'd had the USS Cole bombing in 2000, the attack on the military barracks in the Khobar Towers in Saudi Arabia in 1996, and the first Twin Towers attack in 1993—all by Al Qaeda. But there was also Pan Am flight 103, bombed over Lockerbie, Scotland, in 1988, and the attack on the US Marines' barracks in Lebanon in 1983. The Achille Lauro in 1985. Israel has dealt with a daily onslaught of terrorism for decades. The Irish Republican Army menaced Britain for nearly a century—all while their markets thrived. World War I was started by a terrorist act. The US Marine Corps protected US shipping lines from the North African Barbary pirates in the very early nineteenth century (hence the line from the Marines' Hymn "to the shores of Tripoli"). Simply, the power it has to move markets has been, thus far, fleeting. Yes, September 11 was bigger, but still fleeting in terms of market impact.

Figure 50.1 shows market reactions following some major, more recent terror attacks in the US and globally. On average, stocks are

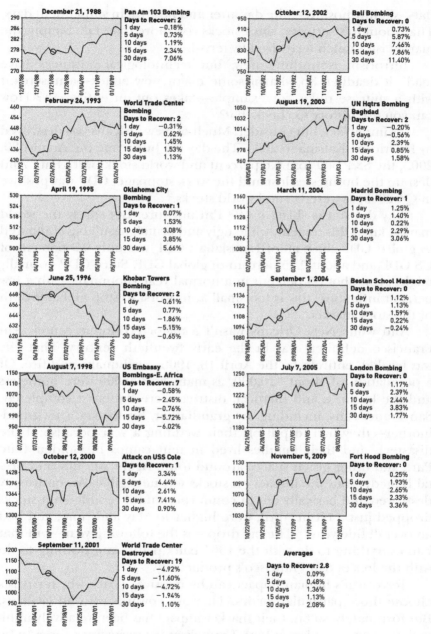

Figure 50.1   Have No Fear—The Market Doesn't

Source: Global Financial Data, Inc., S&P 500 price return.

flat—slightly positive—the day after and positive in subsequent days. That shouldn't surprise, since stocks rise more than fall. Simply, the market isn't much terrorized by terror.

Terrorism is nothing new, but technological advances have made it deadlier. So what if some major new attack—a miscreant with a suitcase nuke, for example—takes out an entire city? How can you use history to check that?

It's imperfect, but consider: Much of New Orleans was destroyed by Hurricane Katrina in 2005. The day the hurricane hit, August 29, 2005, the S&P 500 rose 0.6 percent and world stocks were flat.[8] And despite the businesses lost and the work stoppage, GDP was positive in Q4 2005, as were US and world stocks.[9]

Why did stocks shrug it off? I'm not sure. But surely the world market knew this tragedy, while ugly and brutal, wasn't big compared to global GDP since all of Louisiana's GDP was only 0.9 percent of US GDP and about 0.25 percent of global GDP. Since GDP normally might grow about 5 percent in a normal year (nominal—with a few percent inflation), this is too small at its worst to stop global growth or the stock market.

And while New Orleans wasn't a major economic center, San Francisco definitely was in the early twentieth century. That city was leveled, entirely, by the April 18, 1906, earthquake and fire. Of a population of about 410,000, as many as 300,000 were homeless and the business and financial districts were flattened completely. San Franciscans, including my grandfather, his fiancée (my grandmother—they had to put off their wedding a year because of the disaster), and their families lived in tent camps in Golden Gate Park and other green spaces around town. Again, an ugly and brutal tragedy—but the impact on stocks was negligible. An entire city destroyed and basically out of commission until rebuilt—but stocks dropped just a bit in April, were higher in May and June, and had an overall fine year.[10] The big drop was the following year—but that had everything to do with the 1907 bank panic, and nothing to do with the loss of San Francisco's productivity.

Terrorism's human impact can be massive. That's why terrorists choose those particular tactics. They are cowards who hit civilians. But fortunately, so far, their market impact has been relatively minimal at worst—fleeting at best. Capitalism is too strong a force to be kept back by cowardly thugs.

NOTES

Introduction: Debunkery Made Easy

1. As of 06/30/2010.

Bunk 1: Bonds Are Safer Than Stocks

1. Thomson Reuters, MSCI World Index total return with net dividends.
2. Global Financial Data, Inc.
3. See note 1.

Bunk 2: Well-Rested Investors Are Better Investors

1. Global Financial Data, Inc., USA 10-Year Government Bond Total Return Index from 12/31/2008 to 12/31/2009.

Bunk 5: You Should Expect Average Returns

1. Global Financial Data, Inc., S&P 500 total return from 12/31/25 to 12/31/09.

Bunk 6: "Capital Preservation and Growth" Is Possible!

1. Global Financial Data, Inc., S&P 500 total return from 12/31/1925 to 12/31/2009.

Bunk 7: Trust Your Gut

1. Daniel Kahneman and Amos Tversky, "Prospect Theory: An Analysis of Decision Under Risk." *Econometrica*, Volume 47, Number 2 (March 1979). pp. 263–291.
2. Thomson Reuters, MSCI World Index, price level return.
3. Ibid.
4. Thomson Reuters, MSCI World Index total return with net dividends; Global Financial Data, Inc., S&P 500 total return.
5. Source: MSCI. The MSCI information may only be used for your use, may not be reproduced or redisseminated in any form, and may not be used to create

any financial instruments or products or any indices. The MSCI information is provided on an "as is" basis and the user of this information assumes the entire risk of any use made of this information. MSCI, each of its affiliates and each other person involved in or related to compiling, computing, or creating any MSCI information (collectively, the "MSCI Parties") expressly disclaims all warranties (including, without limitation, any warranties of originality, accuracy, completeness, timeliness, non-infringement, merchantability, and fitness for a particular purpose) with respect to this information. Without limiting any of the foregoing, in no event shall any MSCI Party have any liability for any direct, indirect, special, incidental, punitive, consequential (including, without limitation, lost profits), or any other damages.

Bunk 8: One Big Bear and You're Done

1. Thomson Reuters, MSCI World Index total return with net dividends from 10/31/2007 to 03/09/2009.

Bunk 9: Make Sure It's a Bull Before Diving In

1. See Bunk 7, note 5.
2. Thomson Reuters, S&P 500 total return, MSCI World Index total return with net dividends from 03/09/2009 to 12/31/2009.

Bunk 10: Growth Is Best for All Time. No, Value. No, Small Caps

1. Thomson Reuters.
2. S&P/Citigroup Primary Value index measures the performance of the value style of investing in large cap US stocks. The index is constructed by dividing the top 80 percent of all US stocks in terms of market capitalization into a Value index, using style factors to make the assignment. The Value index contains those securities with a greater-than-average value orientation. The index is market-capitalization-weighted. S&P/Citigroup Primary Growth index measures the performance of the growth style of investing in large cap US stocks. The index is constructed by dividing the top 80 percent of all US stocks in terms of market capitalization into a Growth index, using style factors to make the assignment. The Growth index contains those securities with a greater-than-average value orientation. The index is market-capitalization-weighted.
3. Small cap returns as measured by the Ibbotson Associates SBBI Small Stock Total Return Index, 01/01/1926–03/1/2010, Ibbotson Associates; US stock market returns as measured by the S&P 500 Index, total return, 01/01/1926–03/1/2010, Global Financial Data, Inc.

Bunk 14: Dollar Cost Averaging—Lower Risk, Better Returns

1. Michael S. Rozeff, "Lump-Sum Investing Versus Dollar-Averaging," *Journal of Portfolio Management* (Winter 1994), pp. 45–50.

Bunk 15: Variable Annuities Are All Upside, No Downside

1. AARP.org.
2. Bankrate.com.
3. 2009 Annuity Factbook.
4. Morningstar, Inc., as of 2008.

Bunk 16: Equity-Indexed Annuities—Better Than Normal Annuities

1. Global Financial Data, Inc.
2. Ibid.

Bunk 17: Passive Investing Is Easy

1. *2010 Qualitative Analysis of Investor Behavior*, Advisor Edition, DALBAR, Inc.
2. Global Financial Data, Inc., S&P 500 total return from 12/31/1989 to 12/31/2009.
3. See note 1.
4. Global Financial Data, Inc., Nasdaq Composite, S&P 500 Total Return Index, annualized from 12/31/1995 to 12/31/1999.
5. Thomson Reuters, MSCI World Index total return with net dividends from 03/09/2009 to 12/31/2009.

Bunk 18: Do Better With Mutual Funds by Sending Your Spouse on a Shopping Spree

1. Brad M. Barber and Terrance Odean, "Boys Will Be Boys: Gender, Overconfidence, and Common Stock Investment," *Quarterly Journal of Economics* 116, no. 1 (February 2001).
2. Ibid.

Bunk 19: Beta Measures Risk

1. See Bunk 7, note 5.

Bunk 20: Equity Risk Premiums—Forecasting Future Returns With Ease!

1. Global Financial Data, Inc., USA 10-Year Government Bond Total Return Index, S&P 500 total return from 12/31/1926 to 12/31/2009.

Bunk 21: When the VIX Is High, It's Time to Buy

1. Global Financial Data, Inc., S&P 500 total return from 12/31/98 to 12/31/99.
2. Global Financial Data, Inc., S&P 500 total return from 12/31/94 to 12/31/95.

Bunk 22: Be Confident on Consumer Confidence

1. Thomson Reuters, S&P 500 total return from 03/30/2003 to 03/30/2004.
2. Thomson Reuters, S&P 500 total return from 07/30/2007 to 07/30/2008.
3. Thomson Reuters, S&P 500 total return from 02/29/2008 to 02/28/2009.
4. Thomson Reuters, S&P 500 total return from 10/30/2005 to 10/30/2006.

Bunk 23: All Hail the Mighty Dow!

1. US stock market as represented by the Wilshire 500 Index, Thomson Reuters, Wilshire.com, as of 05/31/2010.
2. Ibid.
3. Thomson Reuters, as of 05/31/2010.
4. Global Financial Data, Inc., S&P 500 total return from 12/31/1964 to 12/31/1982.

Bunk 24: So Goes January

1. Thomson Reuters, S&P 500 total return, MSCI World Index total return with net dividends from 12/31/08 to 1/31/09.
2. Thomson Reuters, S&P 500 total return, MSCI World Index total return with net dividends from 12/31/08 to 12/31/09.

Bunk 25: Sell in May

1. Global Financial Data, Inc., S&P 500 total return from 12/31/1925 to 12/31/2009.
2. Ibid.
3. See note 1.
4. See note 1.

Bunk 26: Low P/Es Mean Low Risk

1. Global Financial Data, Inc., S&P 500 P/E based on 12-month trailing earnings as of 12/31/2008.
2. Global Financial Data, Inc., S&P 500 total return from 12/31/2008 to 12/31/2009; Thomson Reuters, MSCI World Index total return with net dividends from 12/31/2008 to 12/31/2009.
3. Global Financial Data, Inc., S&P 500 P/E based on 12-month trailing earnings as of 12/31/2002.
4. Global Financial Data, Inc., S&P 500 total return from 12/31/2002 to 12/31/2003; Thomson Reuters, MSCI World Index total return with net dividends from 12/31/2002 to 12/31/2003.
5. Global Financial Data, Inc., S&P 500 P/E based on 12-month trailing earnings as of 12/31/1998; S&P 500 total return from 12/31/1998 to 12/31/1999.
6. Global Financial Data, Inc., S&P 500 P/E based on 12-month trailing earnings as of 12/31/1995, 12/31/1996, and 12/31/1997.

7. Global Financial Data, Inc., S&P 500 total return from 12/31/1995 to 12/31/1996, 12/31/1996 to 12/31/1997, and 12/31/1997 to 12/31/1998.
8. Global Financial Data, Inc., S&P 500 P/E based on 12-month trailing earnings as of 12/31/1999.
9. Global Financial Data, Inc. year-end P/Es based on 12-month trailing earnings in 1981, 1982, 1983, and 1984 were 7.9, 11.1, 11.8, and 10.1. S&P 500 total returns were 21.6 percent in 1982, 22.6 percent in 1983, 6.3 percent in 1984, and 31.8 percent in 1985.
10. Global Financial Data, Inc., S&P 500 P/E based on 12-month trailing earnings as of 12/31/1980, S&P 500 total return in 1981 was –4.9 percent.
11. Global Financial Data, Inc., S&P 500 P/E based on 12-month trailing earnings as of year end. S&P 500 total returns were –25.3 percent in 1930, –43.9 percent in 1931, –0.9 percent in 1939, –10.1 percent in 1940, –10.9 percent in 1957, and –7.2 percent in 1976.

Bunk 27: A Strong Dollar Is Super

1. Thomson Reuters, S&P 500 total return from 12/31/2008 to 12/31/2009.
2. Thomson Reuters, International Monetary Fund, as of 12/31/2009.
3. The trade-weighted US dollar index is computed by the Federal Reserve. The base is 1975–1976 = 100 and ten countries are used in computing the index. The index includes the G-10 countries (Belgium, Canada, France, Germany, Italy, Japan, Netherlands, Sweden, Switzerland, and the United Kingdom) weighted by the sum of the country's world trade during the 1972–1976 period.
4. Ibid.

Bunk 28: Don't Fight the Fed

1. Percentage of 2009 GDP. International Monetary Fund, World Economic Outlook Database, April 2010.
2. See Bunk 7, note 5.

Bunk 29: Interest Pays Dividends

1. Bloomberg Finance, L.P.

Bunk 30: Buy a 5% CD for 5% Cash Flow—Easy!

1. Thomson Reuters, Consumer Price Index from 12/31/1989 to 12/31/2009.

Bunk 32: Concentrate to Build Wealth

1. Matthew Miller and Duncan Greenberg, "The Richest People in America," *Forbes*, September 30, 2009.
2. Global Financial Data, Inc., GE total return from 08/28/2000 to 10/09/2002.
3. Global Financial Data, Inc., GE total return, S&P 500 total return from 08/28/2000 to 12/31/2009.

Bunk 34: High Unemployment Is a Killer

1. Global Financial Data, Inc., S&P 500 total return, Thomson Reuters, MSCI World Index total return with net dividends, from 03/09/2009 to 12/31/2009 and from 12/31/2008 to 12/31/2009.
2. Bureau of Economic Analysis, as of 03/31/2009.

Bunk 35: With Gold, You're Golden

1. Thomson Reuters, MSCI World Index total return with net dividends from 11/30/1973 to 2/31/2009.
2. Global Financial Data, Inc., S&P 500 total return from 11/30/1973 to 12/31/2009.
3. Ibid. Global Financial Data, Inc., USA 10-Year Government Bond Total Return Index from 11/30/1973 to 12/31/2009.
4. Global Financial Data, Inc., Gold Bullion Price–New York (US$/Ounce) from 11/30/1973 to 12/31/2009.
5. Ibid.
6. See note 4.
7. Global Financial Data, Inc., Gold Bullion Price–New York (US$/Ounce), S&P 500 total return, MSCI World Index total return with net dividends from 12/31/2008 through 12/31/2009

Bunk 36: Stocks Love Lower Taxes

1. Global Financial Data, Inc., S&P 500 price return from 08/13/1981 to 08/13/1982.
2. International Monetary Fund, World Economic Outlook Database, April 2010; Thomson Reuters.

Bunk 38: Swine Flu, SARS, Ebola, and Other Viral Disasters Make Markets Sick

1. World Health Organization, Executive Board, "Severe Acute Respiratory Syndrome, Report by the Secretariat," January 23, 2004.
2. Thomson Reuters, MSCI World Index total return with net dividends from 12/31/2002 to 12/31/2003.
3. Global Financial Data, Inc., S&P 500 total return.
4. Ibid.

Bunk 39: Consumers Are King

1. Bureau of Economic Analysis, as of 03/31/2010.
2. Bureau of Economic Analysis, real business investment (gross private domestic investment less residential fixed investment) from the low in Q2 2009 through Q1 2010.

Bunk 40: Presidential Term Cycles Are Stock Market Voodoo

1. International Monetary Fund, World Economic Outlook Database, as of 04/30/2010.

Bunk 41: My Political Party Is Best for Stocks

1. Global Financial Data, Inc., S&P 500 total return, from 12/31/2008 to 12/31/2009.
2. Ibid., from 12/31/2007 to 12/31/2008.

Bunk 42: Stock Returns Are Too High and Must Fall

1. Global Financial Data, Inc., S&P 500 total return from 12/31/1989 to 12/31/2009 and from 12/31/1925 to 12/31/1989.

Part 5: It's a Great Big World!

1. International Monetary Fund, World Economic Outlook Database, April 2010.

Bunk 43: Foreign Stocks Just Feel So . . . Foreign

1. Thomson Reuters, as of 03/31/2010.
2. Ibid.
3. Global Financial Data, Inc., S&P 500 total return annualized from 12/31/1969 to 04/30/2010; Thomson Reuters, MSCI EAFE total return with net dividends annualized from 12/31/1969 to 04/30/2010.
4. See Bunk 7, note 5.

Bunk 44: Who Needs Foreign?

1. See Bunk 7, note 5.
2. Thomson Reuters, S&P 500 total return, MSCI EAFE total return with net dividends from 06/30/1994 to 06/30/1999.
3. Thomson Reuters, S&P 500 total return, MSCI EAFE total return with net dividends from 2/28/1985 to 11/30/1988.
4. Global Financial Data, Inc., S&P 500 total return annualized from 12/31/1969 to 04/30/2010; Thomson Reuters, MSCI EAFE total return with net dividends annualized from 12/31/1969 to 04/30/2010.

Bunk 45: Big Debt Is National Death

1. TreasuryDirect, Congressional Budget Office, March 2010 release.

Bunk 48: Trade Deficits Make Deficient Markets

1. Thomson Reuters.
2. Ibid.

3. Ibid.
4. International Monetary Fund, World Economic Outlook Database, April 2010; Thomson Reuters, MSCI USA total return from 12/31/1979 to 12/31/2009.
5. International Monetary Fund, World Economic Outlook Database, April 2010; Thomson Reuters, MSCI UK total return with net dividends from 12/31/1979 to 12/31/2009.
6. International Monetary Fund, World Economic Outlook Database, April 2010.
7. Thomson Reuters, MSCI Japan total return with net dividends from 12/31/1979 to 12/31/2009.
8. Thomson Reuters, MSCI Germany total return with net dividends from 12/31/1979 to 12/31/2009.
9. See note 6.

Bunk 49: GDP Makes Stocks Grow

1. International Monetary Fund, World Economic Outlook Database.
2. National Bureau of Economic Research.
3. Global Financial Data, Inc., S&P 500 total return from 12/31/1980 to 2/31/1981.
4. See note 2.
5. International Monetary Fund, World Economic Outlook Database; Global Financial Data, Inc., S&P 500 total returns from 12/31/1981 to 12/31/1982.
6. See note 1.
7. Global Financial Data, Inc., S&P 500 total return from 12/31/1999 to 12/31/2000.
8. See note 1.
9. Global Financial Data, Inc., S&P 500 total return from 12/31/2007 to 12/31/2008.
10. See note 1; Global Financial Data, Inc., S&P 500 total return from 12/31/2008 to 12/31/2009.
11. Global Financial Data, Inc., S&P 500 total return from 03/09/2009 to 10/31/2009.
12. Global Financial Data, Inc., S&P 500 total return from 12/31/1991 to 12/31/1992.
13. See note 1.
14. Global Financial Data, Inc., S&P 500 total return from 12/31/1994 to 12/31/1995.
15. See Bunk 7, note 5.
16. See note 1.
17. Thomson Reuters, MSCI China, total returns in US dollars from 12/31/2006 to 12/31/2007.
18. See note 1.
19. See note 1.
20. Thomson Reuters, world stock market as measured by the MSCI All Country World Index (ACWI).

Bunk 50: Terrorism Terrorizes Stocks

1. Thomson Reuters, S&P 500 total return from 09/10/2001 to 09/17/2001.
2. Thomson Reuters, S&P 500 total return from 09/10/2001 to 09/21/2001.
3. Thomson Reuters, S&P 500 total return.
4. Thomson Reuters, MSCI Spain total return with net dividends from 12/31/2003 to 12/31/2004.
5. Thomson Reuters, MSCI World Index total return with net dividends from 12/31/2003 to 12/31/2004.
6. Thomson Reuters, FTSE 100 total returns in GBP from 12/31/2004 to 12/31/2005.
7. Thomson Reuters, MSCI World Index total returns with net dividends from 12/31/2004 to 12/31/2005.
8. Thomson Reuters, S&P 500 total returns, MSCI World Index total return with net dividends.
9. Bureau of Economic Analysis, Thomson Reuters, S&P 500 total returns, MSCI World Index total return with net dividends from 12/31/2004 to 12/31/2005.
10. Global Financial Data, Inc.

ABOUT THE AUTHORS

Ken Fisher is best known for his prestigious "Portfolio Strategy" column in *Forbes* magazine, where his over 25-year tenure of high-profile calls makes him the fourth-longest-running columnist in *Forbes'* 90-plus-year history. He is the founder, chairman, and CEO of Fisher Investments, an independent global money management firm with over $32 billion under management (as of June 30, 2010). Fisher is ranked #289 on the 2009 *Forbes* 400 list of richest Americans, and #721 on the 2010 *Forbes* Global Billionaire list. In 2010, *Investment Advisor* magazine named him as one of the 30 most influential individuals of the last three decades. Fisher has authored numerous professional and scholarly articles, including the award-winning "Cognitive Biases in Market Forecasting." He has also written six previous books, including the *New York Times* and *Wall Street Journal* best sellers *The Only Three Questions That Count, The Ten Roads to Riches,* and *How to Smell a Rat,* all published by John Wiley & Sons. Fisher has been published, interviewed, and written about in many major American, British, and German finance and business periodicals. He has a weekly column in *Focus Money,* Germany's leading weekly finance and business magazine.

Lara Hoffmans is a content manager at Fisher Investments, a contributing editor of MarketMinder.com, and co-author of the best sellers *The Only Three Questions That Count, The Ten Roads to Riches,* and *How to Smell a Rat.* She is a graduate of the University of Notre Dame and currently lives in Vancouver, Washington, with husband Aaron and daughter Reagan.

INDEX